Literacy for the New Millennium

I dedicate this series of books to all those who center their professional lives on fostering the development and practice of literacy.

LITERACY FOR THE NEW MILLENNIUM

Volume 3

Adolescent Literacy

Edited by Barbara J. Guzzetti

Praeger Perspectives

Westport, Connecticut
London

Library of Congress Cataloging-in-Publication Data

Literacy for the new millennium / edited by Barbara J. Guzzetti.
   v. cm.
   Includes bibliographical references and indexes.
   Contents: v. 1. Early literacy — v. 2 Childhood literacy — v. 3 Adolescent
literacy — v. 4 Adult literacy.
   ISBN-13: 978–0–275–98969–9 (set : alk. paper)
   ISBN-10: 0–275–98969–0 (set : alk. paper)
   ISBN-13: 978–0–275–98992–7 (v.1 : alk. paper)
   ISBN-10: 0–275–98992–5 (v.1 : alk. paper)
   [etc.]
 1. Literacy.   2. Language arts.   I. Guzzetti, Barbara J.
   LC149.L4987   2007
   302.2'244—dc22   2007018116

British Library Cataloguing in Publication Data is available.

Library of Congress Catalog Card Number: 2007018116
ISBN-13: 978–0–275–98969–9 (set)   ISBN-10: 0–275–98969–0
ISBN-13: 978–0–275–98992–7 (vol. 1)   ISBN-10: 0–275–98992–5
ISBN-13: 978–0–275–98993–4 (vol. 2)   ISBN-10: 0–275–98993–3
ISBN-13: 978–0–275–98994–1 (vol. 3)   ISBN-10: 0–275–98994–1
ISBN-13: 978–0–275–98995–8 (vol. 4)   ISBN-10: 0–275–98995-X

First published in 2007

Praeger Publishers, 88 Post Road West, Westport, CT 06881
An imprint of Greenwood Publishing Group, Inc.
www.praeger.com

Printed in the United States of America

CONTENTS

school and community, tightening control over what is taught in school. English Only initiatives provide one such example. For instance, in Arizona, Proposition 203 eliminates the possibility of building on the dual Spanish/English literacies many students bring to the classroom, despite evidence that doing so can significantly bolster student achievement on standardized tests in English (Menken, 2006). Mandates such as these bar adolescents' literacies and knowledge from the classroom. Beginning with what adolescents know and can do, building on their discourses and passions provides a completely different starting place for literacy learning. The demand for narrowly defined academic achievement has led to the disappearance of experimentation inside of school, marginalizing the opportunities to build on students' interests and knowledge based on their out-of-school practices. Kenway and Bullen (2006) explained that rather than moving toward understanding how to engage youth in schooling, educational systems have adopted "a form of educational fundamentalism that shows an almost complete disregard for who the young are and might become" (p. 532).

Calls for reimagining schools and classroom practices in a globalized world rarely take into account the ways in which many adolescents are already deeply engaged in learning in global communities outside of school. Rather than simply appropriating adolescents' literacy practices and bringing them into classrooms, however, we urge educators to acknowledge adolescents' engagement in out-of-school communities to gain a broader understanding of what students know and can do. In other words, teachers' understandings of adolescents' engagement in literacy on a global scale outside of school can help them reframe their understanding of what students bring to school and their identities as readers and writers.

While many adolescents are engaged in literacy practices outside of school, schools have a special responsibility to provide access to an equitable education, which includes recognition of the global communities in which adolescents are active citizens. Furthermore, schools have the responsibility to create opportunities for critical conversations between and among adults and adolescents around literacy and technology use and provide students with frameworks for exploring the power and limitations of new tools and forms of expression. At the same time, educators working in and out of school settings must rethink citizenship in a global community and the role of literacy in producing global citizens. A. Luke and Carrington (2001) argued for a "critical literacy that envisions literacy as a tool for remediating one's relation to the global flows of capital and information, bodies and images" (p. 62). Perhaps schools and adolescent literacy practices are not robust enough to provide a response to the need to redefine citizenship in a globalized world. That said, they are certainly places to begin.

Sassen, S. (1998). *Globalization and its discontents: Essays on the new mobility of people and money.* New York: New Press.

Schultz, K. (2007). *After the blackbird whistles: Listening to silence in classrooms.* Manuscript submitted for publication.

Skelton, T., & Valentine, G. (1998). *Cool places: Geographies of youth cultures.* London: Routledge.

Soep, E. (2006). Youth media citizenship: Beyond "youth voice." *Afterschool Matters, 5,* 1–12.

Suaréz-Orozco, M. M., & Qin-Hilliard, D. B. (Eds.). (2004). *Globalization: Culture and education in the new millennium.* Berkeley: University of California Press.

Tapscott, D. (1997). *Growing up digital: The rise of the net generation.* New York: McGraw-Hill.

Torres, C. (2006). Democracy, education, and multiculturalism: Dilemmas of citizenship in a global world. In H. Lauder, P. Brown, J. Dillabough, & A. H. Halsey (Eds.), *Education, globalization, and social change* (pp. 524–536). New York: Oxford University Press. (Reprinted from *Comparative Education Review, 42*(4), 1998)

Vasudevan, L., Schultz, K., & Bateman, J. (under review). Beyond the printed page: Multimodal storytelling with urban adolescents.

Wallace, C. (2002). Local literacy and global literacies. In D. Block & D. Cameron (Eds.), *Globalization and language teaching* (pp. 101–114). New York: Routledge.

Chapter Three

POLICY AND ADOLESCENT LITERACY

Bob Fecho, Christine A. Mallozzi, and Katherine Schultz

Chanel Mason, at the time of our writing, was teaching 9th-grade English in a small urban high school in the state of Georgia in the United States. In accordance with her newly opened school's mission, she was attempting to implement more inquiry-based teaching—an approach that encourages students' explorations into and meaning making of subject matter. Despite juggling a fair amount of change, Chanel had started to gain a handle on her inquiry-based teaching, becoming more accomplished at connecting daily inquiry activities into larger explorations driven by questions and capped by performance-based projects. Moreover, she was beginning to feel confident that she, her school administration, and her district were all on the same page in terms of this inquiry focus.

The school had opened in the fall of 2005 with a mandate from the superintendent's office to offer inquiry-based instruction to students within the limits and possibilities of a high school that, in four years, would comprise no more than 400 students. That mandate was supported by structural requirements—25 or fewer students in classes, daily preparation periods with enough time for common planning, a new physical plant, and 100-minute classes meeting every other day—as well as the outside support of a private foundation that provided instructional coaches, professional learning institutes, and other curricular, instructional, and assessment services. In addition, Georgia had adopted performance standards (Georgia Department of Education [GDE], 2005b) that seemed to be user friendly for inquiry-based teachers.

Unlike many teachers, who have to slip inquiry-based instruction into an overstructured curriculum, Chanel sensed that she had the full support of her principal and school district to pursue inquiry teaching. As such, she developed an inquiry unit based on *Romeo and Juliet* and had students delve into Shakespeare's language to consider the possibilities and complications of updating it. Students responded to her challenge with energy and enthusiasm by negotiating several collaborative writing projects that had them rewriting Shakespeare's poetry in the language of hip-hop culture.

However, as she and her students were initiating the exploration, they were faced with the task of preparing for the End-of-Course-Test (EOCT). According to the Georgia Department of Education's Web site (GDE, 2005a), the EOCTs are given

> to improve student achievement through effective instruction and assessment of the standards in the eight EOCT core high school courses. The EOCT program helps to ensure that all Georgia students have access to a rigorous curriculum that meets high performance standards. The purpose of the EOCT is to provide diagnostic data that can be used to enhance instructional programs.

Bowing somewhat to district pressure, the school administration expected class lessons three weeks prior to the test be devoted to preparing students for this traditionally formatted, standardized, multiple-choice examination. Even though the Shakespeare project was developing energy and excitement among her students, Chanel felt pressured to end the inquiry and pursue three weeks of test preparation. Despite her efforts to keep the review inquiry based and critical—for example, she had students write about why they felt they were required to take the EOCTs—she admitted that instructional time would have been better served pursuing the inquiry into the language and themes of *Romeo and Juliet.* Expressing her frustration, she felt caught among conflicting positions: her own inclination to teach from an inquiry stance, her administration's seeming support for such a stance, the fact-based minutiae of the EOCTs, and the political weight her district placed on assessments.

Although the Georgia EOCTs are state and not federally mandated, they are part of the culture of assessment that has been initiated by local and state governments primarily in response to federal educational policy efforts to hold schools and school districts more accountable. Chanel's dilemma—to continue her enthusiastic and district-supported inquiry into language via Shakespeare or to abandon that work to pursue district and state policy that required review and a fact-based, rather than performance-based, assessment—is far too common. Across the state of Georgia and throughout the United States, teachers who are the local implementers of policy frequently sift through contradictory values, support systems, and requirements as they try to put into action what legislators, the distant makers of policy, legislate. Local teachers' voices, students' voices, and parents' voices have been eliminated from discussions of policy; these stakeholders are the experts on the needs of their school community, but their input typically has not been solicited in making policy.

Hence this chapter seeks to discuss what happens and what it means when federal educational policy on literacy leaves no room for local creation and interpretation of policy. We address how policy relates to adolescents and the ways they read and write. In doing so, we discuss the history of federal involvement in education policy, with particular emphasis on literacy policy. We focus on the literacy education policy of the George W. Bush administration, citing critical reaction to that policy and calling into question the apparent lack of local input into that policy. Finally, we suggest ways that current federal policy—indeed, all educational policy—can be more inclusive in construction and implementation.

DEFINING OUR STANCE

It is our belief that healthy policy grows from an ongoing dialogue between centering forces that attempt to unify and standardize public action and outward-tugging forces that seek to individualize and diversify those same public actions. This belief springs from our understanding that language— the medium through which all policy is created—undergoes similar tensions (Bakhtin, 1981). These opposing tensions can be likened to an outdoor tug-of-war game. On one side, the rope is unified and pulled by a composite of government and corporate bodies seeking to standardize language and behavior. On the other side, the rope has frayed into any number of single fibers, each pulled by individuals and communities seeking to use the language and policy in ways that reflect their local needs. Somewhere above, a cosmic mud puddle, the middle-marker ribbon of policy, flutters, pulled more to this side, then tugged more to the other. However, the object of the game is not to pull either side into the mud; instead, it is to keep up enough tension to run the game in perpetuity.

Fair and inclusive policy negotiates that middle ground between the opposing forces. Shifting too far to either extreme creates policy that either ignores the needs of local stakeholders or becomes so subject to those needs that it has no unified core to provide stability. Policy, to be effective, must maintain that ongoing dialogue between standardization and diversification. In this chapter, we take this stance on policy making and implementation and apply it to current federal policy on literacy education, with the intent of calling that policy into question.

A BRIEF HISTORY OF FEDERAL INVOLVEMENT IN EDUCATION

Federal involvement in education is not a new phenomenon. National government and monies have influenced the operations of local schools for decades. Our interest in federal attachment to education stems from what we see as changes in breadth, depth, and intensity of involvement over recent decades. As these policies have widened in scope, the aim seems to have changed from helping local educators with their goal of delivering a satisfactory education to their local constituents to a more top-down approach, in which national mandates are laid on local operations. Current mandates do not simply create an overlay on local affairs, coloring how education looks on the surface, but seep into every minute decision, until the local impetus of decision making is often muffled by the more powerful and better-funded federal initiatives. These trends represent the current state of education and are the most recent manifestations of federal involvement that span time, party lines, political groups, and contexts.

Many policy analyses (e.g., Edmonson, 2000, 2004; Wirt & Kirst, 1997) cite the Elementary and Secondary Education Act (ESEA) of 1965 as one of the first, if not the first, significant legislation of federal policy for education. The path of the ESEA can be traced from the 14th Amendment of the U.S. Constitution (ratified 1868), guaranteeing all citizens equal protection under law; through the U.S. Supreme Court decision for *Brown v. Board of Education*, ruling racial segregation of schoolchildren as illegal; to the attention boost of education in the 1960s Race to Space with the Russians; to the signing of the Civil Rights Act (1964). As part of Lyndon B. Johnson's (D) war on poverty, the ESEA was purported as a guarantee of equal opportunity for students in U.S. public schools. This legislation created special programs, such as Title I and Head Start, two efforts that concentrated on early education to help students in economically disadvantaged areas increase their likelihood of school success. Some criticized the ESEA for playing such an active and specific governmental role in education, but this policy remained a cornerstone of federal education policy, despite the revisions made by several administrations through eight reauthorizations.

In the late 1960s and 1970s, the federal government's focus on addressing domestic poverty and educational opportunities took a backseat to the Vietnam War. The Johnson administration changed its tactic from quality education solving societal problems to increasing job training services, assuming well-paying jobs would come to hardworking people (Edmonson, 2004). This pull-yourself-up-by-your-bootstraps approach lasted as Richard Nixon's (R) and Gerald Ford's (R) administrations moved to disconnect federal legislation and finances from schools by allowing state governments to make decisions on the distributions of federal monies to local districts. The changes continued as Jimmy Carter (D) established the U.S. Department of Education in 1980. Ronald Reagan's (R) reauthorization of the ESEA emphasized less federal control over funds for local education but was paired with a decrease in funds for programs such as Title I (a.k.a. Chapter I). Conversely, the U.S.

Department of Education's National Commission on Excellence in Education (1983) called for more stringent student and teacher standards in the federal report *A Nation at Risk*. A panel during George H. W. Bush's (R) administration, America 2000/Goals 2000, proposed state incentives for students reaching higher standards and achievement by the year 2000.

The role of the federal government was becoming increasingly complex, with a decreased role in funding and decision making, but a strong presence in proposing recommendations and standards. The 1994 reauthorization of the ESEA Improving America's Schools Act during Bill Clinton's (D) administration emphasized Title I, family literacy, professional development for teachers, technology, bilingual education, and provisions for charter schools. In 1996, the federal administration focused on reading by issuing the America Reads Challenge, an initiative with the aim that all children read independently by the end of 3rd grade. The Clinton administration believed that this "'big government' vision of a universally literate U.S. workforce [was] possible through a broad federal policy supported by local community efforts" (Edmonson, 2000, pp. 19–20). A private, conservative think tank, composed of members from the Center for Education Reform, Empower America, the Heritage Foundation, and the Thomas B. Fordham Foundation, but not commissioned or approved by the federal government, wrote a 1998 follow-up report called *A Nation "Still" at Risk* (Thomas B. Fordham Foundation, 1998). Linked to the original 1983 *A Nation at Risk* report in name only, the report contained similar findings and recommendations as the 15-year-old report and fueled a panicked rhetoric of failing U.S. schools.

Although the Clinton administration had planned to pass another authorization of the ESEA, the last major educational legislation under this administration was the Reading Excellence Act of 1998, an amendment to Title II of the Elementary and Secondary Education Act (1965). The four major goals of this act were (1) teaching children to read by no later than 3rd grade, (2) improving the skills of students and teachers using replicable research in reading, (3) expanding family literacy programs, and (4) reducing inappropriate referrals to special education. The bulk of these themes and an increasingly narrow definition of reading would continue into the next millennium due to the "Report of the National Reading Panel" (National Institute of Child Health and Human Development, 2000) and the No Child Left Behind Act (NCLB) of 2001.

Much of the current K–12 federal literacy policy had its basis in reports published by the National Institute of Child Health and Human Development (2000), culminating in a report by the National Reading Panel (NRP). The NRP developed a review of existing reading using a standard of experimental studies, or studies that randomly assigned students to treatment groups, as the only research that qualified as scientifically based reading research (SBRR). The limited description of research named as scientifically based led to a heavily critiqued and narrow definition of reading instruction and assessment, valuing only phonemic awareness, phonics, fluency, vocabulary, and comprehension instruction. Thus the NRP dubbed silent, sustained reading, or periods of time in which students practiced the act of independent reading, as an unsanctioned instructional practice. George W. Bush's administration relied on the "Report of the National Reading Panel" for the most recent reauthorization of ESEA, the NCLB. Emphasizing standardized testing and highly qualified teachers, this legislation was initially enacted at the primary level with Reading First, a grant initiative based on SBRR materials and professional development, with a target of all children reading by 3rd grade by 2014. Currently, the act continues to influence higher grade levels with the Striving Readers initiative (U.S. Department of Education [DOE], 2005a, 2006d, 2006e).

A DISCUSSION OF RECENT FEDERAL POLICY ON LITERACY

As the previous section indicated, federal involvement in education over the last 40 years has fluctuated in terms of constraints and funding. Most of the ESEA reauthorizations, however, maintained or even increased local interpretation and implementation of those policies. The NCLB, the latest reauthorization of ESEA, marked a major shift by eliminating most, if not all, opportunities for local constituencies either to have input into or later interpret the policy. NCLB made an initial impact on education with the Reading First initiative, which set one of its goals as showing all children at the kindergarten through 3rd grades as reading on target grade level by the year 2014. Because it seemed that students who were beginning and developing in literacy were at the forefront, NCLB had erroneously become synonymous with younger learners. The act, which was passed by a bipartisan congressional effort, was in reality crafted from the start to affect schooling in the United States from preschool to postsecondary education and beyond as students entered the workforce (NCLB, 2001; DOE, 2005c). Only recently has interest been pointed toward and dollars been spent on implementing adolescent literacy provisions of the NCLB, making the impact on secondary schools more visible in the public and educational spheres.

President George W. Bush had requested almost $1.5 billion (fiscal year 2007 budget) for what is currently being termed the High School Reform initiative (DOE, 2006b). If granted, this allocation would have surpassed any budgeted money for the Reading First initiative in any given year in its history (DOE, 2006a, 2006c). Although this initiative appeared to be new in the 2007 fiscal year, its roots existed in efforts termed the Preparing America's Future High School Initiative, or simply the High School Initiative (DOE, 2005a, 2005c). In October 2003, at the launch of the High School Initiative, education and policy leaders joined at the National High School Summit in Washington, D.C., to discuss ways to improve the country's secondary schools. Subsequent national and regional summits in 2003 and 2004 provided a setting for the creation of reform plans that met "the vision of the No Child Left Behind Act" (DOE, 2005c), which served as a framework for transforming high schools through intervention, assessment, and literacy instruction.

The profile and history of the High School Reform initiative indicated that the largest portion of requested money was planned for the intervention proposal (DOE, 2005a). The intervention portion of the initiative centers on designs to increase achievement of all high school students and help ensure that students are able to succeed in postsecondary education and in jobs in a global economy. Grants would be distributed to states for the academic improvement of students at risk of not meeting state academic standards and for narrowing the achievement gap between more advantaged and less advantaged students. Although the intervention programs may appear different, the states would still be bound by the narrow definition of scientifically based research education and accountability through evaluation.

The assessment effort marks another major thrust of the High School Reform initiative. This effort calls for expanded assessment in high schools; students would take three annual statewide tests in reading and mathematics during their high school years, instead of the one state test that students are currently required to take between their 10th- and 12th-grade years. Considering that many high schools are four-year institutions, this proposal would result in students being tested three out of four years, in addition to any other national, state, and local assessments. This assessment schedule would be required to be in place for the 2009–2010 school year. Although these assessments could be used to help meet the needs of students, this assessment requirement seems more apt to "strengthen school accountability at the secondary level" (DOE, 2006b).

Issues of accountability have greatly influenced the implementation of NCLB. All states are now required to show student performance through state assessments and make those results available to the public. All states are also required to participate in the National Assessment of Educational Progress (NAEP), periodic assessments conducted by the U.S. Department of Education designed to ascertain what students across the country know and are able to do in terms of school subjects such as math, reading, writing, and the like. After the act's signature into law, a new section 1503 was added to Title I, Part E of NCLB (DOE, 2005b) that required an independent study of state assessments by a research organization to evaluate state accountability systems. The independent researcher would be chosen through a review process of federally chosen peers.

Regardless of the outcome of the independent research on the quality of state accountability systems, the state measures seemed already to be under scrutiny in the public forum. Although many believe that state assessments and the federal NAEP assessment are incomparable, the secretary of the U.S. Department of Education, Margaret Spellings, encouraged the media to look to the discrepancies in percentages of students' state proficiency performances with the percentages of students performing at the basic level on the NAEP (Dillon, 2005). Perhaps unexpected by Spellings, investigations that considered student assessment percentages within the politicized context found important contradictions. Those states that have kept their assessment standards close to the higher federal bar have not been congratulated for their rigor when their students do not achieve required benchmarks. Conversely, those states with lower standards and thus higher assessment scores have been accused of what the Bush administration has termed "the soft bigotry of low expectations" (DOE, 2003). Many legislators and lobbyists have used these comparisons of state and federal tests to show the inadequacies of state standards, laying the groundwork for national standards with national assessments.

A different effort, separate but related to the High School Reform initiative, is the Striving Readers initiative. In 2005 and 2006, the Striving Readers initiative was budgeted $24.8 million and $29.7 million, respectively (DOE, 2006b). The fiscal year 2007 budget included a request for $100 million to support the Striving Readers initiative. This over $70 million increase, one that far outstripped any increase requested at the elementary level, indicated the emphases held in the president's agenda for this effort, which could be termed "Reading First for the Older Grades" (grades 6–12). The $35 million actually approved for this budget, although short of what President Bush requested, still represents a 17.8 percent increase from the previous year (DOE, 2006a). The money from the Striving Readers initiative is granted to school districts and local organizations, sometimes in conjunction with state agencies of education, to implement and evaluate scientifically based researched reading interventions for students reading below grade level (DOE, 2006d, 2006e).

To this point, we have sketched a history of federal policy in terms of literacy education over the last half of the previous century and focused on the ways most recent federal policy prescribed how literacy was to be taught and assessed at the start of the current century. The next section is a critique of that policy, calling into question its needs to standardize and control what formally had been left to state and local districts to manage.

THE IMPACT OF FEDERAL POLICY ON LITERACY, TEACHING, AND LEARNING

One concern with current federal policy on adolescent literacy is that it remains skewed toward forces of standardization and allows for little, if any, local input and interpretation. It is policy intended to narrow definitions, limit critique and interpretation, and constrain the range of resources. The language is one of authority that seeks to monitor content and pedagogy in literacy classrooms through pervasive testing and restriction of resources. Although it purports to give more flexibility to local districts, in fact, that flexibility is dependent on raising test scores to unattainable levels, especially knowing the broad diversity of students and their needs being served by most schools and districts. As McCombs, Kirby, Barney, Darilek, and Magee (2005) indicated, the goal of 100 percent proficiency in reading, using either state tests or the NAEP, seems far-fetched given that few states are even above the 50 percent mark on either form of assessment.

In this section, we discuss the ways that NCLB created a limited view of literacy education, resulting in a range of responses, some disturbing and some proactive, on the part of parents, students, and educators in local districts. We argue that the standardizing pull of NCLB allows little room for a range of individualized, diversifying responses. As such, it prevents teachers, parents, and school districts from finding ways to accommodate local needs and infuse local critique. In short, NCLB provides no room for dialogue. In turn, we're seeing literacy education become less inclusive of diverse perspectives, public schools having their supports diminished, literacy teaching being driven by the narrow confines of state tests, and interested stakeholders suing the federal government for their voices to be heard.

The Politics of Exclusion

As noted earlier, the NRP report of 1998 was seen as a foundation for NCLB. According to Coles (2003) and also Edmonson (2004), the NRP was composed of educational stakeholders, most of whom held the narrow views of literacy education supported by National Institute of Child Health and Development leadership. Only one reading teacher was represented on the panel. Coles (2003) reported that even though public hearings were held, and much testimony was given by local and national educators as to the need to take wider sociocultural and anthropological views of the teaching of reading, the focus of the NRP going into the hearings—phonemic awareness, phonics, fluency, comprehension, and computer technology—remained the same after the hearings, and NCLB contains little in the way of literacy policy that has expanded that base.

An additional concern to us is that the provision that allows parents to remove their children from poorly performing schools and place them into schools that have higher performance indicators is both underfunded and without legal support. The better-performing schools are under no obligation to accept students from the struggling schools and often refuse to do so (Sunderland & Kim, 2004). Constructed primarily by governmental policy makers working within a narrow literacy paradigm, NCLB has a voice and tone that denies the complexities of the lives of those who are poor and disenfranchised.

Undermining Public Schools

Despite a mission that purports to be about supporting all children in their explorations of reading, NCLB routinely undermines schools serving students who are in the most need of support (Darling-Hammond, 2004). Although schools attended by children of the working poor, whether urban or rural, often draw on inadequate tax bases for funding and, consequently, are also resource-poor, few if any provisions in NCLB provide for equity in funding. As reported on National Public Radio (Allen, 2006), a Dade County, Florida, teachers' union spokesperson indicated that tying financial support for schools to test performance undermined the reform efforts of the testing policy. Stripped of resources and autonomy, struggling schools become mired in their inability to attract both human and financial resources to combat their struggles. When such schools performed poorly on standardized tests, their label of "failing school," along with prevailing stereotypes of working in such schools and the rigidity of structures put into place to restructure the school, make it difficult to attract creative, high-quality teachers, who frequently seek placements where a balanced degree of instructional autonomy and a range of resources support their efforts. Darling-Hammond (2004) cited a study by Clotfelter, Ladd, Vigdor, and Diaz (2003) that indicated ways in which the state of North Carolina was encountering difficulties attracting innovative teachers to struggling schools due to the state's labeling schools as not making average yearly progress.

Frequently, the mandates of policy have "potential to put our public schools into a state of chaos and crisis" (Holley-Walker, 2006). This potential for chaos lies in the growing number of schools that are being designated for restructuring, with some estimates as high as 10,000 schools needing restructuring by the year 2011. The consequences of so many schools undergoing major reform or closing are a logistical nightmare and show a deep lack of compassion for the needs of families. For many parents, the thought of their children being bussed from local neighborhoods is abhorrent and seems counter to traditional notions of community and neighborhood. In addition, all too often in the case of rural schools, there are no alternative schools ("Transfers and Tutoring," 2003).

In addition, cultural values differ as to how best to deal with struggling schools. A report by the Pew Hispanic Center (2004) indicated that although Latino families generally tended to support NCLB, they were also more likely to desire keeping struggling schools and their current populations intact and providing resources to those schools. This stance is in contrast to the inclination of many whites and the agenda of NCLB to move children elsewhere. Nothing in NCLB, as it is currently construed, provides for local interpretation of how best to contend with schools whose contexts present overwhelming obstacles to quick-fix reform.

Better Readers or Better Test-Takers?

As the vignette describing Chanel's quandary illustrated, teachers struggle with how to deliver instruction in this era of high-stakes accountability. Frequently, the choice comes down to a dichotomy: do educators teach in ways that will make students better readers, or do they teach in ways that will make students better test-takers? The two results do not necessarily occur through the same means or simultaneously.

An example of this dichotomy is exemplified through an examination of what was originally labeled the "Texas miracle" but, on closer examination, now might be called the "Texas myth" (Coles, 2003, pp. 116–118). As Coles noted, "If students pass a literacy test (e.g. the [Texas Assessment of Academic Skills]), that does not necessarily reveal their reading abilities" (p. 117). Work by Haney (2000) indicated that although TAAS scores had gone up dramatically, 4th-grade and 8th-grade NAEP scores for Texas had remained at the national average, showing virtually no gains. Five years after the Haney study, a report to the Carnegie Corporation (McCombs et al., 2005) raised similar questions. These researchers argued that differences in rigor and definitions of what counts as proficiency between state tests and the NAEP resulted in wildly divergent scores. For instance, Texas 8th graders passed the 2003 TAAS at a rate of 80 percent, although their NAEP scores indicated only 26 percent proficiency.

Aside from variances in rigor and expectations for the two tests, what mostly accounts for such wide divergences is that teachers, when faced with testing that can determine their futures, their schools' futures, and/or their students' futures, teach to the test, frequently to the exclusion of other subject matter (Coles, 2003). Although test-taking skills are important, a little instruction in this area goes a long way. Moreover, rather than a literacy education rich in text, story, and ideas, students are fed a steady diet of decontextualized, short readings for which little engagement is fostered. These activities tend to limit students' abilities to delve into longer, more complex text (Wood, 2004). Teachers like Chanel, who sense that their teaching of language and literacy needs to move students into complex interpretation, application, and synthesis of information, instead feel constrained by policy-initiated pressures to teach the narrow literacy skills measured by most standardized tests. To do otherwise, at least to their perception, puts teachers at jeopardy of losing their positions.

A perhaps more insidious way that schools raise scores is through exclusion of students who might not do well on the tests (Darling-Hammond, 2004). Since the rise of high-stakes testing, school administrations have committed such questionable practices as purging rolls of struggling students who might live outside district boundaries, adding more students to special education classes to gain dispensations that range from test exemptions to lowered benchmarks, holding students back to keep them out of test-taking grades, and encouraging struggling students to drop out of school. All these actions have been done in the name of raising test scores.

A Rise in Critical Response

A growing number of lawsuits by states and educational interest groups against NCLB are one indicator of frustration exhibited by local stakeholders regarding their inability to be heard by federal policy makers. Calling NCLB "the most sweeping intrusions into state and local control of education in the history of the United States," the Republican-controlled Virginia House of Representatives voted 98–1 to ignore NCLB policy, even at the cost of loss of revenues (Becker & Helderman, 2004, p. A1) This lawmaking body felt that NCLB negated or obstructed their own statewide efforts to advance literacy education. The National Education Association (NEA), in concert with six states and the District of Columbia, initiated a civil suit against the U.S. Department of Education with the intent of forcing the federal government not only to fund their mandates, but to reallocate such funding to allow for greater local control of those monies. As the NEA stated, "local communities are simply asking the Bush administration to allow parents to spend hard-earned tax dollars on their children's classrooms—not bureaucracy, paperwork and testing companies" (National Education Association, 2006, p. 2).

Organizations like the National Association for the Advancement of Colored People and the National Council of La Raza, groups representing parents whose children have frequently been left behind in the past, have raised concerns about the effectiveness of NCLB regarding their constituencies and the lack of funding to support the work (National Association for the Advancement of Colored People, 2003; National Council of La Raza, 2002). Simultaneously, professional teaching organizations, such as the National Council of Teachers of English and the International Reading Association, whose rich and broad body of research has largely been ignored by federal policy makers, have raised questions about of the narrowness of NCLB (International Reading Association, 2001; National Council of Teachers of English, 2002).

In addition, there is an ever-growing body of research that indicates that educational reform must take local stakeholders into account (Allington, 2002). For example, a policy brief by a nonprofit research organization described a study that they conducted of recent and tumultuous reform in the Philadelphia School District (Research for Action, 2002). The report cited five lessons learned from that experience, four of which specifically speak to the problems caused when policy makers are unwilling to include a means for dialogue with local stakeholders when making policy (Christman & Rhodes, 2002). The researchers argued that school reform should be forged in the spirit of collaboration, particularly with the intent for reform leaders to value the input of principals, teachers, and parents. Without such invited dialogue, local stakeholders have little substantive access through which to shape policy.

CONCLUSION

Our analysis of current federal literacy policy, particularly as it manifests in the No Child Left Behind Act, leads us to several guidelines for constructing literacy policies for adolescents. First, local, state, and national discussions of educational policy that seek inclusion of the greatest number of diverse voices can produce substantive dialogue that enables the enactment of reflective policy that opens itself to future reconsideration. We envision effective policy as a framework from which all stakeholders continually build new iterations of policy.

Second, policies must be forward looking. They should be responsive to adolescents of the moment, yet contain provisions to address the educational needs of the future. We must stop educating children living in the twenty-first century for contexts and conditions that were operative in the mid-twentieth century. Instead, we should embrace a sense of literacy as a practice that allows all students, particularly students who are marginalized by social and cultural conditions, to use literacy as a means for making meaning of an ever more complex, diverse, technological, and globalized world.

Third, adolescent literacy policies must begin with a careful consideration of the developmental and learning needs of this age group. Policies must resonate with youth's literacy practices both in and out of school. Policy should reflect and prompt young people's interest in new forms of literacy across multiple modalities and a range of new media. Current literacy theory provides a critical knowledge base for conceptualizing the practices and content of this policy.

Finally, policy should create opportunities for dialogue with local stakeholders. We believe that the further the authority is from the constituency it serves, and the greater that constituency is in number, the more general and open-ended the educational policy needs to be. Policy written in Washington, D.C., to serve schools as diverse as those in Patagonia, Arizona, and Philadelphia needs to serve as a discussion point from which local policy can be evolved, rather than as a mandate that all must follow.

In the end, we acknowledge one simple belief: ignoring local voice in the creation, implementation, and refinement of policy does not mean that such voices are stilled. Teachers like Chanel—strong, creative, intelligent teachers who are professionally active and see their classrooms as places of reflection and negotiation—have engaged, do engage, and will continue to engage in dialogue with and locally interpret national policy, even though policy makers may turn a deaf ear to such dialogue. The parents of the students in Chanel's classroom as well as those students themselves will regard or disregard policy as they see fit. The informality of this process—frequently falling off the radar of policy makers—does not negate its existence and eventual impact. Policy that addresses adolescents' literacy learning and their teachers' practices should be responsive to students' and educators' needs as well as to the needs of other local stakeholders. It is incumbent on legislators to reach out to the teachers, students, and parents who embody the life of those schools, embracing their complexities and incorporating their needs and desires into policy that remains ever in dialogue.

REFERENCES

Allen, G. (Reporter). (2006, September 22). *Bush education legacy spices up Florida gov. race* [Radio broadcast]. Washington, DC: National Public Radio. Retrieved October 2, 2006, from http://www.npr.org/templates/story/story.php?storyId=6123055

Allington, R. L. (2002). *Big brother and the national reading curriculum.* Portsmouth, NH: Heinemann.

Bakhtin, M. M. (1981). *The dialogic imagination: Four essays* (M. Holquist, Ed., & C. Emerson & M. Holquist, Trans.). Austin: University of Texas Press.

Becker, J., & Helderman, R. (2004, January 24). Va. seeks to leave Bush law behind: Republicans fight school mandates. *The Washington Post,* p. A1.

Christman, J. B., & Rhodes, A. (2002). *Civic engagement and urban school improvement: Hard-to-learn lessons from Philadelphia.* Philadelphia: Research for Action.

Civil Rights Act, 42 U.S.C. § 241. (1964).

Clotfelter, C., Ladd, H., Vigdor, J., & Diaz, R. (2003, February). *Do school accountability systems make it more difficult for low-performing schools to attract and retain high-quality teachers?* Paper presented at the Annual Meeting of the American Economic Association, Washington, DC.

Coles, G. (2003). *Reading the naked truth: Literacy, legislation, and lies.* Portsmouth, NH: Heinemann.

Darling-Hammond, L. (2004). From "separate but equal" to "No Child Left Behind": The collision of new standards and old inequalities. In D. Meier & G. Wood (Eds.), *Many children left behind: How the No Child Left Behind Act is damaging our children and our schools* (pp. 3–32). Boston: Beacon Press.

Dillon, S. (2005, November 26). Students ace state tests, but earn D's from U.S. *The New York Times.*

Edmonson, J. (2000). *America reads: A critical policy analysis.* Newark, DE: International Reading Association.

Edmonson, J. (2004). *Understanding and applying critical policy study: Reading educators advocating for change.* Newark, DE: International Reading Association.

Elementary and Secondary Education Act, 20 U.S.C. § 70. (1965).

Georgia Department of Education. (2005a). *Georgia end-of-course tests: Information brochure 2005* [Brochure]. Retrieved October 2, 2006, from http://www.doe.k12.ga.us/_doc uments/curriculum/testing/eoct_brochure.pdf

Georgia Department of Education. (2005b). *Georgia standards.org: Gateway to education and professional resources*. Retrieved October 2, 2006, from http://www.georgiastan dards.org

Haney, W. (2000). The myth of the Texas miracle in education: Pt. 7: Other evidence on education in Texas. Retrieved October 2, 2006, from http://epaa.asu.edu/epaa/v8n41

Holley-Walker, D. (2006, September). *The No Child Left Behind Act: Are we saving or ruining our public schools?* Retrieved October 2, 2006, from http://www.susanohanian. org/show_nclb_outrages.html?id=2298

International Reading Association. (2001). *On US government policy on the teaching of reading*. Retrieved March 23, 2004, from http://www.reading.org/resources/issues/posi tions_us_government.html

McCombs, J. S., Kirby, S. N., Barney, H., Darilek, H., & Magee, S. (2005). *Achieving state and national literacy goals, a long uphill road: A report to Carnegie Corporation of New York*. Santa Monica, CA: Rand Education.

National Association for the Advancement of Colored People. (2003). *NAACP opposition to school vouchers*. Retrieved March 23, 2004, from http://www.naacp.org/work/wash ington_bureau/SchoolVouchers093003.shtml

National Commission on Excellence in Education. (1983). *A nation at risk: The imperative for educational reform*. Retrieved November 17, 2006, from http://www.ed.gov/pubs/ NatAtRisk/index.html

National Council of La Raza. (2002). *The No Child Left Behind Act: Implications for local educators and advocates for Latino students, families, and communities*. Retrieved February 13, 2004, from http://www.nclr.org/content/publications/detail/1391/

National Council of Teachers of English. (2002). *NCTE resolution on the Reading First initiative*. Retrieved February 13, 2004, from http://www.ncte.org/about/over/posi tions/category/read/107475.htm?source=gs

National Education Association. (2006). *Stand up for children: Pontiac vs. Spellings*. Retrieved October 2, 2006, from http://www.nea.org/lawsuit/index.html

National Institute of Child Health and Human Development. (2000). *Report of the National Reading Panel. Teaching children to read: An evidence-based assessment of the scientific research literature on reading and its implications for reading instruction: Reports of the subgroups* (NIH Publication No. 00-4754). Washington, DC: U.S. Government Printing Office.

No Child Left Behind Act, 20 U.S.C. § 6301 (2001).

Pew Hispanic Center. (2004). *National survey of Latinos: Education*. Retrieved September 15, 2006, from http://pewhispanic.org/files/factsheets/7.pdf

Research for Action. (2002, Fall). *Lesson from Philadelphia about building civic capacity for school reform* [Policy brief]. Philadelphia: Author.

Sunderland, G. L., & Kim, J. (2004). *Inspiring vision, disappointing results: Four studies on implementing the No Child Left Behind Act*. Retrieved February 15, 2004, from http:// www.civilrightsproject.harvard.edu/research/esea/introduction.pdf

Thomas B. Fordham Foundation. (1998). *A nation "still" at risk: A manifesto*. Washington, DC: Author. (ERIC Document Reproduction Service No. ED422455)

Transfers and tutoring. (2003, Winter/Spring). *Fair Test Examiner, 17* 24–25. Retrieved June 18, 2007, from http://www.fairtest.org/examarts/wint-spring%2003%20double/ transfers_and_tutoring.html

U.S. Department of Education. (2003). *Remarks of Secretary Paige at the Partners in Hispanic Education "Education Fair."* Retrieved May 23, 2006, from http://www.ed.gov/news/speeches/2003/12/12062003.html

U.S. Department of Education. (2005a). *No Child Left Behind: Expanding the promise— Guide to President Bush's FY 2006 education agenda.* Retrieved March 26, 2006, from http://www.ed.gov/about/overview/budget/budget06/nclb/

U.S. Department of Education. (2005b). *Preliminary overview of programs and changes included in the No Child Left Behind Act of 2001.* Retrieved February 21, 2006, from http://www.ed.gov/nclb/overview/intro/progsum/sum_pg5.html

U.S. Department of Education. (2005c). *Welcome to ED.gov/highschool from the Office of Vocational and Adult Education.* Retrieved March 26, 2006, from http://www.ed.gov/about/offices/list/ovae/pi/hs/index.html

U.S. Department of Education. (2006a). *Department of Education fiscal year 2007 congressional action—July 24, 2006.* Retrieved September 29, 2006, from http://www.ed.gov/about/overview/budget/budget07/07action.pdf

U.S. Department of Education. (2006b). *Fiscal year 2007 budget summary—February 6, 2006.* Retrieved May 23, 2006, from http://www.ed.gov/about/overview/budget/budget07/summary/edlite-section1.html

U.S. Department of Education. (2006c). *FY 2007 budget summary: Table of contents, Appendix 1: Summary of discretionary funds, fiscal years 2001–2007.* Retrieved May 23, 2006, from http://www.ed.gov/about/overview/budget/budget07/summary/index.html

U.S. Department of Education. (2006d). *Helping readers achieve and succeed.* Retrieved May 23, 2006, from http://www.ed.gov/nclb/methods/reading/strivingreaders.html

U.S. Department of Education. (2006e). *Striving readers: Purpose.* Retrieved May 23, 2006, from http://www.ed.gov/programs/strivingreaders/index.html

Wirt, F. M., & Kirst, M. W. (1997). *Political dynamics of American education.* Berkeley, CA: McCutchan.

Wood, G. (2004). A view from the field: NCLB's effects on classrooms and schools. In D. Meier & G. Wood (Eds.), *Many children left behind: How the No Child Left Behind Act is damaging our children and our schools* (pp. 33–50). Boston: Beacon Press.

Chapter Four

READING ASSESSMENT FOR ADOLESCENTS

Terry Salinger

There is no shortage of criticism for the amount of testing students experience as they progress through school and for the instruments used to measure their achievement. One need only access the Web site of the National Center for Fair and Open Testing, or FairTest (see http://www.fairtest.org), to find what educators, policy makers, and parents have to say. Rather than enter into the debate about the appropriateness of testing, this chapter strives for objectivity by providing information that may be useful for understanding the most common forms of reading tests students encounter during the middle and high school period. To that end, the chapter discusses the different kinds of tests students in middle and high schools most commonly take, how the tests define reading for adolescents, what the tests measure, why they are administered, and how their data can be used. Details from the state board of education Web site of a southeastern state are used for illustrative purposes, as are the hypothetical experiences of one student in this state. The chapter does not state whether this adolescent student, referred to as Amanda, has taken too many tests, but it docs present the case that at least some of her reading tests have played a significant role in her life as a middle and high school student.

For this chapter, adolescence is defined as the grade 5–12 span. Even though this range may seem a wide range to use as the boundaries of adolescence, there are solid reasons for thinking about assessment across this span. In a 2002 workshop on adolescent literacy sponsored by the National Institute of Child Health and Human Development (2002), participants agreed that extending the term *adolescent* down to 4th or 5th grade made sense, in part because it is at this point in students' progression through school that they must transition to more sophisticated uses of reading and writing as their classes require them to read texts that cover many different topics, vary in readability level, and actually may not be well written (Caldwell & Leslie, 2004).

There is further support for this span of grades in the idea of the so-called 4th-grade slump, which Chall (1967) introduced to the educational vernacular nearly four decades ago. She pointed out that it is at this point that students must move from learning to read to reading to learn. Many students are prepared well enough to avoid this slump and make the transition to more sophisticated reading with ease, but others begin to struggle both in their content work and on the large number of tests that will continue to mark them as poor readers.

DEFINITIONS OF READING FOR ASSESSMENTS

Knowing the underlying definition of reading that guided the development of a test is an important component of understanding what the test actually measures. At the same time, figuring out how to define reading for this age group can be challenging because adolescents read in many different contexts, both in and out of school, and for many different purposes. Adolescents' out-of-school reading may be widely different from in-school reading: they surf the Web, send and receive e-mails, and immerse themselves in comics and graphic novels. The personal relevance of this reading motivates and engages students in ways that textbooks and literature anthologies rarely do. The extent to which these activities strengthen adolescents' skills and enable them to continue to grow as readers, however, is probably idiosyncratic because they may not encourage students to use or develop the entire range of reading strategies that constitute a full reading repertoire.

The fuller repertoire that defines reading for this age group includes skills and strategies that enable adolescents to read complex, extended narrative and expository texts. Strong readers comprehend these texts by understanding the nuances of language and text structure, identifying relationships within and across texts; making generalizations and drawing conclusions; judging authenticity and accuracy; analyzing and evaluating content; and engaging in other sophisticated interactions with text. Indeed, ACT Inc., publisher of the placement and selection tests that many adolescents take, found that this repertoire of reading behaviors is essential if students are going to be ready for the reading demands not just of postsecondary education, but also of the workplace (ACT Inc., 2006). ACT Inc. reached this conclusion after comparing the reading American College Test (ACT) scores of many thousands of students and their levels of success in postsecondary endeavors, including both college study and the workplace. Being ready, according to ACT Inc., means being able to read complex texts, ones that exhibit subtle, involved relationships among ideas or characters; rich and sophisticated information; elaborate structural elements and intricate stylistic elements; and demanding vocabulary. Being able to read texts of this sort in many different content areas is often referred to as academic literacy, to distinguish it from much of the reading students do out of school (Fielding, Schoenbach, & Jordan, 2003).

Academic literacy is the broad construct that most reading tests for adolescents purport to measure, but by no means are all reading tests interchangeable (National Research Council, 1999). Test developers differ widely in how they operationalize this construct through selection of the stimulus materials students will read, the formats and difficulty of items they will answer, and the interpretation that can be made from students' scores on the tests. Furthermore, test users, such as state boards of education, differ in their own interpretation of what adolescent reading means and what level of achievement constitutes reading on grade level or at more broadly defined levels such as basic, proficient, and advanced. These are the levels used on the National Assessment of Educational Progress (NAEP), and even though states may employ this terminology, they do not necessarily adopt the same rigorous expectations for achievement that NAEP uses. States routinely engage teachers and others in a so-called standard setting process that determines how many items students need to get right to pass a test and to score within certain score ranges, and there is a vast difference in how rigorous the standards are (National Research Council, 1999).

As discussed elsewhere in these volumes (see Salinger & Kapinus, 2007), the NAEP in Reading is in many ways the gold standard of reading tests. One important aspect of this model is the rigor of the definition of reading that underpins the NAEP reading tests at grades 4, 8, and 12. Even at grade 4, students are assessed on their ability to make sense of text by inferring, evaluating, analyzing, critiquing author's craft, using information from several parts of a text, and even making comparisons across two texts on the same topic or theme. Certainly there are relatively easy items on each NAEP reading test, but the specifications for the test direct test developers to include lengthy, intact passages and to construct items to measure high levels of thinking.

Many states and commercial test developers have adopted the NAEP model of test development by using fairly long, authentic passages and asking multiple choice and open-ended questions that target different levels of comprehension. However, even though a reading test may superficially seem similar to the NAEP model, there is wide variety in the way in which the construct *reading comprehension* is interpreted (National Research Council, 1999). Depending on what test users want, test developers may take a constructivist stance toward reading and include questions that ask students to think of personal reactions or connections to what they read. Others are more cognitively grounded, even to the extent of basing items on the hierarchy of Bloom's taxonomy of the cognitive domain (knowledge, understanding, application, analysis, synthesis, and evaluation; Bloom, 1956; Krathwohl, Bloom, & Bertram, 1973).

The reading test in the state used for illustrative purposes is aligned to the state standards for reading and consists of items that measure four aspects of reading: cognition, interpretation, critical stance, and connections. Table 4.1 shows how each aspect of reading is described and its percentage of representation on the tests administered in the state at grades 5–8 (North Carolina State Board of Education [NCSBE], 2006c). The descriptions of the aspects of reading are very similar to those included the 1992–2008 National Assessment of Educational Progress in Reading (Council of Chief State School Officers, 1992; Salinger & Kapinus, 2007), suggesting that the test has a constructivist foundation. The reading items are also aligned to the state's thinking skills framework to affirm the value placed on critical thinking and reasoning. The items then reflect both the NAEP constructivist perspective and also a cognitive interpretation of reading.

This state undertook its own test development effort and involved educators in creating a test that would operationalize the standards that tell what students should know and be able to do in reading at each grade level. The tests are criterion-referenced; that is, students' scores are compared against an established list of learning objectives derived from the standards. Criterion-reference tests state a mastery level, that is, a percentage of items that an individual must get correct to indicate mastery of the material assessed. Data derived from the tests help state and local education agencies, teachers, parents, students, and others understand how well students are progressing along a developmental continuum of reading growth.

Other states opt to use a commercial test that has been normed against a nationally representative sample. With such a test, administrators can compare their students' scores against those of students in the same grade who have taken the test nationwide. Commercial testing programs will often tailor a norm-reference test like the Stanford Achievement Test or the Iowa Test of Basic Skills (ITBS) by including sets of items that have been developed by state educators to measure their state standards or by carefully demonstrating the link between items on the test and the state reading standards.

PURPOSES FOR ASSESSING STUDENTS' READING

As stated earlier, many critics oppose any testing at all, and others assert quite appropriately that students are tested far too often. The current emphasis on testing, especially as required by the No Child Left Behind (NCLB) Act of 2001, has meant that many teachers spend a disproportionate amount of time teaching students the specific skills included on a test, rather than teaching them the content, skills, and strategies that will not only prepare them for the test, but will also generalize to other learning situations. Critics and teaching

Table 4.1
Descriptive Information for Grade 7 End-of-Year Reading Test

Category	Description of category	Percent of test items by grade			
		5th	6th	7th	8th
Cognition	Refers to the initial strategies a reader uses to understand the selection. It considers the text as a whole or in a broad perspective. Cognition includes strategies like context clues to determine meaning or summarizing the main points.	35	29	26	29
Interpretation	Requires the student to develop a more complex understanding. It may ask a student to clarify, to explain the significance of, or to extend and/or adapt ideas/concepts.	39	40	42	40
Critical stance	Refers to tasks that ask student to stand apart from the selection and consider it objectively. It involves processes like comparing/contrasting and understanding the impact of literary elements.	20	25	26	25
Connections	Refers to connecting knowledge from the selection with other information and experiences. It involves the student being able to relate the selection to events beyond/outside the selection. In addition, the student will make associations outside the selection and between selections.	6	6	6	6

Source: North Carolina State Board of Education. (2006). *North Carolina end-of-grade test of reading comprehension—Grade 7.* Retrieved October 28, 2006, from http://www.dpi.state.nc.us/docs/account ability/testing/eog/TISG7-2.pdf

to the test aside, there are several important reasons for measuring students' academic literacy. Among the most important is to determine accountability and diagnose reading difficulties. Many adolescents take another kind of reading test, one that is used for selection purposes. These forms of testing are discussed next.

ACCOUNTABILITY TESTING

The state reading assessments whose contents are discussed in Table 4.1 are used to take a measure of how well individual students and groups of students within schools, districts, and the state as a whole are doing in reading. The tests are part of the state's mechanisms for holding districts and schools account-able for teaching students the content included on the state standards. Data from accountability tests, which are often administered near the end of the school year, as in this state, are also reported to the federal government as a measures of schools' adequate yearly progress (AYP). Accountability data can usually be disaggregated to allow for comparisons of different focal groups, for example, according to gender, disability, language status, race/ethnicity, or size of school.

In addition to showing how well individual students are actually learning to read, these comparisons suggest where resources, such as professional develop-ment for teachers or provision of intervention or remedial help for students, should be provided. For example, if data from administration of the reading test at the end of the school year show that the lowest-scoring students in a district are the ones for whom English is a second language, additional profes-sional development might be provided to help teachers improve their skills for working with these students. Likewise, gaps in scores between students in rural or urban areas might motivate policy makers at the state level to expend extra resources to address the differentials.

Accountability tests can be used to generate comparisons of individual students, most appropriately at the school level, and to identify students who might benefit from supplemental services such as attendance in a gifted pro-gram or in an intervention class to improve skills. Provision of an interven-tion class is especially warranted if test scores carry specific consequences with them, as reading test scores often do. Consequences include promo-tion or retention in grade or even conferral or withholding of a high school diploma.

To illustrate at a more personal level how accountability testing can be used, let us consider the hypothetical case of Amanda, a 7th grader in a middle school in the illustrative state. By the time Amanda reached grade 7, she had taken reading tests aligned to the state standards at the end of grades 3–6. The reading test she needed to take at the end of grade 7 was aligned to the fol-lowing reading standards:

> Seventh grade students use oral language, written language, and media and tech-nology for expressive, informational, argumentative, critical, and literary purposes. Students also explore the structure of language and study grammatical rules in order to speak and write effectively. While emphasis in seventh grade is placed on argu-ment, students also:
>
> • Express individual perspectives in response to personal, social, cultural, and histori-cal issues.
> • Interpret and synthesize information.
> • Critically analyze print and non-print communication.

for young adolescents to participate in decision-making" and "encourage collaborative learning and problem solving" (p. 57).

The goal of exploratory programs in the middle schools is "to make the adult world more familiar" (Waks, 2002, p. 37). Exploratory programs offer regularly scheduled classes in a variety of special interest areas. Young adolescents are at an age when they are beginning to learn how to consider options and make informed choices. Exploratory programs are designed to help students in this endeavor as well as learn about and pursue their interests and talents. Students should be free to choose their own exploratory courses and base their choices on their own interests, rather than on the interests and choices of their friends.

Given the changes that middle school students are going through, it is critical that they have teachers who have the necessary training and experience to work with young adolescents. Ideally, this training and experience involve not only course work in adolescent development, but also course work in how to teach young adolescents by taking into account the nature of the curriculum and the needs of young adolescents.

COMPONENTS OF SUCCESSFUL MIDDLE SCHOOL LITERACY PROGRAMS

What do successful middle school literacy programs look like? Successful middle school literacy programs are developed around the key components of successful middle schools previously described. First and foremost, they are developed around the needs of young adolescents and take into account the changes that students are undergoing. In successful middle school literacy programs, interdisciplinary teams of teachers plan ways to incorporate the language arts into their content area lessons. All teachers are knowledgeable not only about their own content area material and how to teach it, but also about young adolescent development, how to teach reading and writing, and how to integrate the language arts into their content areas. Teachers plan together to ensure that the curriculum is integrated and that it focuses on higher-order skills. Successful literacy programs build on the school's exploratory program by allowing students to pursue their own interests and talents and by providing them with opportunities to make choices.

In their report for the Alliance for Excellent Education, Biancarosa and Snow (2004) identified 15 components for successful adolescent literacy programs. These components are as follows:

1. *Direct teaching of comprehension skills.* Comprehension skills are explicitly taught and modeled, and students are provided with time to practice them.
2. *Contextually embedded instruction.* Instruction is implemented within and across content areas and focuses on content area texts and tasks.

3. *Motivation and self-directed learning.* Instruction focuses on developing motivated and self-directed learners.
4. *Collaborative learning.* Instruction focuses on helping students use text to learn in collaboration with other students.
5. *Tutoring.* Struggling or striving readers receive individualized, targeted instruction to promote independent learning.
6. *Text variety.* Students are exposed to a wide variety of texts with different styles, topics, and difficulty levels.
7. *Concentrated writing.* Writing instruction is implemented within and across content areas and focuses on content area texts and tasks.
8. *Technology.* Students learn to use technology as a means of integrating reading and writing into their content area learning.
9. *Formative assessment.* Ongoing assessment is used to guide instruction.
10. *Extended time.* Literacy instruction takes place over several periods and is integrated across the content areas.
11. *Teacher development.* Professional development for teachers is guided by teacher needs and is an ongoing process.
12. *Summative assessment.* Assessment focuses on student progress and is used for program development.
13. *Interdisciplinary teams.* Small groups of teachers from the content areas collaborate to focus on individual student and group needs.
14. *Leadership.* Administrators support the literacy program and promote leadership among teachers.
15. *Comprehensive program.* The literacy program focuses on reading, writing, listening, and speaking within and across the content areas, with a particular emphasis on student needs.

What do literacy programs that are built around these 15 components look like? In successful programs, all teachers promote the language development of young adolescents. This means that communication, dialogue, discussion, and interaction between the teacher and the students, and the students themselves, are crucial elements of learning. Activities in which students interact with the teacher and with each other characterize successful programs. Students play an active role in their learning and use their literacy skills to extend their learning. Students receive formal instruction in effective listening and speaking skills. Activities that integrate reading, writing, listening, and speaking with content area material are essential. Play writing and performances, role-playing, improvisation, poetry readings, journal writing, and peer editing are frequently used to integrate language arts into the curriculum and to capitalize on the social nature of young adolescents.

An important outcome of a successful literacy program is that students engage in reading and writing for enjoyment as well as for learning. Accordingly, opportunities are provided for students to read and write recreationally in all content areas. Recreational reading allows middle school students to read, at their own pace, from sources of their own choosing. Similarly, recreational writing provides students with opportunities to write without having to concentrate on form, punctuation, and spelling and without worrying about sharing their writing with others. When students are read aloud to, the intent is to provide them with informal opportunities to respond and react to what they are hearing. Reading aloud to students also establishes a common starting point for class discussions and other activities.

In successful programs, teachers focus on student learning that makes connections across disciplines, rather than on student learning that focuses exclusively on the memorization of facts within a particular discipline. Teaching occurs in a manner that facilitates students' learning as an active, constructive process, rather than as a passive, reproductive process. Students are active participants in their own learning so that they can learn new material in relevant ways.

ROLE OF CLASSROOM TEACHERS

Teacher quality is perhaps the single most important school-related factor influencing student achievement (Rice, 2003). Given the increasing emphasis on integrated curricula in the middle grades, all teachers, regardless of the subjects they teach, are being called on to integrate the language arts into their subjects. A key recommendation of the NASBE (2006) is that "state plans must target improving literacy skills by teaching them within the context of core academic subjects, rather than apart from challenging content instruction" (p. 5).

Unfortunately, many content area middle school teachers see themselves as content area specialists, and they are reluctant to take time away from their content to teach literacy skills. Also, many teachers have not received sufficient training in how to incorporate the language arts into their teaching. Commendably, many states are in the process of redefining the requirements for pre- and in-service middle school teachers in the area of literacy instruction. Many states are also beginning to offer special certification in adolescent literacy as well as professional development in literacy instruction and literacy mentoring programs (NGACBP, 2005). In terms of professional development for in-service teachers, the NGACBP (2005) recommends that such training be systemic, sustained, and focused on the following activities:

- analyzing student performance data to identify gaps and set school performance goals;
- matching instruction to student needs based on student assessment data;
- promoting collaboration among educators; and
- assigning school personnel roles to support literacy improvement. (p. 8)

What exactly are the roles of effective classroom teachers in a schoolwide literacy program for young adolescents? Farnan (2000) identified four broad roles of effective classroom teachers in a middle school literacy program. First, effective teachers are reflective practitioners who focus on problem-solving and decision making. This means that teachers know the role that literacy plays in the content they teach. They also know the literacy skills students need to learn the content, and they are able to teach and assess those skills. Being a reflective practitioner implies asking questions about your teaching; asking questions is consistent with the view of teachers as researchers who carry out action research projects. Action research can be conducted by individual teachers or by teams of teachers. Using the team approach, ideas for such projects are generated by team members and center on questions and concerns they have about their own practice. Teachers then publish their results in practitioner-oriented journals.

The second role of effective classroom teachers in a middle school literacy program is that of collaborators. This role is particularly important at the middle school level given a focus on interdisciplinary teams. As collaborators, team members plan together to integrate the curriculum and to integrate the language arts into the curriculum. They reflect, solve problems, and make decisions together about student needs and progress. They collect and analyze student data on authentic literacy tasks and then use the results to plan the curriculum. They read and discuss current literacy research together and discuss ways to apply it to their teaching. This notion of teachers as collaborators is ideally suited to help teachers grapple with the complex issues that confront them daily. It is particularly important to beginning teachers as it helps them overcome the feeling of isolation that many of them feel. Farnan (2000) identified several other positive literacy outcomes from teachers working as collaborators, including "increased teacher expertise and professionalism, enhanced student achievement, and an increasing focus on effective classroom practice" (p. 11).

Farnan's (2000) third role for effective classroom teachers is serving as active professionals and leaders. This role implies that content area teachers stay informed and view themselves as lifelong learners. According to Farnan, teachers "attend conferences; read professional journals and books; participate in collegial forums in which ideas, concerns, and insights are exchanged; disseminate information from their action research projects; and participate in graduate programs" (p. 11). Being active professional leaders helps content area teachers incorporate research-based literacy strategies into their teaching. In this role, content area teachers are active in professional organizations, such as the National Science Teachers' Association (NSTA), the National Council for the Social Studies (NCSS), and the National Council of Teachers of Mathematics (NCTM), and they also are well informed about current research in the language arts through the publications of organizations such as the International Reading Association (IRA) and the National Council of

Teachers of English (NCTE). In this role, content area teachers also become familiar with the curriculum standards for middle school English, language arts, and reading, published jointly by IRA, NCTE, and the University of Illinois's Center for the Study of Reading. These standards help content area teachers learn exactly what middle school students should know and be able to do in language arts and what role they, as content area specialists, can play in helping students become proficient in these standards.

The fourth role is that of teachers as mentors. It is well known that the teaching profession has a high attrition rate, with estimates ranging from 30 to 50 percent of new teachers leaving within the first five years of teaching. One cause of this high attrition rate is teacher burnout due to inability to cope with challenges that they view as insurmountable. As Farnan (2000) pointed out, new teachers are still novices who need continued mentoring, and successful teachers can serve as powerful mentors. Many beginning teachers struggle with learning the content and the best ways to teach it, and they sometimes lose sight of the fact that incorporating literacy instruction into their teaching is critical if students are to learn the material. Experienced content area teachers, especially those on interdisciplinary teams, are in a unique position to mentor the beginning teachers in their schools, and especially those on their teams. Simple activities, such as visiting others' classrooms and sharing advice on how to incorporate literacy instruction into the lessons, are typically welcomed by beginning teachers.

ROLE OF THE LITERACY COACH

Given the important roles that content area teachers play in middle school literacy programs, how can they possibly keep up with their own content areas and still find time to stay abreast of the current research in the language arts and how best to incorporate literacy instruction into their teaching? How can the one or two courses in content area reading and writing that teachers take in their teaching training programs prepare them to meet the literacy needs of their students? Fortunately, professional organizations have recognized the enormous challenge that content area teachers face not only to teach their content, but also to help their students develop their literacy skills. IRA, with support from the Carnegie Corporation of New York and in collaboration with NCTE, NCTM, NSTA, and NCSS, has developed standards for middle school literacy coaches. IRA anticipates that the standards will be used by numerous audiences, including administrators, school boards, principals, team leaders, parents, university faculty, and accrediting agencies. According to IRA, literacy coaches should play a critical role in successful middle school literacy programs. What exactly are literacy coaches, and what do they do? We answer these questions in this section.

What Are Literacy Coaches?

Literacy coaches in middle schools are literacy experts who "coach content area teachers in the upper grades who currently lack the capacity and confidence (and sometimes the drive) to teach reading strategies to students particular to their disciplines" (International Reading Association [IRA], 2006, p. 2). Snow, Ippolito, and Schwartz (2006) identified the qualifications for becoming a middle school literacy coach. These qualifications include a strong foundation in literacy, strong leadership skills, working knowledge of adult learning, familiarity with young adolescents, and excellent teaching skills. In addition, it is helpful if literacy coaches have experience in specific content areas, excellent communication and presentation skills, and strong interpersonal skills. Ideally, literacy coaches should have at least a master's degree in literacy or a reading endorsement. The standards for literacy coaches are divided into two areas: three leadership standards and one content area standard:

> Leadership Standard 1: *Skillful Collaborators.* Middle school "content area coaches are skilled collaborators who function effectively in [the] middle school . . . setting" (IRA, 2006, p. 5).
> Leadership Standard 2: *Skillful, Job-Embedded Coaches.* "Content area literacy coaches are skilled instructional coaches for . . . teachers in the core content areas of English language arts, mathematics, science, and social studies" (IRA, 2006, p. 5).
> Leadership Standard 3: *Skillful Evaluator of Literacy Needs.* "Content area literacy coaches are skilled evaluators of literacy needs within various subject areas and are able to collaborate with . . . school leadership teams and teachers to interpret and use assessment data to inform instruction" (IRA, 2006, p. 5).
> Content Area Standard 4: *Skillful Instructional Strategists.* "Content area literacy coaches are accomplished middle . . . school teachers who are skilled in developing and implementing instructional strategies to improve academic literacy in the specific content areas" (IRA, 2006, p. 5).

As IRA (2006) pointed out, the preceding standards represent ideals. Becoming an accomplished literacy coach requires extensive, targeted professional development over several years. It also requires constant professional development over a career.

What Do Literacy Coaches Do?

The primary responsibility of literacy coaches is to provide professional development in literacy to teachers. According to IRA (2006), the professional development that literacy coaches provide should be guided by the following four features of successful professional development:

> grounded in inquiry and reflection; participant driven and collaborative, involving a sharing of knowledge among teachers within communities of practice; sustained,

ongoing, and intensive; and connected to and derived from teachers' ongoing work with their students. (p. 3)

Literacy specialists are responsible for coordinating the schoolwide literacy programs that are developed around the needs of young adolescents. What does this involve? Within the literacy coach standards, IRA delineated seven elements that specify the literacy coach's key responsibilities. They are as follows:

Element 1.1. "Working with the school's literacy team, literacy coaches determine the school's strengths (and need for improvement) in the area of literacy in order to improve students' reading, writing, and communication skills and content area achievement" (IRA, 2006, p. 8). Activities related to this element include working with a literacy team to conduct a schoolwide literacy assessment and communicating the findings to the staff, leading discussions with teachers about problems they face, and working with the staff to align the curriculum to state and district standards.

Element 1.2. "Literacy coaches promote productive relationships with and among school staff" (IRA, 2006, p. 9). Specific activities for this element include becoming familiar with the literacy needs and concerns of the staff, responding to requests for help from teachers, facilitating literacy discussions among teachers, and keeping administrators informed and soliciting their support for the literacy program.

Element 1.3. "Literacy coaches strengthen their professional teaching knowledge, skills, and strategies" (IRA, 2006, p. 11). This element stipulates that literacy coaches read and apply current literacy research, meeting regularly with other coaches, and attend professional conferences and training to keep abreast of the field.

Element 2.1. "Literacy coaches work with teachers individually, in collaborative teams, and/or with departments, providing practical support on a full range of reading, writing, and communication strategies" (IRA, 2006, p. 11). Specifically, literacy coaches help teachers select textbooks, plan instruction around the textbook, and select literacy strategies to support instruction; provide professional development to teachers; and help teachers link research to their practice.

Element 2.2. "Literacy coaches observe and provide feedback to teachers on instruction related to literacy development and content area knowledge" (IRA, 2006, p. 15). Literacy coaches' feedback to teachers should prompt discussion, identify strengths and areas for improvement, and focus on future goals; literacy coaches can also give demonstration lessons to teachers and teams. Demonstration lessons can be videotaped for other teachers in the school and used for simulated recall sessions with groups of teachers.

Element 3.1. "Literacy coaches lead faculty in the selection and use of a range of assessment tools as a means to make sound decisions about student literacy needs as related to the curriculum and to instruction" (IRA, 2006, p. 15). Literacy coaches are responsible for designing the school literacy assessment program, setting test schedules and analyzing the results, and helping teachers design classroom literacy assessments.

Element 3.2. "As dynamic supports for reflection and action, literacy coaches conduct regular meetings with content area teachers to examine student work and monitor progress" (IRA, 2006, p. 16). Literacy coaches help content area teachers find ways to observe student literacy skills, hold meetings with content area teachers to examine and evaluate student work, and help teachers analyze the results of the content area standardized tests.

LITERACY ASSESSMENT IN THE MIDDLE SCHOOL

As the preceding elements indicate, the literacy coach is responsible for helping classroom teachers conduct both formative and summative assessments of students' literacy skills. What exactly does this involve? Literacy coaches help teachers assess the literacy strengths and weaknesses of students, particularly at-risk students, by using a variety of assessment devices.

Perhaps even more important than assessing students' specific strengths and weaknesses is assessing their interests and attitudes toward literacy. Because some students see no use for literacy in their lives, a critical factor in their success is finding some way to connect the school literacy program to students' personal interests and experiences. Successful literacy coaches help teachers recognize and value the cultural and linguistic strengths of all students.

Ensuring that the literacy program is goal oriented is an important assessment responsibility of the literacy coach. Teachers in a successful literacy program should be able to agree on what graduating students should ideally be able to do in the areas of reading, writing, speaking, and listening. Without agreement among teachers on what is important, literacy programs too often end up focusing primarily on improving standardized test scores. While high scores on tests are important, they should not be an end in and of themselves. Goals are equally important. Without goals that are specific to individual schools, teachers have little sense of how to build on what has been taught previously and how to prepare students for what will be taught in the future.

Historically, there have been at least three major goals of middle school literacy. The first is functional literacy, which prepares students to write, read, and speak well enough to compete and succeed in the working world. The second is academic literacy, which enables students to appreciate cultural literature and develop their thinking abilities and appreciation of the world around them. The third is social literacy, which prepares students to change society for the better in accordance with democratic and egalitarian educational ideals. In practice, these three goals overlap considerably and are represented to varying degrees in all successful literacy programs.

ASSESSMENT OF MIDDLE SCHOOL LITERACY PROGRAMS

Successful literacy programs are evaluated and revised regularly, with all stakeholders involved in the process. Coordinating such an effort involves three specific tasks on the part of the literacy coach. First, schoolwide literacy goals and objectives are annually reviewed, revised, and even eliminated, if necessary. For example, just because all students are achieving a certain objective does not mean that the objective remains part of the curriculum—the objective must be relevant to the evolving literacy goals of the program. Second, the literacy coach helps teachers use assessment data to measure student progress toward goals and objectives. This information is then used to make systematic revisions in classroom practice. Third, the literacy coach surveys teachers and students regularly to get their input on the overall strengths and weaknesses of the program as well as on specific features of the program. Regular evaluation and revision of a middle-grade literacy program ensures that it will continue to help students achieve important, lifelong literacy skills.

Literacy coaches are responsible for coordinating the standardized, state criterion–referenced, and classroom literacy tests at the school level. At the state and district levels, this coordination involves helping officials choose and develop assessments that are appropriate for young adolescents. For example, literacy coaches often serve on state and district literacy assessment committees so that they can provide input on the types of assessments that the students in their schools will be required to take. On the local level, literacy coaches are responsible for administering these tests, interpreting the results, and communicating these results to students and parents. Finally, literacy coaches are responsible for helping teachers design their own classroom assessments and use the results to make effective decisions about students.

In successful middle school literacy programs, literacy coaches help teachers integrate authentic assessment into literacy instruction. Unfortunately, many programs are unsuccessful because teachers receive little training in sound assessment practices in general, let alone in authentic types of assessment, such as portfolio and performance assessment, that link literacy instruction and assessment. Although teachers may be familiar with current assessment practices, many are reluctant to use them because of the time involved. In successful programs, literacy coaches work with teacher teams, from the ground up, to design and implement these forms of assessment on a schoolwide basis. The literacy coach meets regularly with teacher teams to discuss their students' performance on the criterion- and norm-referenced tests that they take.

In conclusion, literacy plays a critical role in middle school curricula and instruction. Successful middle school literacy programs are designed around the developmental characteristics of young adolescents and are dependent on a collaborative relationship between classroom teachers and literacy coaches.

REFERENCES

Beane, J. A. (2004). Creating quality in the middle school curriculum. In S. C. Thompson (Ed.), *Reforming middle level education: Considerations for policymakers* (pp. 49–63). Greenwich, CT: Information Age.

Biancarosa, G., & Snow, C. E. (2004). *Reading next: A vision for action and research in middle and high school literacy.* Washington, DC: Alliance for Excellent Education.

Cunningham, A. E., & Stanovich, K. E. (1997). Early reading acquisition and its relation to reading experience and ability 10 years later. *Developmental Psychology, 33,* 934–945.

Farnan, N. (2000). The role of the teacher in the literacy program. In K. D. Wood & T. S. Dickinson (Eds.), *Promoting literacy in grades 4–9* (pp. 3–16). Boston: Allyn and Bacon.

International Reading Association. (2006). *Standards for middle and high school literacy coaches.* Newark, DE: Author.

Joftus, S. (2002). *Every child a graduate: A framework for an excellent education for all middle and high school students.* Washington, DC: Alliance for Excellent Education.

National Association of State Boards of Education. (2006). *Reading at risk: The state response to the crisis in adolescent literacy.* Alexandria, VA: Author.

National Governors Association Center for Best Practices. (2005). *Reading to achieve: A governor's guide to adolescent literacy.* Washington, DC: Author.

National Middle School Association. (2003). *This we believe: Successful schools for young adolescents.* Westerville, OH: Author.

No Child Left Behind Act, 20 U.S.C. § 6301 (2001).

Reading Study Group. (2002). *Reading for understanding: Toward an R & D program in reading comprehension.* Santa Monica, CA: RAND Corporation.

Rice, J. K. (2003). *Teacher quality: Understanding the effectiveness of teacher attributes.* Washington, DC: Economic Policy Institute.

Snow, C., Ippolito, J., & Schwartz, R. (2006). What we know and what we need to know about literacy coaches in middle and high schools: A research synthesis and proposed research agenda. In *Standards for middle and high school literacy coaches* (pp. 35–49). Newark, DE: International Reading Association.

U.S. Department of Education. (2003). *National assessment of adult literacy.* Washington, DC: Author.

Waks, L. J. (2002). Exploratory education in a society of knowledge and risk. In V. A. Anfara & S. L. Stacki (Eds.), *Middle school curriculum, instruction, and assessment* (pp. 23–40). Greenwich, CT: Information Age.

Chapter Eight

CONTENT LITERACY: READING, WRITING, LISTENING, AND TALKING IN SUBJECT AREAS

David W. Moore

The following is a fictional account of a 9th-grade solar system unit of instruction. This account is written in the form of a journal and reflects on the content literacy practices that occurred in this teacher's classroom. It is a reference point for this chapter on content literacy: reading, writing, listening, and talking in the subject areas.

I explored the solar system with my 9th-grade science class during the last two weeks. I launched this unit of instruction by reading aloud a few inspiring excerpts on space travel, showing a brief NASA video of its accomplishments, then having students call up what they already knew about the solar system. Next, I displayed and read aloud the following prompt that would guide students' thinking through this unit:

You are the commander of a space shuttle that recently traveled through the solar system. Now that you have returned, you are to report on your journey to members of the U.S. Congress, people who know very little about the details of your trip or what you experienced. Describe your journey so that Congress will fund more money for the space program.

I explained that everyone would have many opportunities to gather information on the solar system for his or her presentation. Then I presented the unit's five objectives so everyone knew the basic expectations: (1) analyze the solar nebular hypothesis, the most widely accepted theory of the origin of the solar system; (2) describe prior explorations of the solar system; (3) portray the distinguishing characteristics, locations, and motions of the principal objects in the solar system; (4) compose a persuasive multiparagraph presentation; and (5) deliver a polished speech that uses visual aids and technology to clarify and defend positions.

As usual, I included objectives for subject matter as well as language arts. My students and I regularly work to develop both areas in my classes. I always share my objectives this way so that students know the essentials they are expected to learn and so that they can take an active role in monitoring their learning. I also presented the assessments we will use to determine how well our teaching and learning is progressing. Doing this at the beginning helps us keep focused.

To begin students' inquiries into the solar system, I reviewed the basic differences between planets and dwarf planets, satellites, asteroids, meteors, and comets. Even during this review, I focused attention on word-learning strategies. For instance, I noted that the root word of *asteroid* is *astro,* meaning "star," as in *astrology, astronomy,* and *astronaut,* and that *meteor* comes from *meta* and *aoro,* meaning "beyond air."

I called attention to the various references available in the class—brochures, nonfiction library books, newspaper clippings, CDs, and the Web—that provided various ways to learn the unit's subject matter. I had gone through the science department's resource center and the school's media center, pulling together reading materials on the solar system so that students could choose passages that fit their interests and abilities.

Students acquired much information for this unit through a computer simulation that models travel through the solar system. The graphics are quite vivid, and the information is abundant and accurate. The game-like aspect of the simulation involves exploring as much of the solar system as possible within an allotted time. Because the positions of the planets relative to each other are constantly changing, the simulation is somewhat different each time it is played.

I devoted five days to students individually or in small groups, gathering ideas and information from the available materials. At the beginning of each class period, I conducted brief lessons on the solar system as well as on the language arts competencies addressed during this unit. At the end of each period, I held whole-class discussions about the students' inquiries, sharing insights into the solar system and tips on composing their presentations.

One day, when the class had formed into pairs, I noticed Victor and Theresa, two students with limited English proficiency, seated together. When I asked whether or not their pairing was by their choice, they said yes. Victor told me, "This way, if we get stuck trying to understand and explain what we're learning in English, we can switch to Spanish." "OK," I said, "first talk through the subject matter as much as you can—and help each other—in English, but use Spanish mainly to get through any rough spots."

On several occasions, I had individuals write out the beginnings of their presentations on an overhead transparency, then the class talked about what they liked about each introduction and inquired into unclear ideas. When an introduction was confusing, either a classmate or I asked something like, "Why are you including _____ ?" or "What support do you have for _____ ?" I insisted on all questions and comments being respectful. I also made sure that the class's gender and ethnic groups were represented fairly when nominating individuals to share their introductions.

On the seventh day of the unit, I reminded the class that this was an opportunity to work full-time to finish their presentations. As I circulated about the room, I answered numerous substantive questions about the solar system, space travel, and multiparagraph presentations and speeches. The class seemed well engaged with science concepts and language arts competencies.

The culmination of this unit consisted of students presenting their reports in small groups. After each presentation, the group collaboratively assessed it by using a scoring guide, or rubric. Each presenter then attached the group's consensus assessment and a self-assessment to his or her printed material for my rating. We debriefed the presentations as a whole class, concluding with a discussion of the immensity of the solar system and the possibility of one day actually exploring all of it with manned spacecraft.

INTRODUCTION

The fictional account of classroom instruction just presented suggests how subject matter and language arts can be brought together. It depicts content literacy in action. Content literacy refers to "the ability to use reading and writing for the acquisition of new content in a given discipline" (McKenna & Robinson, 1990, p. 184). As the fictional account shows, students can use reading, writing, listening, and talking to learn about the solar system. Reading brochures and library books, interacting with computer simulations, talking through unclear ideas, and composing and listening to peers' presentations are powerful tools for acquiring new subject matter knowledge. Students' reading, writing, listening, and talking can be improved when they are engaged in topics like the solar system.

Content literacy goes by names like *academic literacy, content area reading and writing, disciplinary reading and writing,* and *literacy across the curriculum.* Content literacy links attention to reading, writing, listening, and talking with attention to school subjects, such as biology, geometry, history, literature, physical education, and theater, to name a few. Teachers who work to improve their students' content literacies help them use language like biologists, mathematicians, historians, novelists, athletes, actors, and so on. Content literacy is in contrast with the reading and writing people do while conducting their personal lives, running their households, performing their jobs, and acting as citizens. It is the literacy of school.

BACKGROUND

The content literacies of youth have been receiving more attention recently. While pockets of reading educators have realized the importance of secondary school content literacy instruction for years, influential U.S. educational policy makers are just beginning to recognize its value.

Reading Educators

Educators' attention to content literacy in the United States can be traced to the early 1900s. At that time, many educational theorists began questioning the traditional goals of oral reading and rote learning and began realizing the importance of silently reading for meaning. For instance, a noted psychologist and philosopher of this era, William James, told of students who could recite that "the interior of the earth is in a condition of igneous fusion" (James, 1923, p. 150), but who could not say whether the bottom of a very deep hole would be hotter or colder than the top. Progressive educational philosophers such as John Dewey and reformers such as William Heard Kilpatrick and Colonel Francis Parker in the early 1900s advocated teaching students how to understand and remember meaningful ideas.

Pioneering calls for reading instruction in the high schools occurred in the early 1940s as a few educators began realizing that many high school readers struggled at this level. Those involved in the study of child development, such as Ruth Strang, promoted reading instruction that changed across the life span, leading to the catch phrase "First children learn to read, then they read to learn." During this time, William S. Gray initiated the slogan "Every teacher a teacher of reading" to indicate that all high school teachers should play a role in youth's reading development. About three decades later, Harold Herber (1970) published *Teaching Reading in Content Areas,* the first text devoted exclusively to this topic. Current textbooks devoted to the content literacy of youth include titles such as *Content Reading and Literacy* (Alvermann, Phelps, & Ridgeway, 2006) and *Developing Readers and Writers in the Content Areas* (Moore, Moore, Cunningham, & Cunningham, 2006). An online Google search of the term *content literacy* produced 97,500 hits at the time of this writing.

While a small portion of the professional educational literature has addressed content literacy for more than a century, actual content literacy practices implemented in middle and high school classrooms have been comparatively limited. Classroom surveys and observations suggest that past middle and high school teachers rarely focused on their students' literacies while examining subject matter (Cuban, 1993). Up until now, secondary school teachers have concentrated on students' subject matter learning and generally neglected their literacy learning.

Educational Policy Makers

U.S. educational policy makers' attention to what many have called a reading crisis or a literacy crisis (e.g., McQuillan, 1998) is due in large part to reading test score reports. For instance, the National Assessment of Educational Progress (NAEP), commonly called the nation's report card, shows about 25 percent of U.S. 8th graders reading below basic, the lowest level of the test (Livingston, 2006). The NAEP also shows 12th-grade readers' scores declining slightly from 1992 to 2002. U.S. students' performance on international educational comparisons typically presents a substandard picture for older readers. U.S. nine-year-olds typically score higher than their international peers on reading assessments; however, 15-year-olds typically score about the same as their international peers on reading assessments, and U.S. adults' literacy scores are below several other industrialized countries' scores.

In 2003, 19 states administered mandatory high school exit exams, reading tests students must pass to graduate from high school, and five states are phasing in such exams by 2008 (Gayler, Chudowsky, Kober, & Hamilton, 2003). Exit exam pass rates vary from state to state, but all place considerable numbers of youth at risk of not passing. Practically every state has established academic standards, expectations of what youth are to accomplish in school, and content literacy standards normally are included.

A recent survey of employers' perceptions of high school graduates' readiness for the workforce revealed that many believe these graduates lack the skills needed for success (Casner-Lotto & Barrington, 2006). While many employers considered high school graduates to be adequate with information technology, openness to diversity, and collaborative teamwork, many considered them deficient in reading comprehension and writing. Finally, ACT Inc. (2006), a principal publisher of college entrance exams, considered only about half of the seniors they tested in 2005 to be ready for college-level reading. ACT also reported slight declines in older youth's reading achievement, with more students in the 8th grade headed for college-level reading than those in the 12th grade.

The No Child Left Behind Act of 2001 (NCLB; cf. http://www.ed.gov/nclb/landing.jhtml), which the federal government enacted in 2002, calls for all U.S. students to be proficient in reading (as well as math and science) by the 2013–2014 academic year. By including the mandate for *all* students to be proficient, NCLB focuses on eliminating the substantial gaps in academic achievement demonstrated along racial, ethnic, and income lines. This focus is noteworthy because according to the NAEP, the average 8th grader who is African American or Hispanic or who is from a low-income family reads three to four grade levels below those students who are white or better advantaged. Youth with such underdeveloped literacies often find themselves in non-college-bound high school courses, and those in urban high schools often have graduation rates below 50 percent (Barton, 2003).

In response to reports such as these on U.S. adolescents' literacy performance, many highly visible and influential educational policy makers have called for content literacy instruction. Groups recently advocating such instruction in the secondary school subject areas include the U.S. Department of Education (n.d.), the National Association of State Boards of Education (2006), the National Governor's Association Center for Best Practices (2005), the National Association of Secondary School Principals (2005), and the Carnegie Corporation of New York in conjunction with the Alliance for Excellent Education (Biancarosa & Snow, 2004). Secondary school teachers of all subject areas now are becoming responsible for all students attaining high levels of literacy.

RATIONALE

If you are like many who are new to the idea of content literacy instruction in secondary schools, you might wonder why the response to U.S. adolescents' reading achievement involves subject matter teachers. You might ask something like, "I'm convinced of the need to improve adolescents' literacy performance, but shouldn't this be done during English or special reading classes?" If you are a middle or secondary school teacher, you might think only elementary teachers should teach literacy, wondering something like, "Shouldn't lower-grade teachers be the ones to concentrate on improving students' reading and writing so upper-grade teachers can present their content?" Three compelling reasons for linking youth's reading, writing, listening, and talking with subject matter study follow: (1) subject matter consists of language, (2) the language of subject matter differs, and (3) the demands of subject matter language continually increase.

Subject Matter Consists of Language

Biologists, historians, and astronomers use language to construct and convey meaning about what they examine. Even when scientists investigate concrete natural phenomena, they work with words to form concepts and explain conceptual relationships about the phenomenon. Think how various subject matter specialists would examine a large boulder they might come across in the outdoors: how a paleontologist would think and talk about any fossils that shed light on prehistoric plant and animal life, how an anthropologist would comment on any pictographs and petroglyphs that reveal information about ancient cultures, and how a geologist would refer to its mineral content. Each subject matter specialist would employ a particular perspective on the identical boulder, using language to advance that perspective.

Acting like a biologist, historian, astronomer, paleontologist, anthropologist, or geologist means using language in particular ways to think about particular aspects of the world. Among other things, it means being proficient in reading the journal articles, textbooks, brochures, and scholarly books of the specialization as well as writing the observation notes, transcripts, reactions to experiences, reports, and so on that characterize the specialization.

Subject matter teachers are best able to support students who are challenged by subject matter language. Instruction typically benefits learners the most when they want to accomplish something specific. Teaching students to take notes about history content generally is most appropriate when students have the desire to understand and remember history. Teaching students how to solve mathematics word problems is done best in math class when students want to solve such problems. Content literacy learning occurs best in content area classrooms when students have the need to know and where teachers are expert in the language of the subject.

The Language of Subject Matter Differs

A single word often means different things when used in different subjects. For instance, in English class, *base* refers to the central word to which prefixes and suffixes are attached, yet in chemistry, *base* is the word for the compound that reacts with acids to form salts. In economics, *base* represents the lowest price of a publicly traded stock, while in mathematics, *base* refers to the source of numbering systems. Then consider *table*. Is it used to refer to a water table, a kitchen table, or a multiplication table? Does someone want to table a motion or table a set of information?

The following words demonstrate the reality of single words having several meanings: *base, table, principal, power, prime, radical, square,* and *set.* When used in mathematics, these words have very specific, technical meanings that differ from their meanings when used outside of math. Youth benefit from deep understanding of words' different meanings according to the subject areas where they are used.

Language of the Subject Area Texts

Take note of the poem "The Eagle," presented below.

The Eagle

He clasps the crag with crooked hands;
Close to the sun in lonely lands,
Ringed with the azure world, he stands.
The wrinkled sea beneath him crawls;
He watches from his mountain walls,
And like a thunderbolt he falls.
Alfred, Lord Tennyson (1851)

What does this lyric poem mean? Is it a portrayal of a significant event in a raptor's life? Is it actually referring to a person rather than an eagle? Or is Tennyson talking about the British military in a manner similar to his "Charge of the Light Brigade" ("Theirs not to reason why, / Theirs but to do and die")? Perhaps "The Eagle" is meant to be ambiguous and multilayered so that readers will access multiple meanings and think about multiple aspects of their natural and social worlds.

Note the music of Tennyson's words. The structure of the first line is an eight-syllable, iambic tetrameter that provides notable rhythm. The alliteration in this line (clasps, crag, crooked) and the later rhymes (hands, lands, stands; crawls, walls, falls) suggests a certain majesty. And the descriptive language of the poem (azure world, wrinkled sea, thunderbolt) appeals rather vividly and compellingly to the senses.

Now compare "The Eagle" with the following passage about angles.

Angles

An angle is the union of two rays that do not lie on the same line. When the sum of the measure of two angles is 90°, the angles are complementary; when the sum of the measure is 180°, the angles are supplementary. (Moore, Moore, Cunningham, & Cunningham, 2006, p. 5)

Did you find yourself having to mentally shift gears when reading the angles passage after "The Eagle"? Did you need a different mind-set, a different way of thinking and reading? The meaning of the angles passage is much more exact and constrained than what just preceded it. There is little room for multiple defensible interpretations. This passage tersely tells what an angle is and what to name the sums of angles' measures. It exemplifies scholarly mathematical conceptualizations of physical space.

The angles passage has none of the musicality found in "The Eagle"; it is presented in a forthright, no-nonsense manner that gets straight to the point. Its precise, painstakingly sequenced description guides readers unequivocally.

Furthermore, the vocabulary of the angles passage is distinctive, including the symbol for degree and the multiple-meaning words *ray, complementary,* and *supplementary.*

The Magna Carta selection presented below offers another glimpse into the language differences among subject matter.

Magna Carta

In 1215, a group of barons forced King John of England to sign the Magna Carta. The barons wanted to restore their privileges; however, the Magna Carta grounded constitutional government in political institutions for all English-speaking people. (Moore et al., 2006, p. 5)

This passage seems to present concepts more explicitly than "The Eagle" but less explicitly than the angles passage. It offers some room for interpretation. It presents English history factoids, implies the time span of the notion of constitutional government, and suggests how human actions often have unintended consequences. The language of the Magna Carta passage fits the genre of nonfiction narrative, rather than the poetic or procedural genres of the other passages. It exemplifies the way social scientists present cause-effect relationships among social, economic, and political events. And it assumes readers will be familiar with the terms *barons, privileges, constitutional government,* and *political institutions* because if offers no clarifications.

"The Eagle" and the passages on angles and the Magna Carta suggest how the language of subject matter differs. These reading selections show why subject matter teachers are the logical choice for teaching content literacy. Subject matter teachers know the mind-sets of those who produced such materials, the special vocabulary of the materials, their structures, and generally, what it takes to make sense of them.

Language of the Subject Area Classrooms

Along with the language of the subject, the language of the classroom matters. Teachers do well when they clarify the forms of language, thought, and action that students need to participate effectively in their classrooms. For instance, math teachers might expect students to solve problems by calculating data precisely and recording the findings in meticulous order. A government teacher might expect these same students to solve problems by examining hypothetical situations, forming opinions about appropriate courses of action, and advocating their opinions during open-ended debates. To do well, these students need to act like meticulous problem-solvers in the math class and adventurous debaters in the government class.

An English language arts teacher then might expect this same group of students to participate in teacher-student writing conferences as a sign of being serious writers. When this happens, teachers are at risk of mistakenly considering those who prefer to not participate to be second-rate writers. Finally, a science teacher might expect these students to act like bankers of information who, when tested, accurately recover what was deposited during class lectures.

Regardless of the subject area, teachers tend to reward those who communicate as expected. Youth sometimes have difficulty in school because they do not apply the fine points of acting like particular readers, writers, listeners, and speakers in particular classrooms. These youth might lack the language of a classroom because they are unaware of the verbal customs sanctioned there. Or these youth might decide willfully not to participate in classroom language for personal and cultural reasons, disdaining the academic customs of mainstream classrooms.

Educators who acknowledge the role of classroom language seek ways to explicitly inform youth of their classroom language expectations. They also seek ways to inform youth's decisions to participate because they realize that youth ultimately decide the extent to which they develop their content literacies.

The Demands of Subject Matter Language Continually Increase

As students progress through school, they read more and more expository material about more and more complicated ideas. They might read stories about neighborhood helpers in the primary grades, textbook passages about world geography in the middle grades, and primary sources comparing governmental systems in high school.

The two columns presented in Table 8.1 hint at the increase in word difficulty that students experience as they progress through the grades. To be specific, all the words are derived from bases or roots, but each word in the left column contains two syllables, the base word appears fully in each (i.e., delete the *y* in each and the base remains), and all the words represent somewhat familiar, simple, and concrete things.

On the other hand, the words in the right column also all end with *y*, but they contain up to seven syllables, and all have roots rather than bases—their central elements cannot stand alone. The Greek and Latin roots *chrono* (time),

Table 8.1
Derived Words

Relatively Easy	Relatively Difficult
dirty	chronology
cloudy	dermatology
fruity	heterogeneity
hilly	monogamy
rainy	philanthropy
sleepy	sedimentary

derm (skin), *gen* (type), *gam* (marriage), *anthrop* (man), and *sed* (settle) require a prefix or suffix to appear in English. These words represent somewhat unfamiliar, complex, and abstract phenomena.

The ever-increasing difficulty of what students read, as exemplified by these columns of words, indicates the need for continual support across the subjects at all grade levels. Just as primary-grade students benefit from peeling off the *y* of certain words and examining their bases, secondary school students benefit from removing multiple prefixes and suffixes, knowing the meanings of the foreign roots, and combining these elements into sensible concepts. And to be sure, the sentences, paragraphs, and longer discourse that students encounter across the grades increase in complexity in their own ways.

In summary, students deserve content literacy instruction across the subject areas and throughout their school careers. Extended instruction over time in subject matter reading, writing, listening, and talking enables individuals to handle the dramatic changes they experience in learning about the world.

INSTRUCTION

Organizing instruction to promote reading, writing, listening, and speaking along with subject matter learning is complex; indeed, entire textbooks are devoted to this enterprise (see, e.g., Moore et al., 2006). This section presents six features of content literacy instruction that provide a good starting point for planning it. The six features are (1) instructional units focusing on big ideas, (2) objectives linked with assessments, (3) materials that students can and want to read, (4) guidance through challenging tasks, (5) explicit instruction in strategies, and (6) differentiation and collaboration.

Instructional Units Focusing on Big Ideas

Classroom units of instruction are a productive framework for bringing together language and subject matter. Units divide the school year among topics and blocks of time, lasting from a few days to a few weeks The fictional unit at the beginning of this chapter focused on the solar system, a common topic. Table 8.2 presents other common topics that high school instructional units center about.

Table 8.2
Units of Instruction

English	Algebra	Biology	American history
Beloved (novel)	Number system	The cell	Precontact America
Poetry (genre)	Rational numbers	Heredity	European exploration
Angelou (author)	Properties	Interdependence	Colonies
Identity (theme)	Equations	Evolution	Nation forming
Essay (skill)	Linear functions	Energy flow	Westward expansion

After selecting a unit topic, focusing attention on its big ideas helps to link language and subject matter. With regard to the novel *Beloved*, a big idea could be what it means to be beloved. If precontact America were the topic of an American history unit, a big idea could be whether Native Americans were better off before or after European contact. Rather than relying on a question, the solar system unit's big idea asked the student to produce a composition that would "describe your journey so that Congress will fund more money for the space program."

Big ideas are meant to provoke and sustain students' thinking, use of language, and subject matter learning. They glue together what students encounter during day-to-day unit activities. When focusing on big ideas, students still need to grasp the numerous facts associated with a topic, but these facts become the building blocks of thought and language. The open-ended aspect of big ideas permits all high- and low-achieving students to form acceptable responses, although their sophistication might vary.

Objectives Linked with Assessments

By stating what is to be learned during a unit, objectives direct students' and teachers' actions. Objectives, which have gone by the names of *goals, aims, curriculum standards,* and *content outcomes,* designate what is to be accomplished. Linking units' subject matter and language objectives places a focus on content literacy. For instance, the fictional solar system unit contains two literacy objectives ("Compose a persuasive multiparagraph presentation …" and "Deliver a polished speech …"). The presence of these two in a science unit calls for instruction that attends to both, developing language in the service of learning subject matter.

Assessments, measures of what students know and can do, can be productive teaching and learning tools. As the fictional unit portrayed, showing early on how reading and writing will be assessed and having classmates use scoring guides while responding to one another's presentations clarifies expectations and signals what is important. The scoring guides, checklists, and tests help teachers and students keep their eyes on their subject matter and content literacy objectives.

Materials That Students Can and Want to Read

Youth who spend time reading and writing connected text tend to increase their word knowledge, fluency, and reading comprehension, along with their knowledge of the world and attitude toward literacy (Krashen, 2004). Providing students accessible and interesting materials, time to read them, and support for their reading promotes literacy.

Materials written at different levels of difficulty and in different genres give students a chance to get subject matter that is personally meaningful. As the solar system unit showed, teachers can provide various types of reference material—brochures, nonfiction library books, newspaper clippings, CDs, and the Web—obtained from classroom supplies as well as department and media center collections. Some teachers pair picture books with advanced reading materials, thinking that the simpler materials provide stepping-stones to the more complex ones. These teachers believe that some of the time spent helping students understand their textbooks might be time better spent getting understandable materials into students' hands.

Guidance through Challenging Tasks

Challenging tasks, ones that call for special effort but are not defeating, improve learning (Bransford, Brown, & Cocking, 1999). Challenging tasks are neither too easy nor too demanding. They are assignments that students cannot accomplish on their own, but can accomplish with reasonable support. Delivering a polished speech promoting solar system exploration, as the fictional unit expected, would challenge most 9th-grade students yet be within their grasp.

Guidance through challenging language tasks has discernible beginnings, middles, and endings. For instance, if students are expected to understand a challenging passage, teachers might begin by connecting its unfamiliar vocabulary and ideas with subject matter encountered earlier. They might have students take notes or ask and answer questions while reading. After reading, they might have students produce a written response then receive feedback. This sequence of guidance leads to teachers uncovering—rather than covering—subject matter.

Guidance through challenging tasks helps youth develop understandings of the particular topic at hand as well as future ones. Guidance promotes knowledge of the world, which is crucial background for making sense of new ideas. As students develop their understandings of the solar system and persuasive speech presentations, for example, they bring this new knowledge to future reading and subject matter learning. They learn about the world incrementally, continually connecting new ideas and information with what they already know.

Explicit Instruction in Strategies

Explicit instruction in how to accomplish what youth are expected to accomplish promotes their comprehension and learning (Nokes & Dole, 2004). If a unit plan calls for students to obtain information online, and they are not already adept at searching for information online, then effective teachers would present the strategies for accomplishing that task. With the solar system unit, teachers would demonstrate how to access the Web, locate appropriate sites in the solar system, and record pertinent information before having students do it on their own.

Strategies enable individuals to learn on their own, when no guidance is available. Strategies teachers commonly address during content literacy instruction include graphically organizing ideas, thinking aloud while reading, discussing ideas in cooperative learning groups, and maintaining journals or learning logs (Bacevich & Salinger, 2006).

An effective instructional practice is to introduce strategies such as these with materials unrelated to the current unit of instruction, then quickly integrate the strategies into ongoing course work. This provides students with the opportunity to take control of their learning. It shows that thinking deeply about subject matter and learning it is not a matter of being innately smart, but a matter of applying proper strategies.

Differentiation and Collaboration

Differentiating instruction means accommodating the strengths and needs of diverse learners. Teachers who differentiate instruction know that not everyone learns the same way and that individuals have preferred ways of processing subject matter as well as different cultural backgrounds, career aspirations, and identities. They assume that individuals follow different pathways to learning.

Collaboration is a powerful practice for differentiating instruction, especially for English language learners. As the solar system unit portrayed, some students who are learning English might benefit from working alongside another who speaks the same first language. Such collaboration permits learners to talk through their confusion and emerging understanding. It provides opportunities for participants to think of things they otherwise might not have considered. Collaborative discussions are powerful tools for helping learners come at subject matter differently and obtain new insights and perspectives.

A FINAL WORD

Youth who begin to read, write, listen, and talk like subject matter specialists go far toward achieving the high levels of language needed for the twenty-first century. Secondary school subject matter classrooms are a prime location for instruction along these lines. Content literacy, the literacy of school, deserves the attention of those wishing to promote literacy and subject matter learning.

REFERENCES

ACT Inc. (2006). *Reading between the lines: What the ACT reveals about college readiness in reading.* Iowa City: Author.

Alvermann, D. E., Phelps, S., & Ridgeway, V. G. (2006). *Content reading and literacy: Succeeding in today's diverse classrooms* (5th ed.). Boston: Allyn and Bacon.

Bacevich, A., & Salinger, T. (2006). *Lessons and recommendations from the Alabama Reading Initiative: Sustaining focus on secondary reading.* Washington, DC: American Institutes for Research.

Barton, P. E. (2003). *Parsing the achievement gap: Baselines for tracking progress.* Princeton, NJ: Educational Testing Service.

Biancarosa, F., & Snow, C. E. (2004). *Reading next: A vision for action and research in middle and high school literacy—A report to Carnegie Corporation of New York.* Washington, DC: Alliance for Excellent Education.

Bransford, J. D., Brown, A. L., & Cocking, R. R. (Eds.). (1999). *How people learn: Brain, mind, experience, and school.* Washington, DC: National Academy Press.

Casner-Lotto, J., & Barrington, L. (2006). *Are they really ready to work? Employers' perspectives on the basic knowledge and applied skills of new entrants to the 21st century U.S. workforce.* New York: Conference Board, Corporate Voices for Working Families, Partnership for 21st Century Skills, and Society for Human Resource Management.

Cuban, L. (1993). *How teachers taught: Constancy and change in American classrooms, 1890–1990.* New York: Teachers College Press.

Gayler, K., Chudowsky, N., Kober, N., & Hamilton, M. (2003). *State high school exams put to the test.* Washington, DC: Center on Education Policy.

Herber, H. (1970). *Teaching reading in content areas.* Englewood Cliffs, NJ: Prentice Hall.

James, W. (1923). *Talks to teachers on psychology, and to students on some of life's ideals.* London: Longman.

Krashen, S. (2004). *The power of reading* (2nd ed.). Englewood, CO: Libraries Unlimited.

Livingston, A. (Ed.). (2006). *The condition of education 2006 in brief* (Report No. NCES 2006-072). Washington, DC: National Center for Educational Sciences.

McKenna, M. C., & Robinson, R. D. (1990). Content literacy: A definition and implications. *Journal of Reading, 34,* 184–186.

McQuillan, J. (1998). *The literacy crisis: False claims, real solutions.* Portsmouth, NH: Heinemann.

Moore, D. W., Moore, S. A., Cunningham, P. M., & Cunningham, J. W. (2006). *Developing readers and writers in the content areas: K–12* (5th ed.). Boston: Allyn and Bacon.

National Association of Secondary School Principals. (2005). *Creating a culture of literacy.* Reston, VA: Author.

National Association of State Boards of Education. (2006, July). *Reading at risk: The state response to the crisis in adolescent literacy.* Alexandria, VA: Author.

National Governor's Association Center for Best Practices. (2005). *Reading to achieve: A governor's guide to adolescent literacy.* Washington, DC: Author.

No Child Left Behind Act, 20 U.S.C. § 6301 (2001).

Nokes, J. D., & Dole, J. A. (2004). Helping adolescent readers through explicit strategy instruction. In T. L. Jetton & J. A. Dole (Eds.), *Adolescent literacy research and practice* (pp. 162–182). New York: Guilford Press.

Tennyson, A. (n.d.). *The eagle.* Retrieved October 4, 2006, from the Poems Library Web site: http://www.poemslibrary.com/alfred-lord-tennyson/142

U.S. Department of Education. (n.d.). *Striving readers.* Retrieved May 14, 2006, from http://www.ed.gov/programs/strivingreaders/index.html

Chapter Nine

EXEMPLARY YOUNG ADULT LITERATURE: THE BEST BOOKS FOR ADOLESCENTS

James Blasingame Jr.

I recently found myself inescapably encircled by 200 rowdy, teenaged girls, all wearing plastic vampire teeth and identical black "Bite Me" T-shirts, as they mobbed best-selling author Stephanie Meyer, or as she is more often known, the "vampire lady." Stephanie's most recent book, *New Moon* (Little, Brown, 2006), the sequel to her teenage vampire thriller *Twilight* (Little, Brown, 2005), spent 11 weeks as number one on *The New York Times* bestseller book list in the category of children's chapter books.

Stephanie was appearing at Changing Hands Bookstore in Tempe, Arizona, and anyone failing to arrive at least 90 minutes early was out of luck. Teen readers around the world are enthralled with her protagonists, Edward Cullen (the handsome but aloof teen vampire) and Bella Swan (the adventurous high school junior looking for her place in the world). The popularity of these books even extends to international fan sites, which are Web sites created by young fans of Stephanie's work, such as TwilightLexicon.com, a very stylish and technologically savvy Web site with a wealth of pages on everything from vampire mythology, to detailed chapter summaries, to discussion boards where fans can chat.

What makes the books of a certain author so popular with young readers? On the surface, it may look as if they are just enthusiastic participants in the latest fad, but an examination beneath the surface reveals that quality young adult literature rises to the top for good reasons, and the reasons are rooted in the nature of adolescence itself.

Young adult readers have very definite opinions about books. A few years ago, at age 13, my niece Katelin had amassed a considerable collection of young adult books autographed to her by various famous authors, including Phyllis Reynolds Naylor, Sharon Draper, and Vicki Grove. As a student at the University of Kansas at that time, under the tutelage of renowned adolescent literature expert John Bushman, I had the opportunity to meet with 20 or more outstanding authors as they visited campus. After hosting the authors around the campus for two days, I always scored a set of autographed books for my nephews and niece, Alex, Nick, and Katelin.

These three were not only avid readers, but discriminating readers as well. As her 8th-grade school year began, I asked Katelin what they would be reading this year in English class. She responded, "I don't know what we're going to be reading yet, Uncle Jim, but I hope it's the good, interesting stuff and not the dumb, boring stuff." Among the books that Katelin would read that year from the "good, interesting stuff" were Vicki Grove's *Crystal Garden* (Putnam, 1995), Carolyn Cooney's *Face on the Milk Carton* (Delacorte, 1990), Christopher Paul Curtis's *The Watson's Go to Birmingham: 1963* (Delacorte, 1995), Sharon Draper's *Tears of a Tiger* (Atheneum, 1994), and Karen Hesse's *Letters from Rifka* (Henry Holt, 1992). All these books have won multiple awards, and all have been recognized as among the very best in young adult literature.

CHARACTERISTICS OF EXEMPLARY YOUNG ADULT LITERATURE

What are the hallmarks of the very best in literature for adolescents? Exemplary literature for young adults becomes something very special when the reader interfaces with it; it becomes a sort of user's guide to life, a guide with great influence over how the reader grows as a human being. Perhaps a better way to ask the question would be, What kind of books do young adults need in their lives?

The answer to this question might be reduced to these five principles:

1. Young adults need books with characters and situations to which they can relate.
2. Young adults need books that treat the issues that adolescents face respectfully.
3. Young adults need books that are accessible to them.
4. Young adults need books that reflect the diversity of their world.
5. Young adults need books that help them make sense of their own lives.

I will explore each of these five principles as well as good examples of books that are exemplars of each. At the end of the chapter, I will include some lists of recommended works that also fit these principles. Let us look at the first, second, and fifth principles together. In their best-selling book on adolescent literature, *Literature for Today's Young Adults*, Alleen Nilsen and Ken Donelson (2004) placed readers on a continuum of stages of literary appreciation, stages they progress through as they mature. Readers are generally in the third stage as they enter adolescence, the stage of "losing oneself in literature" (p. 39), when reading becomes a pleasant escape from everyday life. As adolescence overtakes them, however, they progress into the fourth stage, the stage of "finding oneself in literature" (p. 39). To do this, they need literature with characters with whom they can connect, characters with whom they can easily and strongly identify.

As Mel Glenn, winner of the American Library Association's (ALA) Best Books Award for *Class Dismissed! High School Poems* (Clarion, 1982), explains, "When a reader can say, 'Hey, I feel what that character is going through,' a tangible connection has been made between printed word and human recipient, or in other words, what is that character to me or me to that character that I should care so; the reader and the protagonist intertwine" (Blasingame, 2007, p. 174). It is this connection between the reader and the characters, especially the connection with the protagonist, that is so crucial in high-quality young adult literature.

READER RESPONSE THEORY

This connection is surely the one that Louise Rosenblatt, the founder of reader response theory, first wrote about in her landmark work *Literature as Exploration* in 1938. Rosenblatt's theory was that when a text and a reader come together, something is created that never existed before because each reader is a unique individual and

> brings to the work personality traits, memories of past events, present needs and preoccupations, a particular mood of the moment, and a particular physical condition. These and many other elements in a never-to-be-duplicated combination determine his response to the peculiar contribution of the text. (pp. 30–31)

According to Rosenblatt, the meaning of a text is created in a transaction that takes place between the text and the reader.

THEORIES OF ADOLESCENT DEVELOPMENT

The significance of this transaction is especially high, considering the physical, emotional, and psychological development that takes place during adolescence. Moral and personality development are in high gear for teens at this time, as theorized by noted developmental psychologists Lawrence Kohlberg and Erik Erikson. In his 1981 work *Essays on Moral Development,* Kohlberg describes stages of moral development in which human beings form consciences, including how these consciences operate and change as children mature. In his 1950 work *Childhood and Society,* Erickson theorizes eight stages of human development, each describing the tensions between two polar opposite states of psychological development. For example, in stage 5 (12–18 years of age), "Identity versus Role Confusion," teens ask the question, Who am I? Erikson is famous for coining the phrase *identity crisis* in referring to this stage. The individual attempts to determine personal beliefs, values, and roles in life such as gender roles and social roles. During this time, adolescents are experimenting with identities, trying on different ways of being, and seeing how well they fit.

Books can enable young readers to experiment safely and vicariously through the trials and tribulations of characters like them. Far better that when a young reader encounters a certain life-changing decision or dilemma for the very first time, it is in a book, rather than in real life. As Newbery Medal winner Katherine Paterson contends,

> that's what books do for you. They give you practice doing difficult things in life. In a way, they prepare you for things that you are going to have to face or someone you know and care about is going through. They sort of help you know how it feels—though not exactly. It is the remove that gives you a deep pleasure rather than a total pain. (Scholastic Inc., 2005)

CHARACTERS AND SITUATIONS CLOSE TO THE LIVES OF YOUNG ADULTS

Books that fulfill these requirements (relatable characters and events and stories that help young people make sense of their own lives) may look very different from each other on the surface. For example, the five books in Gary Paulsen's *Hatchet* (Bradbury, 1987) series have entirely different settings and conflicts from Laurie Halse Anderson's *Speak* (Farrar, Straus and Giroux, 1999). After being marooned in the Canadian wilderness, Paulsen's protagonist, Brian, spends most of his time just trying to stay alive, while Anderson's Melinda Sordino spends most of her time at school or at home after having been secretly raped at a high school party. Yet Brian and Melinda are not so different: they both feel alone and hopeless, without power and without purpose, floundering in a hostile environment. Feeling alone, feeling somehow different from everyone else, is a commonality among teenagers, and books with characters who also experience these feelings are helpful to them. Award-winning author and counselor to dysfunctional families Chris Crutcher (1992) explains, "Stories can help teenagers look at their feelings or come to emotional resolution, from a safe distance.... I have never met a depressed person, or an anxious person, or a fearful person who was not encouraged by the knowledge that others feel the same way they do. 'I am not alone' is powerful medicine" (p. 39).

As young readers follow the ups and downs of characters much like themselves, they wrestle with the protagonist's issues side-by-side with him or her.

These issues may be as innocuous as working up the nerve to ask someone out on a date, or as heart wrenching as helplessly watching as a terminally ill sibling declines, such as in *Drums, Girls and Dangerous Pie* (DayBue, 2004), New Jersey middle school teacher Jordan Sonnenblick's first successful novel. Sonnenblick wrote *Drums* after learning that one of his students was dealing with a terminally ill sibling. He knew full well the power of literature for healing and for helping young people make sense of the world, but the right book for his student, a book about living with a terminally ill brother or sister, was not available, and so he set out to write it: "I saw a void. I loved this kid, and I wrote the book that wasn't there for her. People say they climb Mt. Everest because it's there, well I wrote this book because the need was there" (Blasingame, 2006, p. 61).

Sonnenblick also understood the need for authenticity and accuracy, and as he worked on the plot details of *Drums,* his goal was 100 percent believability: "It needed to be perfect. A very special reader was trusting me to tell her the truth, and when someone hands you the ball of their trust, you don't drop the ball" (Blasingame, 2006, p. 62). Sonnenblick turned to a lifetime friend, an oncologist, for information about cancer symptoms, medicine, side effects, and treatments. Good young adult authors display the utmost respect for their readers.

Young readers love the gritty details that come from an author's personal experience, too. Consider two of their favorites, Will Hobbs and Gary Paulsen. In Hobbs's *Wild Man Island* (HarperCollins, 2002), 14-year-old Andy Galloway is marooned on Alaska's Admiralty Island while sea kayaking. Will wrote that book after he and his wife, Jean, sea kayaked that very same area and saw for themselves many of the obstacles that Andy would encounter in the book, including whales, sea lions, and giant brown bears. Gary Paulsen wrote *Woodsong* (Bradbury, 1990) and *Dogsong* (Bradbury, 1985), two books steeped in the facts of running dogsleds, very soon after personally running the Iditarod, Alaska's annual 1,150-mile dogsled race from Anchorage to Nome.

REFLECTING DIVERSITY IN YOUNG ADULT LITERATURE

Adolescents also need books that reflect the diversity of who they are. It is imperative that *all* young people see themselves in their reading and that all adolescents see the total diversity of the human race in their reading as well. When adolescents do not see themselves in their reading, they are likely to infer, consciously or subconsciously, that they do not count or do not matter. In her 2006 article "The Voices of Power and the Power of Voices," scholar of Native American literacy Marlinda White-Kaulaity described the consequences suffered by young readers who never see their own ethnic or cultural heritage reflected in their classroom reading. She stated that "when certain voices are excluded … teachers deprive young readers of one purpose of literature: to read and learn about themselves and others in life" (p. 8).

In addition to omitting a group, stereotyping members of that group as being all alike (good or bad) further marginalizes the group and is grossly inaccurate. For example, in debunking the myth of the romanticized, noble Native American as portrayed in so-called enlightened books and films, Native American author Cynthia Leitich Smith stated that the romanticized stereotype is nearly as bad as the old cowboys and Indians movie image of a fearsome savage: "The problem is that it's equally dehumanizing. Literature must show us in our full complexity, and that includes flaws and, in some cases, perspectives that might make others uncomfortable" (Blasingame, 2007, p. 163). Multicultural children's literature scholar Virginia Loh (2006) further explained the problem with stereotyping of any kind, positive or negative:

> The main caveat seems to be attributing characteristics and traits to an entire group without considering individuals and the multiplicity of culture and ethnicity even though there are consistencies among cultural groups. No one image is enough to create stereotypes, but pervasive images do, which are then reinforced by culture and/or society. (p. 48)

One author who is especially adept at showing people in their full complexity is Gary Soto, a National Book Award finalist and winner of the Literature Award from the Hispanic Heritage Foundation. Just a few of Soto's books include *Buried Onions* (Harcourt, 1997), *Jesse* (Harcourt, 1994), *Living Up the Street* (Strawberry Hill Press, 1985), *A Fire in My Hands* (Turtleback Books, 1990), *Baseball in April* (Harcourt, 1990), and *Petty Crimes* (Harcourt, 1998). Soto's books often revolve around teen characters growing up Latino in his hometown of Fresno, California. Soto creates characters who are as complex as their counterparts in the real world, an important quality for young readers who are beginning to understand that people are generally neither all bad nor all good nor all anything, but are, instead, complex and not always easy to understand.

Voices from diverse ethnic/cultural heritages are important, and so are voices of the individuals who all too often receive negative attention or no attention at all. Jack Gantos, winner of the Michael Printz Honor Award and the Newbery Honor Award, is famous for his beloved protagonist Joey Pigza and his adventures in *Joey Pigza Swallowed the Key* (Farrar, Straus and Giroux, 1998), *Joey Pigza Loses Control* (Farrar, Straus and Giroux, 2000), *What Would Joey Do?* (Farrar, Straus and Giroux, 2002), and *I Am Not Joey Pigza* (Farrar, Straus and Giroux, 2008). Joey is an early teen who suffers from attention-deficit/hyperactivity disorder (ADHD). Over the course of the series, as Joey comes to terms with his own ADHD, he also attempts to provide stability for the maladjusted adults in his dysfunctional family. Gantos charmingly portrays Joey as a boy who does not judge those around him and does his best to make the world a better place for everyone.

Depression, just like ADHD, is very much a part of the lives of young people or their peers. According to a report from the Substance Abuse and Mental Health Services Administration (2006),

> population studies show that at any one time between 10 and 15 percent of the child and adolescent population has *some* symptoms of depression. The prevalence of the full-fledged diagnosis of major depression among all children ages 9 to 17 has been estimated at 5 percent.

One of the best recent novels to address this aspect of adolescence is *Damage* (HarperCollins, 2001), by A. M. Jenkins. Her protagonist, Austin Reid, is the star quarterback of the Parkersville High School Panthers, who secretly suffers from depression and suicidal impulses caused by a chemical imbalance. Ultimately, Austin will have to accept that he is who is and must love himself enough to look for help.

Young readers not only need to read about characters like them, but also characters different from them. Young adult books have an imperative to help young people grow to understand the world they live in and all its peoples. As White-Kaulaity explains, all young readers, from all walks of life, "need cross boundary knowledge, interaction and experiences to live in an interdependent world. Literature can help achieve such goals" (p. 10). As former president of the Assembly on Literature for Adolescents of the National Council of Teachers of English, author, and editor Michael Cart says, "Literature teaches empathy, tolerance, and respect for the dignity and worth of every human being" (Blasingame, 2007, p. 130). Cart (2006) shared further words about the power of literature to help readers understand the lives of others in his masterful work *From Romance to Realism: Fifty Years of Growth and Change in Young Adult Literature*:

> Fiction gives us not only an external view of another life, however, but an internal one, as well, through its empathic immediacy, the emotional rapport that it offers the reader; it enables us, in short, to eavesdrop on someone else's heart. Yes we can get statistical profile of the adolescent problem drinker from a report in *Time* magazine, but to emotionally comprehend the problem, to understand how it feels to be trapped in that skin, we turn to Robert Cormier and his novel, *We All Fall Down*. ... To understand the emotional plight of impoverished, single-parent families, we look to Virginia Euwer Wolff's *Make Lemonade*. (p. 269)

Literature has great power to put the reader in the shoes of the characters in ways that touch emotions, values, and beliefs.

Many outstanding authors are writing wonderful books today, supplying the requisite variety of voices, and voices that all young readers need to hear.

A list of recommended authors providing these voices can be found at the end of this chapter.

ACCESSIBLE LITERATURE

One final principle of the five remains to be addressed: accessibility. None of the good things that young adult literature holds in store for readers are available to them if they cannot or will not read it. As Nicholas Karolides contended in his 1991 edited collection *Reader Response in the Classroom: Evoking and Interpreting Meaning in Literature*, in his own essay "The Transactional Theory of Literature,"

> the language of a text, the situation, characters, or the expressed issues can dissuade a reader from comprehension of the text and thus inhibit involvement with it. In effect, if the reader has insufficient linguistic or experiential background to allow participation, the reader cannot relate to the text, and the reading act will be short-circuited. (p. 23)

Two of the quickest paths to short-circuiting students' reading are stories that are not interesting because they are not at the students' maturity/experiential level in content and stories that are too high above students' reading ability. Young people who read substantially below grade level may find the majority of books written for their age frustratingly difficult to read. Conversely, most books written at their reading level may not be age-appropriate in content. Five possible solutions to this dilemma are (1) high/low books, which have high-interest topics written at lower reading levels; (2) series books, which maintain the same characters and setting from book to book; (3) graphic novels, with storyboard graphics to go with the text; (4) short story collections, which are sets of stories centered on a common theme; (4) poetry collections, usually centered on a theme; and (5) narratives told in verse.

Publishers such as Orca, James Lorimer and Company, and Townsend Press are committed to providing young adult literature in a variety of content areas through books with high interest and low reading difficulty. Orca's *Juice* (2006), by Eric Walters, for example, is the story of a high school football star pressured to use anabolic steroids by his coach. This is very mature subject matter, but the readability level of the book averages at about the third grade level, and the book is only 112 pages long. The Bluford books from Townsend Press, and now in reprint by Scholastic Inc., comprise one of today's most successful book series for teen readers. These 13 books are set at fictitious Guion Bluford High School (named for the first African American U.S. astronaut) in southern California, and the stories revolve around the lives of students at Bluford High, an urban school with a primarily African American and Latino student body.

Graphic novels can also entice struggling readers. Research shows that they improve reading (Krashen, 1993), and many of them are very complex and sophisticated. Graphic novels provide the reader with additional context clues to the text embedded in the cartooning. Recently, the genre was acknowledged for its true potential when Gene Yang's *American Born Chinese* (First Second, 2006) was a National Book Award finalist in the regular category of young people's literature. Other outstanding graphic novels, just to name a few, include the entire Age of Bronze series (Image Comics, 2001) by Eric Shanower; Alan Moore's *Watchmen* (DC Comics, 1995) and his *V Is for Vendetta* (DC Comics, 1988); Art Spiegelman's *Maus* (Pantheon, 1986); Will Eisner's *Contract with God* (Titan Books, 1989); Neil Gaiman's Sandman series (DC Comics, 1993); Daniel Clowes's *Ghost World* (Fantagraphic Books, 1997); Craig Thompson's *Blankets* (Top Shelf, 2003); and Jeff Smith's Bone series (Cartoon Books, 1996).

Short stories appeal to readers of all abilities through quickly developed plots and conflict resolutions. Several short story collection editors stand out through the quality of their work: Don Gallo, Michael Cart, Jerry and Helen Weiss, and Lori Carlson, who collect stories from the best writers, and Gary Soto, Chris Crutcher, Lawrence Yep, Jane Yolen, Graham Salisbury, and Sherman Alexie, who have put together collections of their own work. Additional recommended authors and short story collections are listed at the end of the chapter.

Poetry collections and stories told in verse can also appeal to the struggling and advanced reader alike. Some of the best collections today come from Sarah Holbrook, Alberto Rios, Naomi Shihab Nye, Pat Mora, Paul Fleischman, Nikki Grimes, and again, Lori Carlson. Poetry has the benefit of strong image and feeling.

Young readers love the sound and performance aspects of poetry, and many of them are performance poets, often slam/hip-hop poets. Slam poetry is "a form of spoken word performed at a competitive poetry event, called a 'slam,' at which poets perform their own poems (or, in rare cases, those of others) that are 'judged' on a numeric scale by randomly picked members of the audience" (Wikipedia, 2006). An excellent book of slam poems compiled from the national poetry slam competition is *From Page to Stage and Back Again, 2003 National Poetry Slam* (Wordsmith Press, 2004), edited by Michael Salinger, a performance poet. An additional place to find slam poetry written by poets 19 years of age or younger is at Poetic License's Youth Online Poetry Journal (http://www.itvs.org/poeticlicense/youth_flash.html).

Narratives written in verse can be especially powerful. The story and the rhythm of the language can work together to enhance the reader's understanding. Some of the very best of today's young adult authors work in this medium, including Sharon Draper, Mel Glenn, Nikki Grimes, and Karen Hesse. Some of their best are *Bronx Masquerade,* by Nikki Grimes (Dial, 2002); *Class Dismissed: High School Poems,* by Mel Glenn (Clarion, 1982); *Dark Sons,* by Nikki Grimes (Jump at the Sun, 2005); *Out of the Dust,* by Karen Hesse (Scholastic, 1996); *Split Image,* by Mel Glenn (HarperCollins, 2000); and *Who Killed Mr. Chippendale: A Mystery in Poems,* also by Mel Glenn (Lodestar, 1996). The quality of these works is fantastic, such as Karen Hesse's *Out of the Dust,* which won the Newbery Medal.

ADDITIONAL GENRES

All the genres of literature are present in young adult literature. A few additional genres popular with young readers are historical fiction, fantasy, mystery, and science fiction. The best of these genres merit acknowledgment.

Cast Two Shadows (Harcourt, 1998) is one of renowned historical fictionist Ann Rinaldi's best works. The protagonist, Carolyn Whitaker, is the teenaged daughter of a rich plantation owner and a slave during the American Revolutionary War. Reading about the life of a biracial child may be especially relevant for young readers coming to understand their own heritage. Additional recommended works of historical fiction are listed at the end of the chapter.

The majority of young adult fiction on the market today is fantasy. The attraction for young readers may have much to do with the archetypal plotline in fantasy. Typically, protagonists in fantasy fiction are unappreciated and misunderstood at home and must venture out into the wider universe to discover their true talents. This journey generally involves a grand quest, with the fate of the world, planetary system, or universe hanging in the balance. Consider J.R.R. Tolkien's *The Lord of the Rings* trilogy, in which Frodo Baggins must overcome supernatural forces to save Middle Earth, despite the fact that he is not very big, not very experienced, and not at all feared and respected. Bilbo's story is surely the quintessential tale of adolescence. Additional recommended fantasy works are listed at the end of the chapter.

Although young adult mysteries are far outnumbered by fantasies, there are some very good ones, such as Kevin Brooks's *The Road of the Dead* (Scholastic, 2006). Brooks's protagonist, 14-year-old Ruben Ford, and his 17-year-old brother Cole, set out to solve the mystery of their sister's horrible murder in the remote area of Dartmoor, England. Ruben can hear the thoughts and feel the feelings of other people, even at great distances, and even when he would prefer not to. He can even feel himself inside his sister's killer's mind. Young readers will find themselves identifying heavily with both Ruben and Cole. Additional recommended mysteries are listed at the end of the chapter.

Science fiction fans are passionate, and National Book Award winner Pete Hautman has written an excellent young adult science fiction book titled *Hole in the Sky* (Simon and Schuster, 2001). In this futuristic tale, Earth has been ravaged by a super influenza virus, leaving most of the world's population dead. The few who survive live in constant fear of a psychopathic cult called the Survivors. Hautman tells the story from the point of view of four teenaged protagonists, and it is filled with chase and escape, safety and danger, life and death action. Additional recommended science fiction authors and works are listed at the end of the chapter.

A few additional authors well known for excellent books on particular topics include Joan Bauer, writer of humorous stories about young women growing such as *Rules of the Road* (Putnam, 1998) and *Best Foot Forward* (Putnam, 2005); Francesca Lia Block, writer of innovative urban fairy tales for the hip such as *Weetzie Bat* (HarperCollins, 1989); Edward Bloor, writer of social satires such as *Story Time* (Harcourt, 2004); Sharon Creech, writer of fictional narratives such as *Walk Two Moons* (HarperCollins, 1994); Sara Dessen, writer of realistic fiction such as *Dreamland* (Viking, 2000); John Green, writer of realistic fiction such as *Looking for Alaska* (Penguin, 2005); S. E. Hinton, one of the true pioneers of young adult literature, whose work involves coming of age under tough conditions such as *The Outsiders* (Viking, 1967) and *Rumble Fish* (Delacorte, 1976); Robert Lipsyte, writer of sports books such as *The Contender* (HarperCollins, 1967); David Lubar, writer of humorous stories of young men successfully making the best of life such as *Dunk* (Clarion, 2002) and *Sleeping Freshmen Never Lie* (Dutton, 2005); Gordon Korman, writer of humorous stories of young men in interesting situations such as *Son of the Mob* (Hyperion, 2002) and *No More Dead Dogs* (Hyperion, 2002); Richard Peck, writer of narrative fiction with autobiographical elements such as *A Long Way from Chicago* (Dial, 1998) and *A Year Down Yonder* (Dial, 2000); Rodman Philbrick, writer of realistic fiction such as *Freak the Mighty* (Scholastic, 1993); Jerry Spinelli, who writes about quirky characters who teach lessons about life such as in *Maniac Magee* (Little, Brown, 1990) and *Stargirl* (Knopf, 2000); Janet Tashjian, writer of humorous political satire such as *The Gospel According to Larry* (Holt, 2001) and *Vote for Larry* (Holt, 2004); Virginia Euwer Wolff, who writes about making the most of life's difficulties such as in *Make Lemonade* (Holt, 1993); and Ned Vizzini, who takes humorous looks at the problems of adolescence such as in *Be More Chill* (Miramax, 2004) and *It's Kind of a Funny Story* (Miramax, 2006). There are many, many others; my apologies to those I have omitted.

AWARDS

Exemplary young adult literature is recognized for its excellence through the bestowing of many awards, some with a very specific accomplishment in mind, such as the Coretta Scott King Award, which is given to authors of African descent representing an appreciation of the American dream (American

Library Association, 2006), or the Scott O'Dell Award, which is specifically for "a meritorious book … for children or young adults" with a "focus on historical fiction" (ScottOdell.com, 2006). A few of the more prestigious awards include all of the various ALA awards (http://www.ala.org/ala/yalsa/booklistsawards/ booklistsbook.htm), the Booklist Editors' Choice, the Boston Globe–Horn Book Award, the Margaret A. Edwards Award, the National Book Award, the Newbery Medal, the Printz Award, Publishers Weekly Best Book of the Year, the Pura Belpré Award (portraying and celebrating the Latino experience), VOYA Books in the Middle, and the YALSA Popular Paperback for Young Adults.

As a culminating activity in the search for exemplary young adult literature, let us return to that black T-shirted mob of teenaged girls I found myself engulfed in as I began this chapter. Why are these teenagers so emotionally engaged with Stephanie Meyer's vampire novels about Isabella (Bella) Swan and her love interest, the handsome, eternally teenaged vampire Edward Cullen? In her article titled "Vampires, Changelings, and Radical Mutant Teens: What the Demons, Freaks, and Other Abominations of Young Adult Literature Can Teach Us About Youth," Elaine O'Quinn (2004), professor of English at Appalachian State University, examined this very issue: why are adolescent readers so drawn to such unusual characters? O'Quinn explained that teens are constantly struggling with the people whom they are changing into, physically, emotionally, and psychologically. As they struggle with concepts of right and wrong, with newfound talents and vulnerabilities, they are very much like the vampire and werewolf protagonists, who are also "caught up in the pursuit of self, community, and humanity; trying to balance a newfound physicality with emotional awareness, intellectual consciousness, and moral perception; and attempting to negotiate a world strung somewhere between farce and tragedy" (p. 52). O'Quinn further explained that adolescents and their favorite supernatural characters share in the basic issues of maturing such as "how to deal with profound feelings of alienation and loneliness" (p. 54). For some young readers, realistic fiction works just fine for letting a protagonist carry life's burden for a while, but others may need something else, stories with even more distance from reality to safely examine their own life issues.

Whether it is fantasy, modern realism, outdoor adventure, mystery, horror, biography, or autobiography, the important thing is this: young people need to hear *their* stories. It may happen on a distant planet in a future century, or it may have happened in a concentration camp in a world war 65 years ago, it may even happen to a teenaged vampire, but they will recognize themselves and their stories in the authors' creations. By telling their stories, authors validate and honor young readers' lives. In her acceptance speech for the Astrid Lindgren Award, Katherine Paterson (2006) said,

What I want to say to isolated, angry, fearful youth—to all the children society has regarded as disposable, children who cannot love others because they have not yet learned to love themselves, all the sad, the lonely, the frightened who might read my books is this: you are seen, you are not alone, you are not despised, you are unique and of infinite value in the human family. As a writer I can try to say this through the words of a story.

Exemplary young adult literature is available to adolescents in thousands of titles and by hundreds of excellent authors. These authors and their works meet adolescents' need for literature in which they can see themselves and their life experiences as well as seeing the life experiences of teens representing other walks of life with which they may not be familiar. The best books will ring true to young readers because of authentic plots and accurate details. No matter what issues of adolescence authors write about, they must always treat these issues with respect. The best books will be those written so that the text is accessible to teen readers, who may then fold their reading into their maturation process, using the experiences of the characters to help them form their own values, beliefs, and perspectives on life—and have a little fun along the way.

RECOMMENDED LITERATURE

Authors Whose Books Reflect the Diversity of the Human Experience

Sherman Alexie: *The Lone Ranger and Tonto Fistfight in Heaven* (Atlantic Monthly Press, 1993), *Reservation Blues* (Warner, 1996), *The Toughest Indian in the World* (Grove Press, 2001); Julia Alvarez: *How Tia Lola Came to Stay* (Knopf, 2001), *How the Garcia Girls Lost Their Accents* (Algonquin, 1991); Rudolfo Anaya: *Bless Me, Ultima* (TQS Publications, 1972); Laurie Halse Anderson: *Speak* (Farrar, Straus and Giroux, 1998), *Catalyst* (Viking, 2000), *Twisted* (Viking, 2007); Maya Angelou: *I Know Why the Caged Bird Sings* (Random House, 1969); Judy Blume: *Are You There, God? It's Me, Margaret* (Bradbury, 1970), *Forever* (Bradbury, 1975); Coe Booth: *Tyrell* (Scholastic, 2006), Joseph Bruchac: *Heart of a Chief* (Dial, 1998), *Code Talker* (Scholastic, 2005), *Jim Thorpe—Original All-American* (Dial, 2006); Sandra Cisneros: *The House on Mango Street* (Random House, 1984), *Caramelo* (Knopf, 2003); Chris Crowe: *Mississippi Trial, 1955* (Fogelman, 2002); Christopher Paul Curtis: *The Watsons Go to Birmingham, 1963* (Delacorte, 1995), *Bud, Not Buddy* (Delacorte, 1999), *Bucking the Sarge* (Wendy Lamb Books, 2004); Sharon Draper: *Copper Sun* (Atheneum, 2006), *Tears of a Tiger* (Atheneum, 1994), *Forged by Fire* (Atheneum, 1997); Nancy Garden: *Annie on My Mind* (Farrar, Straus and Giroux, 1981), *Endgame* (Harcourt, 2006); K. L. Going: *Fat Kid Rules the World* (Putnam, 2003), *St. Iggy* (Harcourt, 2006); Bette Greene: *The Drowning of Stephan Jones* (Bantam, 1991); Laila Halaby: *West of the Jordan* (Beacon, 2003); Virginia Hamilton: *The House of Dies Drear* (Simon and Schuster, 1968), *M.C. Higgins the Great* (Simon and Schuster, 1974); Valerie Hobbs: *Stefan's Story* (Farrar, Straus and Giroux, 2003), *Letting Go of Bobby James or How I Found My Self of Steam* (Farrar, Straus and Giroux, 2004); Francisco Jiménez: *Breaking Through* (Houghton Mifflin, 2001), *Circuit: Stories from the Life of a Migrant Child* (University of New Mexico Press, 1997); Angela Johnson: *Heaven* (Simon and Schuster,

1998), *First Part Last* (Simon and Schuster, 2003), *Toning the Sweep* (Orchard, 1993); Cynthia Kadohata: *Kira-Kira* (Atheneum, 2004), *Weedflower* (Atheneum, 2006); M. E. Kerr: *If I Love You, Am I Trapped Forever?* (HarperCollins, 1973), *Deliver Us from Evie* (HarperCollins, 1994); Ron Koertge: *Arizona Kid* (Little, Brown, 1988), *Margaux with an X* (Walker, 2004), *Spaz and Stoner* (Candlewick, 2002); David Levithan: *Boy Meets Boy* (Knopf, 2003), *The Realm of Possibility* (Knopf, 2004), *Wide Awake* (Knopf, 2006); Lois Lowry: *Number the Stars* (Houghton Mifflin, 1989); Victor Martinez: *Parrot in the Oven* (Joanna Cotler, 1996); Janet McDonald: *Spellbound* (Farrar, Straus and Giroux, 2001), *Twists and Turns* (Farrar, Straus and Giroux, 2003); Ben Michaelson: *Touching Spirit Bear* (HarperCollins, 2001); Walter Dean Myers: *Monster* (HarperCollins, 1999), *The Beast* (Scholastic, 2003), *Fallen Angels* (Scholastic, 1988); An Na: *A Step from Heaven* (Handprint, 2001); Naomi Shihab Nye: *Nineteen Varieties of Gazelle: Poems of the Middle East* (Greenwillow, 2002), *This Same Sky* (Simon and Schuster, 1992); Linda Sue Park: *A Single Shard* (Clarion, 2001), *The Kite Fighters* (Clarion, 2000), *When My Name Was Keoko* (Clarion, 2002); Pam Muñoz Ryan: *Esperanza Rising* (Scholastic, 2000), *Becoming Naomi Leon* (Scholastic, 2004); Alex Sanchez: *Rainbow Boys* (Simon and Schuster, 2001), *So Hard to Say* (Simon and Schuster, 2004); Cynthia Leitich Smith: *Rain Is Not My Indian Name* (HarperCollins, 2001), *Indian Shoes* (HarperCollins, 2002); Greg Leitich Smith: *Ninjas, Piranhas, and Galileo* (Little, Brown, 2003), *Tofu and T-Rex* (Little, Brown, 2005); Gary Soto: *Buried Onions* (Harcourt, 1997), *Jesse* (Harcourt, 1994), *Accidental Love* (Harcourt, 2006); Mildred Taylor: *The Road to Memphis* (Dial, 1990), *Roll of Thunder Hear My Cry* (Dial, 1976), *Let the Circle Be Unbroken* (Dial, 1981); Terry Trueman: *Stuck in Neutral* (HarperCollins, 2000), *Cruise Control* (HarperCollins, 2004), *Inside Out* (HarperCollins, 2003); Victor Villaseñor: *Macho* (Delta, 1997), *Walking Stars: Stories of Magic and Power* (Piñata Books, 1994); Jeanne Wakatsuki: *Farewell to Manzanar* (Laurel Leaf, 1983); James Welch: *Fool's Crow* (Viking, 1986); Rita Williams-Garcia: *Like Sisters on the Homefront* (Lodetar, 1995), *Blue Tights* (Puffin, 1996); Ellen Wittlinger: *Hard Love* (Simon and Schuster, 1999), *What's in a Name* (Simon and Schuster, 2000); June Rae Wood: *The Man Who Loved Clowns* (Putnam, 1992), *Turtle on a Fence Post* (Putnam, 1997); Jacquelyn Woodson: *Miracle's Boys* (Putnam, 2000), *I Hadn't Meant to Tell You This* (Laurel Leaf, 1995), *From the Notebooks of Melanin Sun* (Scholastic, 1995).

Recommended Works of Historical Fiction

Crispin, Cross of Lead, by Avi (Hyperion, 2002); *Eyes of the Emperor,* by Graham Salisbury (Wendy Lamb Books, 2005); *Grasslands,* by Deb Seely (Holiday House, 2002); *Island of the Blue Dolphins,* by Scott O'Dell (Houghton Mifflin, 1960); *The Land,* by Mildred Taylor (Fogelman, 2001); *The Last Mission,* by Harry Mazer (Delacorte, 1979); *The Legend of Bass Reeves,* by Gary Paulsen (Wendy Lamb Books, 2006); *Mary, Bloody Mary,* by Carolyn Meyer (Gulliver, 1999); *Nightjohn,* by Gary Paulsen (Delacorte, 1993); *Out of the Dust,* by Karen Hesse (Scholastic, 1996); *Sarny: A Life Remembered,* by Gary Paulsen (Delacorte, 1997); *Sing Down the Moon,* by Scott O'Dell (Houghton Mifflin, 1970); *A Single Shard,* by Linda Sue Park (Clarion, 2001); *Soldier's Heart,* by Gary Paulsen (Delacorte, 1998); *Under the Blood-Red Sun,* by Graham Salisbury (Delacorte, 1994).

Recommended Short Story Collections

American Dragons, by Lawrence Yep (HarperCollins, 1993); *Athletic Shorts,* by Chris Crutcher (Greenwillow, 1991); *Baseball in April,* by Gary Soto (Harcourt, 1990);

Dreams and Visions: Fourteen Flights of Fantasy, edited by Jerry and Helen Weiss (Starscape, 2006); *First Crossing: Stories about Teen Immigrants,* edited by Don Gallo (Candlewick, 2004); *Island Boyz,* by Graham Salisbury (Random House, 2002); *Moccasin Thunder: American Indian Stories for Today,* edited by Lori Carlson (HarperCollins, 2005); *Necessary Noise: Stories about Our Families As They Really Are,* edited by Michael Cart (HarperCollins, 2003); *On the Fringe,* edited by Don Gallo (Dial, 2001); the Rush Hour series, edited by Michael Cart (Delacorte, 1997–2007); *Ten Little Indians,* by Sherman Alexie (Grove, 2003); *Tomorrowland: 10 Stories about the Future,* edited by Michael Cart (Scholastic, 1999); *Toughest Indian in the World,* by Sherman Alexie (Atlantic Monthly Press, 2000); *Vampires: A Collection of Original Stories,* by Jane Yolen (HarperCollins, 1991).

Recommended Poetry Collections

Chicks Up Front, by Sarah Holbrook (for young women in their upper teen years) (Cleveland State University Poetry Center, 1998); *Cool Salsa: Bilingual Poems on Growing Up Latino in the United States,* edited by Lori Carlson (Holt, 1994); *Joyful Noise: Poems for Two Voices,* by Paul Fleischman (HarperCollins, 1998); *My Own True Name,* by Pat Mora (Arte Publico, 2000); *Nineteen Varieties of Gazelle: Poems of the Middle East,* by Naomi Shihab Nye (Greenwillow, 2002); *The Smallest Muscle in the Human Body,* by Alberto Rios (Copper Canyon Press, 2002); *Walking on the Boundaries of Change,* by Sara Holbrook (Boyds Mills, 1998).

Recommended Fantasy Works

Abarat, by Clive Barker (Joanna Cotler, 2002); *The Amber Spyglass,* by Philip Pullman (Knopf, 1999); the Artemis Fowl series, by Eoin Colfer (Hyperion, 2001–2006); *City of the Beasts,* by Isabel Allende (HarperCollins, 2002); *Dragonflight,* by Anne McCaffrey (Atheneum, 1976); *Ella Enchanted,* by Gail Carson Levine (HarperCollins, 1997); *Eldest,* by Christopher Paolini (Knopf, 2005); *Eragon,* by Christopher Paolini (Knopf, 2003); *Farthest Shore,* by Ursula Le Guin (Atheneum, 1972); *The Golden Compass,* by Philip Pullman (Knopf, 1996); *The Goose Girl,* by Shannon Hale (Bloomsbury, 2003); the Harry Potter series, by J. K. Rowling (Arthur A. Levine Books/Scholastic Inc., 1997–2004); *Heir Apparent,* by Vivian Vande Velde (Harcourt, 2002); *The Hobbit,* by J.R.R. Tolkien (Allen and Unwin, 1937); *Inkheart,* by Cornelia Funke (Scholastic, 2003); *Inkspell,* by Cornelia Funke (Scholastic, 2005); *Kingdom of the Golden Dragon,* by Isabel Allende (Rayo, 2004); *The Lord of the Rings,* by J.R.R. Tolkien (Allen and Unwin, 1954); *The Magic Circle,* by Donna Jo Napoli (Dutton, 1993); *A Sending of Dragons,* by Jane Yolen (Delacorte, 1987); *The Subtle Knife,* by Philip Pullman (Knopf, 1997); *The Thief Lord,* by Cornelia Funke (Scholastic, 2002); *The Tombs of Atuan,* by Ursula Le Guin (Atheneum, 1972); *A Wizard of Earthsea,* by Ursula Le Guin (Parnassus, 1968).

Recommended Science Fiction Works

47, by Walter Mosley (Little, Brown, 2005); *Dune,* by Frank Herbert (Chilton, 1965); *Ender's Game,* by Orson Scott Card (TOR, 1985); *Feed,* by M. T. Anderson (Candlewick, 2002); *House of Stairs,* by William Sleator (Dutton, 1974); *House of the Scorpion,* by Nancy Farmer (Atheneum, 2002); *Interstellar Pig,* by William Sleator (Dutton, 1984); *The Last Book in the Universe,* by Rodman Philbrick (Blue Sky Press, 2000); *Mr. Was,* by Pete

Hautman (Simon and Schuster, 1996); *Parasite Pig,* by William Sleator (Dutton, 2002); *Stranger in a Strange Land,* by Robert Heinlein (Putnam, 1961).

Recommended Mysteries

The Body of Christopher Creed, by Carol Plum-Ucci (Harcourt, 2000); *I Am the Cheese,* by Robert Cormier (Knopf, 1977); *I Know What You Did Last Summer,* by Lois Duncan (Archway, 1975); *The Other Side of Dark,* by Joan Lowery Nixon (Delacorte, 1986); *Séance,* by Joan Lowery Nixon (Harcourt, 1980); *Summer of Fear,* by Lois Duncan (Little, Brown, 1976); *Who Killed Mr. Chippendale: A Mystery in Poems,* by Mel Glenn (Dutton, 1996).

REFERENCES

Amazon.com. (2006). *Drums, girls and dangerous pie.* Retrieved December 10, 2006, from http://www.amazon.com/Drums-Girls-Dangerous-Jordan-Sonneblick/dp/096689409X

Blasingame, J. (2006). Venturing into the deep waters: The works of Jordan Sonnenblick. *ALAN Review, 33*(2), 60–64.

Blasingame, J. (2007). *Books that don't bore 'em: Young adult books that speak to this generation.* New York: Scholastic.

Cart, M. (2006). *From romance to realism: Fifty years of growth and change in young adult literature.* New York: HarperCollins.

Crutcher, C. (1992). Healing through literature. In D. Gallo (Ed.), *Author's insights: Turning teenagers into readers and writers* (pp. 33–40). Portsmouth, NH: Boynton Cook.

Erickson, E. (1950). *Childhood and society.* New York: W. W. Norton.

Karolides, N. J. (1991). The transactional theory of literature. In *Reader response in the classroom: Evoking and interpreting meaning in literature* (pp. 3–25). White Plains, NY: Longman.

Kohlberg, L. (1981). *Essays on moral development* (Vol. 1). San Francisco: Harper and Row.

Krashen, S. (1993). *The power of reading.* Englewood, CO: Libraries Unlimited.

Loh, V. (2006). Quantity and quality: The need for culturally authentic trade books in Asian American young adult literature. *ALAN Review, 34*(1), 36–53.

Nilsen, A. P., & Donelson, K. L. (2004). *Literature for today's young adults.* Boston: Pearson, Allyn and Bacon.

O'Quinn, E. (2004). Vampires, changelings, and radical mutant teens: What the demons, freaks, and other abominations of young adult literature can teach us about youth. *ALAN Review, 31*(3), 50–56.

Paterson, K. (2006). *Astrid Lindgren Lecture.* Retrieved December 10, 2006, from http://www.alma.se/page.php?realm=625

Rosenblatt, L. (1938). *Literature as exploration.* New York: Century Appleton.

Scholastic Inc. (2005). *Katherine Paterson's biography.* Retrieved December 10, 2006, from http://books.scholastic.com/teachers/authorsandbooks/authorstudies/authorhome.jsp?authorID=80&collateralID=5257&displayName=Biography

ScottODell.com. (2006). *The Scott O'Dell Award for Historical Fiction.* Retrieved November 10, 2006, from http://www.scottodell.com/index.html

Substance Abuse and Mental Health Services Administration. (2006). *Depression and suicide in children and adolescents.* Retrieved December 10, 2006, from http://mental health.samhsa.gov/features/surgeongeneralreport/chapter3/sec5.asp

White-Kaulaity, M. (2006). The voices of power and the power of voices: Teaching with Native American literature. *ALAN Review, 34*(1), 8–16.

Wikipedia. (2006). *Slam poetry.* Retrieved December 24, 2006, from http://en.wikipedia. org/wiki/Slam_poetry

Chapter Ten

MOTIVATING ADOLESCENTS IN LITERACY

Jeanne Swafford

Adolescents have a reputation for being difficult to live with, being bored with everything (particularly things suggested by teachers or parents), and being full of raging hormones. Perhaps aspects of this reputation are well founded, but there is much more to adolescents than these negative attributes. Adolescents are passionate individuals. They care deeply about their relationships with their peers and spend much time building relationships with them, face-to-face and electronically. Much of what they do revolves around activities with their peers, such as sports, gaming, music, and, yes, even occasional academically related pursuits. Adolescents care very much about how their peers perceive them and about fitting in with their peer groups. This allegiance to their peers represents a shift from when they were younger and adult influence and support were viewed as most important. Motivation to engage in school-related tasks also declines in the years surrounding adolescence. For decades, various sources have noted that the numbers of students who are alliterate (they can read but choose not to) are higher than expected (Guthrie, McGough, Bennett, & Rice, 1996). The challenge for teachers is to figure out how to capitalize on the strengths adolescents bring to school to make education—and literacy learning, in particular—more motivating, meaningful, and engaging.

MOTIVATIONS

The multifaceted construct of motivation has been a topic of much interest to researchers for years (e.g., Wigfield & Guthrie, 1997). Various explanations of motivation have been proposed and investigated. In this section of the chapter, I draw from writings from both psychology and education to describe different aspects of motivation. These aspects are not to be seen as definitive, but as illustrative of the complexity of the construct. First, I briefly describe the traditional intrinsic and extrinsic dimensions of motivation. Next, I describe the attributes adolescents often credit for their success or failure, thus influencing motivation. I also examine the kinds of achievement goals that contribute to motivation. Last, I describe social goals, the most recent element to be researched in relation to motivation. Although I refer to motivations to read, these motivations also apply to other aspects of literacy such as writing.

Intrinsic Motivation

Traditional explanations of motivation include discussions of intrinsic and extrinsic motivations. Intrinsic motivation has typically been described as coming from within an individual and is related to the satisfaction or pleasure a person gets from engaging in a task. Intrinsic motivation is often described as it relates to a learner's feelings of self-efficacy (competency) and autonomy (self-direction or self-determination).

Self-Efficacy

Intrinsic motivation has been linked to self-efficacy (Wigfield & Guthrie, 1997) or feelings of competency. Self-efficacy is important for understanding an individual's motivations to choose, attempt, sustain, and complete tasks (Pajares & Schunk, 2001). Adolescents who possess high self-efficacy believe that they are capable of successfully reading difficult texts. When they are challenged by a text, they will persist and put forth more effort because they are confident that they possess strategies they need to negotiate a text successfully. Adolescents who demonstrate high self-efficacy are more intrinsically motivated to read challenging texts, especially relating to topics about which they are passionate. The challenge and the satisfaction of learning something new or understanding a difficult text would be motivating in and of itself. If adolescents have low self-efficacy, they probably will not engage in reading texts they perceive as difficult. If they do begin to read a text and find it difficult, they will not persist.

Self-efficacy should not be viewed as an either-or proposition. It depends on many conditions, which include, but are not limited to, the type or difficulty of text/s, the purpose for reading, and a reader's schema and interest about a topic. For example, an individual may have high self-efficacy when reading a text for which he or she has a well-developed schema. On the other hand, a reader may experience low self-efficacy when reading about random topics to answer questions on a standardized test. A reader's perceptions of self-efficacy (competency) will definitely influence motivation to read.

Autonomy

Autonomy is also related to intrinsic motivation. When adolescents have a sense of autonomy, they believe that their behaviors are self-directed or self-determined (Reed, Schallert, Beth, & Woodruff, 2004). They make their own choices about their purposes for reading, what to read, when to read, where to read, with whom to read, and what strategies to use before reading, during reading, and after reading. When readers are autonomous, they self-direct their reading.

When students experience autonomy, they may read for the sheer joy of reading, or they may choose to read because they are particularly curious about a topic or issue. Autonomous readers often lose themselves in their reading, whether its purpose is for pleasure or for information (which can also be for pleasure). Some writers liken this kind of involvement to what Csikszentmihalyi (1990) called flow: students become so enthralled or immersed in what they are reading that they do not know what is going on around them. They tune out everything, except the world of the text; they lose track of time, and nothing else matters. Not only do individuals enjoy losing themselves in a book to experience pleasure, but they also experience freedom and fulfillment. This is the ultimate experience of autonomous reading.

Extrinsic Motivation

Extrinsic motivation is described as coming from outside the individual and is traditionally associated with tangible rewards such as grades, privileges (e.g., pizza parties, free time), or punishments. External motivation typically has not received rave reviews in educational literature. Research has demonstrated that students will engage in behaviors as long as rewards are present. When those rewards are withdrawn, intrinsic motivation is undermined, and behavior diminishes (Deci, Koestner, & Ryan, 2001). Thus extrinsically motivated behaviors tend to be short term. Nevertheless, tangible rewards are an important part of many classroom reading incentive programs.

The early work related to intrinsic and extrinsic motivation was grounded in behaviorism (psychology of human behavior, which posits that behavior results from consequences of past behavior). Since that time, researchers from various traditions have continued to explore the construct of motivation in an attempt to explain why people behave the way they do. Ryan and Deci (2000) suggested that extrinsic motivation varies depending on the degree of autonomy (i.e., self-direction, self-determined behavior, or self-directed goal orientation) related to a task. For example, if Suzy strives to get good grades because her parents threaten to take away her cell phone, she is motivated to avoid punishment. This motivation is characterized by low autonomy (i.e., self-direction). On the other hand, if Sarah makes good grades because she wants to go to college and she knows good grades are necessary, then her goal is more self-directed (autonomous).

Ryan and Deci (2000) took their explanation of extrinsic motivation a step further and suggested that the extent to which students internalize or integrate the values of a classroom influences their motivation or lack of motivation. In the example mentioned above, Sarah, who makes good grades because she knows it is important for getting into college, has internalized values related to school. If she also studies hard because she understands the power of knowledge for today and in the future, then perhaps she has integrated school values with her own. As the values of school are integrated to become a personal commitment, extrinsic motivation is enhanced. In other words, Ryan and Deci suggested that extrinsic motivation can be viewed as a continuum, from low autonomous motivators to high autonomous motivators, rather than with an either-or perspective.

In the previous discussion of intrinsic motivation, autonomy was related to intrinsic motivation. Yet, in the discussion of extrinsic motivation, Ryan and Deci (2000) also referred to autonomy. I believe these seemingly contradictory ideas are the result of the fuzzy understanding of the construct of motivation. Ryan and Deci seem to suggest that almost all motivations are extrinsic, but some motivations are situated closer toward the intrinsic end of the continuum than others. In an attempt to simplify my use of the word *autonomy*, I refer to autonomy as it relates to intrinsic motivation (or the intrinsic side of the continuum).

Attributes of Success

Motivation also depends on factors that a person attributes to his or her success. These factors include effort, ability, task difficulty, or luck (Pressley, 1998). Adolescents who believe that effort determines success or failure take more responsibility for their successes and failures. They believe that they have personal control over tasks (autonomy), and as long as they feel capable (efficacious), they will be motivated to work hard, study, practice, or do whatever it takes to be successful. Failure (an extrinsic motivator) can quickly change an individual's belief about the usefulness of effort, however.

Other individuals believe that their success depends on their ability (or lack of ability). If students believe that their lack of success is because they are not smart enough, they may not expend much—if any—effort. For example, if students have experienced enough failure, especially when others experience success, they may attribute their failure to their lack of ability. Adolescents who have been labeled "at risk" or who have participated in special reading instruction have likely identified themselves as having less ability than others in their class. If individuals believe that they do not possess the ability to read well (related to low self-efficacy), they believe that they are powerless to complete a task successfully. As a result, they may not be motivated to read.

Others attribute success to how difficult they believe a task is. If adolescents believe a task is just too difficult to accomplish, they will not expend much effort. For example, suppose the task is to read and understand a poem. Imagine that a student typically has little trouble reading but has had difficulty understanding poetry in the past. If the student attempts to read the poem and experiences the least little bit of confusion, she may quit reading because she believes that understanding the poem (the task) is just too difficult. Success is attributed to how easy or how difficult a student perceives a task to be.

Still others attribute success to luck. If luck is the cause of success or failure, then the individual is not responsible. If students successfully complete a task, they are lucky. If they are not successful, they are simply unlucky. If individuals believe that success is simply the luck of the draw, they are powerless. When individuals feel powerless to control their destiny, so to speak, they are not motivated to engage in tasks that are the least bit challenging.

Regardless of what an adolescent believes is responsible for his or her success or failure, Pressley (1998) contended that academic motivation is a "fragile commodity" (p. 229). Adolescents must be successful to perceive themselves as successful and to possess high self-efficacy. As success declines, lack of motivation will surely follow.

Achievement Goals

Individuals' achievement goals may also contribute to their motivation to read. What texts adolescents choose to read and how long they engage in reading are driven by their personal achievement goals. In addition, memories related to pleasurable literacy-related tasks may also motivate an individual to set particular goals (Reed et al., 2004). Ruddell and Unrau (2004) described achievement goals as mastery oriented or ego oriented. Mastery-oriented goals are related to intrinsic motivation: a learner is motivated to engage in inquiry about a topic or stick with reading a challenging text because he or she wants to learn. An individual who is mastery oriented will be apt to put forth additional effort when a task becomes difficult so that he or she can accomplish a task. In contrast, ego-oriented goals are related to extrinsic motivation: the focus is on seeking recognition for accomplishing a goal. For example, an individual may brag about reading a very long book in a very short time to impress his or her peers.

Social Goals

Adolescents are also motivated by their social goals (Baker & Wigfield, 1999). As noted earlier in the chapter, adolescents care very much about their relationships with their peers, and they are motivated by the desire to share with and be accepted by their friends. Because they have similar interests, they read texts about topics that are appealing to their friends (i.e., affinity groups).

Reading that occurs outside of school is often socially motivated and is usually unrelated to academic interests. Literacy-related activities that adolescents engage in outside of school may involve face-to-face or electronic interactions. For example, when studying adolescent girls who wrote zines (self-published alternatives to commercial magazines) outside school, Guzzetti and Gamboa (2004) found that the girls' affinity groups (both online and face-to-face) motivated them to "initiate and sustain ... writing against gender stereotypes and for social justice" (p. 432). Chandler-Olcott and Mahar's (2003b) study of Rhiannon, who wrote her own fan fictions (fiction written by fans of an original work, using the same characters and/or setting) and constructed anime-focused Web pages (Japanese-style animation), and Eileen, who participated in an art-related anime mailing list, demonstrated motivation from their online affinity groups to further develop their fan fictions.

MOTIVATION AND ENGAGEMENT

The relationship between motivation and engagement is an obvious one. To become engaged in an activity, individuals must be motivated to become involved. Without motivation, engagement would not occur. In the 1990s, research at the National Reading Research Center on reading motivation and engagement laid the foundation for much of the research that is being done today. This research was precipitated in part by the results of a national survey, which revealed that teachers' number one concern was how to motivate students to read (Gambrell, Palmer, Codling, & Mazzoni, 1996).

The construct of motivation was described earlier. But what, exactly, is engagement? This answer is not an easy one. Some researchers describe engagement in terms of student outcomes: enjoyment of reading for its own sake (intrinsic motivation), getting lost in reading (intrinsic motivation, flow), and on-task behavior (Guthrie & Wigfield, 2000). Still others suggest that engagement is a combination of factors related to self-efficacy (intrinsic motivation), purposeful reading, relevancy, lack of anxiety, and a positive relationship with the teacher (Cambourne, 1995). Although researchers define engagement in different ways, they all agree that motivation is necessary for engagement to occur. Guthrie and Wigfield (2000) wrote, "A person reads a word or comprehends a text not only because she can do it, but because she is motivated to do it" (p. 404). Although motivation is an essential component of engagement, motivation alone is not sufficient for engagement. Guthrie and Wigfield stated that the cognitive and social dimensions of engaged reading are also critical components of engagement. The following quote describes engaged readers by showing the relationship between motivation, cognitive dimensions (strategic and knowledgeable reader), and social dimensions of engagement: "Engaged readers are motivated to read for a variety of personal goals, strategic in using multiple approaches to comprehend, knowledgeable in their construction of new understanding from texts, and socially interactive in their approach to literacy" (Guthrie & Wigfield, 2000, p. 403).

LOOKING BACK, LOOKING FORWARD

Although much has changed over the more than 30 years I have been teaching, some things seem to stay the same. Adolescents keep us on our toes. They are energetic and delightful and exasperating, all at the same time. They are less motivated to read and engage in school-related tasks than they were when they were younger. Some adolescents continue to embrace the goals of their parents and teachers and make good grades, even if they are not intrinsically motivated to learn for learning's sake. Others, however, who may or may not have been successful in elementary school, decide for one reason or another not to place studying, reading, and schoolwork as a high priority. Perhaps school-related tasks are not motivating, or perhaps these adolescents do not know how to juggle the multiple demands and pleasures in their lives.

Also the same, after all these years, is that many teachers strive to create classroom activities intriguing enough that even the least interested student will become curious and motivated to take part. Every now and then, there will be a glimmer of interest demonstrated by a student who does not typically engage in schoolwork. Other teachers feel helpless and lament that they do not know what to do with the student who is "so capable but does not try" or the student who is "so far behind, they'll never be able to make it." All these things are still as real today as they were many yesterdays ago.

What has changed in the last decade is how researchers have conceptualized and are studying adolescent literacies (Alvermann, Hinchman, Moore, Phelps, & Waff, 1998). Now they are learning about adolescent literacies from adolescents themselves—researchers are finding out what students are up to and are focusing on their perspectives, not just on those of teachers, about schooling. Today, researchers and teachers are not only concerned with the literacies adolescents use to be successful in school, but also with the personal literacies that adolescents use in their lives outside of school. From recent, in-depth case studies, much has been learned about the multiple literacies adolescents use outside of school. Research about motivation, engagement, and adolescents' multiple literacies provides clues about how to motivate adolescents in school.

WHAT'S A TEACHER TO DO?

How can teachers build on what is known about motivation and adolescents to create classroom environments and literacy-related tasks that will engage adolescents? Hinchman, Alvermann, Boyd, Brozo, and Vacca (2003–2004), members of the International Reading Association's Commission on Adolescent Literacy, suggest the following ideas, based on their review of research.

Adolescents As Competent Individuals

First, adolescents need to see themselves as competent (efficacious) and having something to offer. When students believe they are competent, they will be more likely to engage successfully in school literacy practices. Research suggests that adolescents competently use multiple literacies outside of school. For example, Smith and Wilhelm's (2002) study of adolescent boys revealed that they read magazines, newspapers, cookbooks, movie reviews, music lyrics, and other texts. Alvermann and Heron (2001) reported that Robert, an adolescent who participated in after-school Read and Talk (R&T) Clubs in a public library, professed a disinterest in reading. Yet in this context outside of school, he not only read and summarized elaborate episodes of Dragon Ball Z (a Japanese anime series about the adventures of Goku, who protects the earth and other planets from fierce enemies), he also described the characters and explained the complicated plots.

To design environments and literacy tasks that support and build on students' competencies, teachers need to know about adolescents' interests and out-of-school activities. The importance of showing an interest in adolescents' activities outside of school cannot be underestimated. For example, Bambino, a wrestling expert who participated in Smith and Wilhelm's (2002) study, said, "The teachers don't know you, care about you, recognize you. So why should you care about them or the work they want you to do?" (p. 99). Simply acknowledging Bambino's interest and expertise or asking about a wrestling match would have gone a long way with this adolescent boy. Similarly, Eric, a 6th grader who coauthored the first chapter of *Reconceptualizing the Literacies in Adolescents' Lives* (Alvermann, Hinchman, Moore, Phelps, & Waff, 2006), indicated that if teachers recognized Eric's interest in writing—which he did outside of school—it would show that they valued the choices he made. Alvermann (2006) suggested that this interest "encourages a reciprocal teaching-learning relationship in which teachers take seriously—are even instructionally guided by—the literate identities students choose to share" (p. 8). Girls who wrote zines outside of school suggested that teachers could support in-school writing assignments that encourage "students to write about their own values, experiences, and ideas" (Guzzetti & Gamboa, 2004, p. 433), a characteristic of zines. If, however, teachers do not know that students read and write zines, they would miss this opportunity to build on students' strengths and interests. For example, Chandler-Olcott and Mahar (2003a) wrote about Rhiannon and Eileen, two adolescent girls who routinely engaged in reading, writing, and illustrating quite elaborate fan fictions. The girls considered their "fanfics" much better writing than their somewhat formulaic school writing and spent more time writing fanfics than academic writing. Although the writing was done for themselves, not for a public audience, it may have been interesting for teachers to see the kind of writing Rhiannon and Eileen did outside of school, not for evaluation purposes or as an effort to include fanfic writing in school, but to get to know the girls and their writing from a different perspective.

It is important that teachers and parents know what interests adolescents outside the classroom. Listed below are questions that might help adults become more consciously aware of the kinds of activities adolescents choose to do outside of school. Many of these questions are guided by what I see my son and his friends doing and by ideas found in the literature related to adolescents and adolescents' literacy activities.

Do students work after school or on weekends? If so, what jobs do they do? What special knowledge do they have that enables them to do their jobs? Are they responsible for their younger siblings while their parents are not home, or do they babysit regularly for others? What extracurricular activities do they participate in? Do they play a sport, dance, play in a band, or act in local theater productions? Do they compose music or write song lyrics or raps? Do they enjoy photography, modeling, styling hair, or designing their own clothes? Do they volunteer at an animal shelter or train and show horses? Are they 4-H members? Perhaps they build their own computers and create Web pages for themselves and others. Are they gaming enthusiasts? Are they members of online communities that expand their friendships across the globe? Are they anime fans or collectors? Do they go to the opening night of movies that appeal to them? Do they make their own CDs and videos? Are they artists or designers of graphics for T-shirts or local tattoo artists? Are they wrestling enthusiasts or reality TV fans? Perhaps they are interested in the armed forces and train regularly to prepare for a military career. Are they into talk radio and have a favorite celebrity host? Where do they hang out after school? What do they do? Are they university or professional sports fans? Do they collect memorabilia? Perhaps they are car, skateboarding, motorcycle, or moped enthusiasts. Do they run marathons or train at a gym? Do they write zines? Do they have their own book clubs? Are they involved in activities for improving the local community? The list could go on and on.

Next, think about the kinds of specialized skills and knowledge adolescents must possess to participate in these activities. What kinds of literacies do young people engage in when participating in after-school activities? What do they read? What kinds of writing or drawing do they do? Consider the idea that reading is not just about reading books. Adolescents may read text messages, information from the Internet, e-mail, blogs, letters, magazines, advertisements, catalogs, recipes, guidebooks, flyers, directions, zines, newspapers, and poetry. Perhaps they listen to books on tape or read CD lyrics. When adults really start listening to and observing adolescents, it will be easier to understand what interests them and what issues matter to them.

A word of caution is necessary here: adolescents may be suspicious of a teacher's or parent's sudden interest in them and be less than open to queries. Even adolescents who are so-called good students may not readily reveal what brings them pleasure outside of school. The questions could be seen as encroaching on their personal lives. This may especially be the case before adults gain an adolescent's trust. If young people do share bits of information about themselves, savor those and put them to good use. Be careful to respect, rather than critique or trivialize, what adolescents reveal.

Personally Relevant Connections

The second recommendation for creating engaging literacy instruction is to help adolescents make personally relevant connections between their academic literacies and their lives outside of school. Adolescents' interests can be used as a guide for providing them with such texts as magazines, newspapers, novels, informational texts, manuals, song and rap lyrics, and electronic texts in the classroom. These texts can be used as alternatives to textbooks to teach content related to curriculum standards. For example, to demonstrate how writers' voices differ in different contexts, rap lyrics, an article from a popular magazine, and a newspaper clipping can be used. Students will be more motivated, interested, and willing to read texts that are personally relevant.

When helping adolescents make personally relevant connections between themselves and school learning, it is important to build on and recognize students' funds of knowledge from their homes, communities, peers, and popular culture (Moje et al., 2004). Moje and her colleagues found that "pop Latino, gangster rap, and traditional Mexican music" (p. 60) were reflected in Latino students' developing identities and the texts they read (e.g., magazines) and wrote. News media, television, and movies helped students feel more like a part of the global Latino community. Surprisingly, the researchers also found that students used popular culture texts to make connections with and think about science concepts.

Another way to connect students' lives with the school curriculum is to think about the issues about which they are concerned and use those as the focus of inquiry and discussion. Some inquiries may come directly from students' experiences. Fairbanks (2000) invited 6th-grade students to engage in inquiries about social issues that affected them personally. They investigated such topics as homelessness (one girl had a friend who was homeless and wanted to know more), violence (a boy was concerned about gangs in his neighborhood), and abusive home situations and alcoholism (two students were dealing with these issues at home). Students were motivated to pursue these inquiries because they chose to study issues of crucial importance to them. In relation to motivation, classroom engagements such as these foster intrinsic motivation (i.e., self-efficacy, autonomy) and support mastery-oriented goals. In addition, students would be more likely to attribute their success to effort than other attributes.

A Caution

Adolescents and researchers alike caution teachers about how they use adolescents' popular culture to make connections in classrooms. First, students engage in multiple literacies outside of school to relax, have fun, relieve stress, and accomplish their own purposes (Chandler-Olcott & Mahar, 2003a; Guzzetti & Gamboa, 2004)—all intrinsic motivations. The adolescent girls in the Guzzetti and Gamboa study did not think it was a good idea to suggest that students write zines in school because it would negate the pleasures associated with them; rather, they suggested it would be worthwhile to bring the do-it-yourself ethic of zines and support the freedom of topic choice and sharing or not sharing into the classroom. These practices would bring in the element of autonomy, thus supporting aspects of intrinsic motivation. Second, when teachers use popular culture as a reward or to hook or trick students into engaging in classroom activities, students may view teachers' motives as inauthentic.

Choice

I would be remiss if I did not include the importance of choice as it relates to motivating adolescents to engage in academic literacy. This is not a new idea. One of the most inspiring education-related books I remember reading as an undergraduate was *Hooked on Books* (Fader & McNeil, 1968). My recollection is that a teacher was concerned because his students could not read. He took them to a large book warehouse, gave them empty bags, and told them to choose any books they wanted. His students filled up their bags and wanted more. The teacher learned that not only did the students know how to read, but when they chose what they wanted to read, they read voraciously. (My apologies to the author if my recollection is not quite accurate.) More than 30 years later, 6th-grade students were asked what motivated them to read (Ivey & Broaddus, 2001). Their request was loud and clear: let them read what they choose, and give them access to interesting reading materials.

Choice is also important in terms of how activities within a classroom are structured. In a study done by Alvermann, Young, Green, and Wisenbaker (1999) of a R&T Club, Athene (an adolescent girl in the club) mentioned that one of her teachers sometimes allowed them to choose a more freestyle discussion, rather than a typical turn-taking, teacher-directed discussion.

Giving students a choice—whether it is a choice about what text to read, what to write about, what inquiry to pursue, or the discussion style—is motivating to adolescents. The choices give them a feeling of autonomy (a motivator associated with intrinsic motivation). Choices also motivate students to engage in tasks for which they are likely to experience high self-efficacy. Honoring students' choices also promotes connections between school and personal literacies. The choices adolescents make are likely to reflect the strengths they bring with them from outside of school.

Active Learning Environment

A third suggestion for creating engaging literacy classrooms is to use active, "experiential and participatory approaches" (Hinchman et al., 2003–2004, p. 306). Because of adolescents' social nature, they are more inclined to engage in activities in which they can actively participate. Gone are the days when the teacher, the so-called sage on the stage, delivers a carefully prepared and fascinating lecture to students, who hang on every word and take copious notes for the shear joy of learning; rather, students need to be engaged actively in thinking about ideas.

One way to encourage active involvement is to use role-play. For example, when studying about prejudices of all kinds, students could take examples from their own lives and role-play the situation for the class. This activity capitalizes on the third recommendation (making personally relevant connections) as well as the recommendation that approaches need to be participatory. Collaborative group work for solving problems or discussing alternative perspectives and student-controlled discussions encourages students to consider ideas actively. Providing students with opportunities to use their multiple literacies to represent their understandings of content is another way to engage students. For example, students can develop multimedia projects, documentaries, or posters and write raps or poetry to communicate what they have learned.

Approaches that support active, participatory, or experiential learning may motivate students in several ways. Students' self-efficacy may be enhanced when a variety of approaches to learning, not just traditional paper-and-pencil tasks, are honored. When there is no right or wrong answer, but room for interpretation—like in a role-play—students' mastery-oriented goals may also motivate them. Also, when students work together in self-chosen groups to create a product, they are partially motivated by their social goals.

Instructional Support

A fourth recommendation is to provide adolescents with instructional support so that they know how to locate accurate information easily and critique its usefulness (Hinchman et al., 2003–2004). Think about the skills and strategies students are motivated to use outside of school. Then point out to students how these same skills can be useful in school-related tasks (Alvermann, Huddleston, & Hagood, 2004). Comparing and contrasting these skills and showing young people how they can be modified to suit different purposes should help students transfer skills from one context to another.

In a classroom that honors students' multiple literacies, it is important that many types of texts and other resources are accessible for inquiries. The traditional print resources, such as trade books and reference books, represent only a small portion of what is available. Students have access to the Internet and all its reputable (and disreputable) resources. Primary source documents are at their fingertips at Web sites such as the Smithsonian Institute. Current and back issues of newspapers, magazines, and television broadcasts are also often available on the Internet. With access to digital photography, cell phones with video capability, and other electronic devices, adolescents can easily gather data from the field.

With the mountains of potential resources at their fingertips, students will need to be taught effective search strategies for locating information in different kinds of sources. Locating information in the table of contents or index in a print resource is very different from using a search engine. As students begin to find information, they will need assistance to sort through that information and critically evaluate the sources to determine if they are reliable.

Alvermann (2006) recommended that students need instructional support to evaluate the critically texts they read, view, and hear. This relates, of course, to determining the usefulness of resources. She contended, however, that much more is involved to teach adolescents to develop a critical awareness when reading. Students need to understand that there is often more to a text than meets the eye and that subtexts (implicit meanings) influence readers to think in particular ways.

When adolescents are given the instructional support they need, they can competently approach tasks by critically evaluating them in terms of accuracy, point of view, and how they are meant to influence the reader. These accomplishments promote self-efficacy. In addition, students will be more likely to attribute their success to their effort because they have confidence in the skills and strategies they have used in tasks outside of school and have learned in school.

Embedded Strategy Instruction

The fifth recommendation is to embed systematic strategy instruction in a context where relevant connections are made between school topics and students' knowledge, experiences, and interests developed outside of school.

Strategy instruction also needs to occur within the context of content area (e.g., social studies, science) instruction and in an environment that supports collaborative work (Alvermann, 2006). This recommendation is in direct opposition to the kind of instruction that involves students reading short paragraphs and then using a strategy to answer a question; rather, embedded strategy instruction takes place within the context of the texts students are reading. The strategies that promote "organizing, integrating, and reflecting on informational texts and/or narrative texts" (Alvermann, 2006, p. 9) are effective when taught overtly and systematically. Reciprocal teaching was also found to be effective. This approach involves the teacher and students in a discussion that includes making predictions, clarifying information or ideas, summarizing, and asking questions.

Hinchman and colleagues (2003–2004) suggested that teachers need to practice a teaching model that uses a gradual release of responsibility to guide their strategy instruction, always within the context of conceptual learning. For example, when students are studying about an issue of concern to them, they would need instruction to summarize information from a variety of sources. Summarizing is a complex task that can be broken down into its different parts. To write a summary, adolescents must read and make decisions about what information is most important. Then they must know how to take notes in an organized way. Finally, they use those notes to write a summary.

To teach students this process, using the gradual release of responsibility teaching model, teachers first model and think aloud about how they make decisions about what information is most important. Then they show students how they take notes. Next, it is the students' turn to read and take notes, collaborating with their peers. The teacher provides responsive guidance, as needed. After guided note taking, the class reconvenes. The students discuss the notes they took, the decisions they made when reading and taking notes, and why they made their decisions. The teacher scaffolds throughout the discussion, making important teaching points to help students hone their strategy use. When students are ready to read and take notes independently, they do so, with the teacher supporting them, as needed. All this work is done within the context of learning content through reading and writing (and other literacies as well).

Students learn how to use strategies in the context of content area learning and with overt and systematic teaching within a supportive, collaborative learning environment. As students need to learn new strategies or use old strategies with different kinds of texts, the teaching process continues. How much time is spent modeling and guiding students' practice depends on the students' needs.

Showing students how and then supporting them as they learn literacy strategies are essential for student success. Regardless of how motivating a topic is, there are points when students may need assistance to approach a task strategically and sustain their work.

The importance of embedded strategy instruction, within the context of content area learning, and in a collaborative environment, cannot be underestimated as it relates to motivation. Without adequate instructional support by the teacher and the social support of peers, students feel out of control and experience low self-efficacy. Students may attribute their lack of success either to their lack of ability or to an impossibly difficult task. All these factors combined could contribute to students' lack of motivation and potentially to academic failure.

CONCLUSION

What motivates adolescents to engage in literacy learning in school? This is a complex question, and the answer is even more complex. Perhaps the better question is, How can teachers create learning environments where students will be motivated to engage in literacy learning in school? I believe the following quote provides the best answer we have to date:

> As teachers, we need to take stock of what students already are able to do in the name of literacy. Most are engaging in significant literacy activities in their everyday lives outside of school. Forming bridges that connect school-based literacies with students' out-of-school literacies can support more nuanced thinking in both worlds. Supporting students' development of strategic approaches suitable for both contexts will enable them to be more successful in our increasingly complex society. (Hinchman et al., 2003–2004, p. 309).

Motivation is a complex and multifaceted construct. Researchers and theorists have hypothesized that many factors contribute to motivation, yet it is unclear how to motivate adolescents to engage in literacy-related activities. What researchers, teachers, and parents do know is that young people are motivated and passionate about engaging in personal, multiple literacies outside of school. In this chapter, several factors have been discussed that may help adults better understand what may motivate adolescents to engage in literacy-related activities both inside and outside of school. By observing, listening to, and valuing adolescents' personal literacies, adults can better understand how to design academic contexts in which literacies will be valued by adolescents.

REFERENCES

Alvermann, D. E. (2006). Youth in the middle: Our guides to improved literacy instruction? *Voices from the Middle, 14*(2), 7–13.

Alvermann, D. E., & Heron, A. H. (2001). Literacy identity work: Playing to learn with popular media. *Journal of Adolescent and Adult Literacy, 45,* 118–122.

Alvermann, D. E., Hinchman, K. A., Moore, D. W., Phelps, S. F., & Waff D. R. (Eds.). (1998). *Reconceptualizing the literacies in adolescents' lives.* Mahwah, NJ: Lawrence Erlbaum Associates.

Alvermann, D. E., Hinchman, K. A., Moore, D. W., Phelps, S. F., & Waff D. R. (Eds.). (2006). *Reconceptualizing the literacies in adolescents' lives* (2nd ed.). Mahwah, NJ: Lawrence Erlbaum Associates.

Alvermann, D. E., Huddleston, A., & Hagood, M. C. (2004). What could professional wrestling and school literacy practices possibly have in common? *Journal of Adolescent and Adult Literacy, 47,* 532–540.

Alvermann, D. E., Young, J. P., Green, C., & Wisenbaker, J. M. (1999). Adolescents' perceptions and negotiations of literacy practices in after-school read and talk clubs. *American Educational Research Journal, 36,* 221–264.

Baker, L., & Wigfield, A. (1999). Dimensions of children's motivation for reading and their relations to reading activity and reading achievement. *Reading Research Quarterly, 34,* 452–477.

Cambourne, B. (1995). Toward an educationally relevant theory of literacy learning: Twenty years of inquiry. *Reading Teacher, 49,* 182–190.

Chandler-Olcott, K., & Mahar, D. (2003a). Adolescents' anime-inspired "fanfictions": An exploration of multiliteracies. *Journal of Adolescent and Adult Literacy, 45,* 556–566.

Chandler-Olcott, K., & Mahar, D. (2003b). "Tech-savviness" meets multiliteracies: Exploring adolescent girls' technology-mediated literacy practices. *Reading Research Quarterly, 38,* 356–385.

Csikszentmihalyi, M. (1990). *Flow: The psychology of optimal experience.* New York: HarperCollins.

Deci, E. L., Koestner, R., & Ryan, R. M. (2001). Extrinsic rewards and intrinsic motivation in education: Reconsidered once again. *Review of Educational Research, 71,* 1–27.

Fader, D. N., & McNeil, E. B. (1968). *Hooked on books.* Oxford, NY: Pergamon Press.

Fairbanks, C. M. (2000). Fostering adolescents' literacy engagements: "Kid's Business" and critical literacy. *Reading Research and Instruction, 40,* 35–50.

Gambrell, L. B., Palmer, B. M., Codling, R. M., & Mazzoni, S. A. (1996). Assessing motivation to read. *Reading Teacher, 49,* 518–533.

Guthrie, J. T., McGough, K., Bennett, L., & Rice, M. E. (1996). Concept-oriented reading instruction: An integrated curriculum to develop motivations and strategies for reading. In L. Baker, P. Afflerbach, & D. Reinking (Eds.), *Developing engaged readers in school and home communities* (pp. 165–190). Mahwah, NJ: Lawrence Erlbaum Associates.

Guthrie, J. T., & Wigfield, A. (2000). Engagement and motivation in reading. In M. L. Kamil, P. B. Mosenthal, P. D. Pearson, & R. Barr (Eds.), *Handbook of reading research* (Vol. 3, pp. 403–422). Mahwah, NJ: Lawrence Erlbaum Associates.

Guzzetti, B. J., & Gamboa, M. (2004). Zines for social justice: Adolescent girls writing on their own. *Reading Research Quarterly, 39,* 408–436.

Hinchman, K. A., Alvermann, D. E., Boyd, F. B., Brozo, W. G., & Vacca, R. T. (2003–2004). Supporting older students' in- and out-of-school literacies. *Journal of Adolescent and Adult Literacy, 47,* 304–310.

Ivey, G., & Broaddus, K. (2001). "Just plain reading": A survey of what makes students read in middle school classrooms. *Reading Research Quarterly, 36,* 350–377.

Moje, E. G., Ciechanowski, K. M., Dramer, K., Ellis, L., Carrillo, R., & Collazo, T. (2004). Working toward third space in content area literacy: An examination of everyday funds of knowledge and discourse. *Reading Research Quarterly, 39,* 38–70.

Pajares, F., & Schunk, D. H. (2001). Self-beliefs and school success: Self-efficacy, self-concept, and school achievement. In R. Riding & S. Rayner (Eds.), *Perception* (pp. 239–266). London: Ablex.

Pressley, M. (1998). *Reading instruction that works: A case for balanced teaching.* New York: Guilford Press.

Reed, J. H., Schallert, D. L., Beth, A. D., & Woodruff, A. L. (2004). Motivated readers, engaged writer. In T. L. Jetton & J. A. Dole (Eds.), *Adolescent literacy research and practice* (pp. 251–282). New York: Guilford Press.

Ruddell, R. B., & Unrau, N. J. (2004). The role of responsive teaching in focusing reader intention and developing reader motivation. In R. B. Ruddell & N. J. Unrau (Eds.), *Theoretical models and processes of reading* (5th ed., pp. 954–978). Newark, DE: International Reading Association.

Ryan, R. M., & Deci, E. L. (2000). Intrinsic and extrinsic motivations: Classic definitions and new directions. *Contemporary Educational Psychology, 25,* 54–67.

Smith, M. W., & Wilhelm, J. D. (2002). *"Reading don't fix no chevies": Literacy lives of young men.* Portsmouth, NH: Heinemann.

Wigfield, A., & Guthrie, J. T. (1997). Relations of children's motivation for reading to the amount and breadth of their reading. *Journal of Educational Psychology, 89,* 420–432.

Chapter Eleven

CRITICAL LITERACY AND ADOLESCENTS

James R. King, Steven Hart, and Deborah Kozdras

In this chapter, we define and explain critical literacy by providing an analysis of the term *critical literacy* and the way this term is used in the professional literature in reference to adolescents. We report on the ways the term is used differently for different audiences and the variations in the use of the term *critical literacy*. We suggest a systematic way of understanding critical literacy in situated contexts that involve adolescent learners. We intend to provide direction for further implementation of critical literacy with adolescents.

This overview was guided by a focus on critical theory articulated by the Frankfort School (Habermas, 1973). At the University of Frankfurt, in Germany, a group of scholars formulated an approach to social criticism that came to be known as the Frankfort School of thought. Critical theory based on the Frankfort School seeks to trip the levers of power to establish a dialectic between the construction of the individual and social structure. In language, particularly written language, critical theory seeks to reveal the forms that are privileged by various social hierarchies.

In our review, we were guided by Fairclough (1995), Rogers (2004), and Wodak and Meyer (2000) in their approaches to critical discourse analysis (CDA). CDA is an approach to the study of language use, especially within the use of texts, as well as other cultural and social practices. According to Gee (1996), all these language systems can be referred to as D/discourses, with *discourses* referring to everyday, shared language use and *Discourses* referring to special, insider uses of language that delimit identities (truckers, valley girls, physicists). In particular, the Discourses are ideological, resistant to self-criticism and interrogation, used as standpoints from which to speak, center on viewpoints and objects with given perspectives while marginalizing others, and relate to power and its circulation. CDA looks at how power is exercised through language to construct representations of the world, of social identities, and of relationships.

Our study drew heavily from Fairclough's (1995) three-dimensional framework of local (a particular text or event), institutional (social institutions that enable and constrain the local domain), and societal (policies and metanarratives that shape and are shaped by the institutional and local domains). This framework provided a way to continually examine how the concept of critical literacy was articulated within particular texts, the forces that shaped this situated use, and the social actions the texts attempted to produce.

Our investigation of critical literacy as it pertains to adolescents revealed several thematic descriptors that appear to represent the multiple lenses through which critical literacy is viewed in situated local contexts. These descriptors are identity, popular culture, project-based learning, reflexive text analysis, and media literacies. We discuss these categories separately as a way to present distinct features of particular themes. Our analysis demonstrates that each of these themes does not exist in isolation; rather, the themes are interrelated and mutually influence one another.

IDENTITIES

From a semiotic perspective, habits, clothes, friends, and idioms are all texts that reveal the subjectivities or multiple layers that students use to talk about themselves. Progressive educators in writing pedagogy (Atwell, 1987; Graves, 1983) have advocated that when students have more choice over their writing topics, they have more voice in their classroom writing. From this approach, voice leads to students' ownership and subsequent empowerment through their writing. Finally, the students represent their understanding of their subjective experiences in their writing.

More recent theorizing in identity formation offers more complex views into who is and who is not in the class. Hagood (2002) suggested that this is not a dichotomous in or out of the class decision. In fact, students always have each of their identities present. Furthermore, the selection of a particular identity is also not discrete. In any case, the formation of self or subjectivities of self is seen as vital to the use of critical literacy. As Hagood stated, "The coupling of critical literacy and formations of the self address[es] how conceptions of self are formed through an interrogation of texts" (p. 248). So to know an individual, it is necessary to listen to the responses that person generates as he or she engages with a particular text, a subsequent text, and so on. Here, as with most of the chapter, *text* is broadly conceived to include talk, scripts, gestures, traditional texts, visual presentations, and so on.

Hagood (2002) continued with reasoning that makes our quick rephrase a problem. She stated, "This coupling, however, is a tricky matter because neither term *[critical literacy, formations of self]* is unitary in its conceptualization nor singular in its manifestations" (p. 248). People represent their multiple identities through such means as response, lack of response, gesture, and so on. Hagood made the point that critical literacy is premised on liberation, socially situated practice (and therefore political), and societal change, all of which influence constructions of self through texts:

> What is central to critical literacy that focuses on identity is the influence of the text and specifically identities in texts on the reader . . . [and] that the identities produced in texts are often normative and stable, stereotypical, and hegemonic, inscribing for adolescent readers identities for emulation that serve to perpetuate dominant, mainstream images of the status quo. (p. 248)

Therefore a critical response to these textual identities entails or enables a student's critical analysis of self.

If adolescents are invited to share their lives as contexts for learning literacy, what are teachers' obligations for having issued such an invitation? When students comply with teachers' requests for their lives as contexts for teacher-mediated learning, what are the possible forms of reception? A case in point is the rather recent attention played on adolescent masculinities as they are produced in texts and in discourses related to texts. Moje, Young, Readence, and Moore (2000) suggested that critical literacy might productively offer activities for adolescents' exploration of their own gender identities. To make matters more complex, Young (2000, 2001) as well as Young and Brozo (2001) targeted versions of masculinities that were seemingly at odds. While Young promoted activities that draw boys' focus to gender inequities as they are portrayed in texts, Brozo (2002) advocated iterative versions of Jungian archetypes (e.g., the lover, the warrior) for reparative masculinities (Lingard & Douglas, 1999). In a review of texts on masculinities and literacies, King (in press) pointed out that the ideology behind the "masculinity" makes for very different intentions on the part of teachers and outcomes for students. For example, students' responses to adolescent fiction that portrays class and race struggles, such as *Tangerine* (Bloor, 1997), may differ by virtue of the stance that each takes toward being male. In the case of Young, it was reasonable to infer a masculinity that is based on feminist understandings of gender (Lingard & Douglas, 1999), which would, in turn, allow for multiple meanings for the masculine. For Brozo (2002), the masculinity appeared to be premised on a reparative version of the mythopoetic men's movement, the reclamation of so-called wild man masculinity (Bly, 1990). Both these literacy theorists lay claim to promoting a sensibility toward young boys' (and girls') gender development as it is deployed in literature. Each expects a very different version of masculinity as an outcome, however. Reparative masculinities would enhance the privilege of the male protagonists. Feminist-informed masculinities would critique the privilege that they enjoy. Consequently, the acceptable identities that are made available for young men are very different. True to Hagood's (2002) cautions, each of the identity spaces is multiply conceived. Similar examples could be presented from different perspectives on females' identities. Likewise, examinations of school practices from perspectives based on race, social classes, abilities strata, and other social groupings could be presented. It is possible that teachers do no more and no less than make students aware of multiplicities. Insisting on a particular instantiation of masculinity is merely another type of oppression for youth to suffer.

In lieu of seeking an answer to which kind of masculinity is the best, adolescents and their teachers more productively engage in media critiques of the various representations of multiple masculinities as they appear in media. Critical theory analyzes patterns of power differentials and aims to reverse positions in power relationships. The degree to which an individual can accomplish reversal of power positioning through texts is central to the efforts of critical literacy. Reversal of power can be based on the knower/known, as in Wigginton's (1986) example with a troublesome 9th grader in *Foxfire* (cf. chapter 9). Often, the reversal is personified in the identity of a male who is challenging and subsequently supportive of his teachers.

Lankshear and Knobel (2002) offered several media-based strategies for interrogating texts. Their list included meme-ing (personalized, attention-gaining icons); scenariating (recasting current circumstances into new, imagined situations and allowing for play-out); culture jamming (reusing media icons and images in a countercultural way), and transfer (arranging for links to so-called hot properties so that an individual's work will be accessed). How and should these strategies be included in adolescents' literacy? It is really a moot point as the students already control these strategies. These strategies, as literate competence, are made part of the students' identity kits. That competence is transferable and portable and can be deployed outside of classrooms.

Reversal requires an expectation for difference on the part of the teacher. Felman (1997) argued that for the most part, teachers in classrooms ask questions and conduct their teaching inquiry from a stance of confirming the known; that is, they know the answers to the questions they ask. Students are positioned to offer the teacher the answer that the students perceive is wanted by the teacher. Vacca and Vacca (2002) called this teaching "guess what's in my head." In reversal, teachers are indeed the unknower and depend on the student-as-knower to teach. Therefore an expectation for difference is required. This can be a decentering experience for a teacher and an empowering one for adolescents. It is also important that these experiences with reversal are real, yet inviting students to this difference space is not without its own complexities.

Albright (2001) wrote at length about the resistance that teachers may encounter as part of their critical literacy work with adolescents (as well as any other work). He is careful to distinguish resistance and opposition. Albright muses, "Why students refuse to accept their teacher's invitations to engage in literate activities is a question that I believe haunts many literacy teachers' practices" (p. 648). While this question rings true, it is resistance to constitutive texts and tasks that is the very work of critical literacy. It is a double bind for teachers who intend to practice a critical dialectic with their students. It is not acceptable for empowerment to be to the point of convenience for the teacher; that is, once begun, the process of empowerment for students can sometimes be uncomfortable for teachers. Albright looks for larger frames of understanding to alleviate the potential conflicts that may arise between teachers and students. "Many discourses, especially in schools, reward rationality and manage conflict" (p. 653). Part of a critical approach that would at least address this conundrum would be "foregrounding issues of power and desire" (p. 653) that appear in literacy conflicts (teachers', students', texts', media's, etc.).

Students' resistance to traditional and more progressive literacy practices inside schools can also position them as marginal students. Students' resistant behavior (interpreted as opposition) can place them in remedial instruction, solitary schooling, and repetition of an academic year. In contrast, resistance can be the very tool to understand the ways that literacy is used to colonize and marginalize adolescents' identities in schools. Albright sees these sites of conflict as resistant openings and not as oppositional endings. In a discussion of the use of the movie *American Pie* with adolescent males, Ashcraft (2003) also referenced resistance. In a reversal of stereotypic representations, the males in Ashcraft's study who were discussing *American Pie* addressed the pressures they felt to engage in activities and discourses that were oppressively sexist. When students do reverse, however, they are often uncomfortable, feel that they will get into trouble, or that they will be ridiculed in some way. These are risky behaviors for adolescent students.

One difficulty in using popular culture in the classroom is the allegiance a devoted fan might hold for a pop star. Much has been written about adolescents' obsessive attention to rap, pop, movie, and media stars. Alvermann, Moon, and Hagood (1999) suggested that a transaction across media texts creates fan-star dyads, and subsequent intertextual networks of like-minded fans, who are linked by shared media space. Idolatry simply cannot abide criticism. For example, in a recent presentation on a rap artist, an undergraduate student did not mention the artist's multiple arrests, violent and misogynistic lyrics, or gang membership; rather, the presentation featured bling, (expensive looking, visible jewelry), the artist's girlfriends, and symbols of his fame. The values of the student relative to the artist, and how the student intended those values to be read by his classmates, are revealed in what was chosen and what was suppressed in the student's presentation. A comparison of the represented and absent characteristics might start a critical investigation of the artist as text. From a more distanced perspective (such as writing about the event for a book chapter), these differences are intriguing, productive, and could lead to a critical self-awareness. This is often intractable work that might be refused by a devotee, however. While this interrogation may *seem* productive, the role of the student-as-fan in fan-star discourses (Alvermann & Hagood, 2000) suggests that the student will not engage in this critical inquiry. In short, a fan-star relationship may preclude critical analysis because of the student's idolatry. Positioning adolescents as media consumers in fan-star transactions leads to inclusion of popular culture in classroom discourses.

POPULAR CULTURE

One way that young people's attention has been drawn to school-based literacy is through framing literacy within students' interests. Often, attempts to include students' interests in classrooms are based on popular culture, which may include texts such as television, video, movies, music, and other youth-oriented media. The inclusion of youth culture as contexts for literacy is a decision that is rife with opportunities for examination. Consider the fact that adolescents are warned that sexually oriented talk, behavior, and gestures are not acceptable in school discourses. Yet when these students leave school, they are bombarded with sexually informed and directed messages. School is either a safe place or a lame place.

It is not our intent to sexualize school, but rather to point out the duplicity experienced by youth. Sexuality and its discourses comprise but one so-called objectionable theme. Because of their adult status, teachers are allowed the very things that they try to keep from their students. The list of privileges is endless. Adults' access to these forbidden pleasures must create adolescents' resentment. It is probably most pronounced when teachers silence the emergence of unpopular popular culture in classrooms. Yet teachers themselves enact the subtleties of these desires. For example, during our observations , a young man was seen flirting with a young woman in class; he was admonished by his teacher to keep flirtation outside of school. Later on, in the class, the same teacher referred to this same striking young man as "our Calvin Klein model." The student was reinforced for a sexuality that he may not even have claimed. Adults' talk in the presence of youth is always monitored, evaluated, and appropriated. For example, when the coach teaches math, the athletes in the class are granted more attention. We are not suggesting that anything be done differently, only that our habits and talk related to the unpopular are always instructive, whether or not it is our intent to do so.

Walkerdine (1991) argued that elementary grade teachers function as "containers of rationality," where their classrooms are oases of order in a chaotic world. Walkerdine is critical of the practice of teachers' containment because of the costs it enacts on these teachers. Nevertheless, early-grade teachers hold back the chaos of the outside world to facilitate the emergence of the child. With some minor revisions, there is an apparent analogy to adolescents' classrooms. Teachers are constructed, and subsequently represent themselves as mediators for the infusion of popular culture and the everyday lives of their students. From a critical theory approach to media literacy, Alvermann et al. (1999) argued for infusion of popular culture to develop adolescents' abilities to analyze "the social, political, and economic messages" that are embedded within media. Alvermann, Hagood, and Williams (2001) also explored the complexity of adult-student roles when popular culture is introduced as academic text:

> Just as adults position themselves as more knowledgeable about meaning youth will make with popular culture, we also position ourselves as naïve about or oblivious to popular culture.... Interestingly, [research has] illustrated that youth are usually quite willing to share their likes and to teach others about their interests if adults show a willingness to listen and learn from them.

From our perspective, this is clearly different from pandering to students' interests to cajole them to do schoolwork. The interjection of popular culture disrupts business as usual long enough to redirect the learning path. For example, we heard a middle school student object, "Miss, we can't bring our music in here." The student was objecting because songs that play well outside of school may cause students embarrassment when they are replayed in schools. Lyrics become charged with strange importance inside of school because of everyone's awareness of their disruptive potential. Our previous finger-pointing at the duplicity of teachers is now pointing to the student, who is, in this case, self-censoring. Student-as-self with friends on the outside becomes student-as-student with peers and teacher in a classroom, or even student-as-student with a teacher alone. This happens to us all. How many of us have enjoyed a movie with one set of friends, only to be embarrassed viewing it with another set? The problem here for critical literacy is that students will not tell their teachers what was the best part of *American Pie* in the same way that they tell friends the best part because it is simply not acceptable within school discourses to do so (Ashcraft, 2003).

A first problem with the attribution of the connection between youth and popular culture is that it essentializes or stereotypes all youth attention, while it equates and levels all genre and quality of popular culture. There is a presumption that all adolescents use or consume the same media texts in the same ways. A second notion that is problematic is that once the popular media is incorporated into schoolwork, its value is suspect because of its collocation with academic literacies. A third issue is that students may distrust teachers' intentions with popular culture. Teachers who may need to document their students' academic work may compromise the pleasure that students would have derived from engagement with popular media. Fourth, teachers' choices of media for classroom consumption constitute an instantiation of the students' choices. The teacher may be inaccurate about students' interests. Students must be included in the process of selecting which themes, stories, texts, songs, pictures, and movies are used as classroom texts.

Arguably, teachers serve as mediators between popular culture texts and classroom discourses. Teachers who work to use popular culture as a context for critical literacy are faced with decisions about which texts to allow and which to prohibit. The dilemma is based in understanding how the decisions to include or exclude particular texts impact the value students will hold for such texts. Texts championed by teachers may lead to students' dismissal of these texts solely because of the teachers' sponsorship. Prohibiting an objectionable text can have the effect of increasing its currency or value. Through a shared process of text selection, teachers and students can negotiate the risk factors in the text and discuss how the text may be used productively within a particular project. By focusing the process of deciding which media texts to include and exclude on textual analysis, teachers and students can work to uncover the power structures that privilege or marginalize particular literate practices and products.

PROJECT-BASED LEARNING

Literacy acts are best accomplished when literacy serves a tool for accomplishing a larger measure, rather than literacy learning being the goal itself (Harman, 1985). If a learner has a specific, personal goal in mind that includes his or her social orientation, that student is likely to be more motivated to learn the incidental use of a literate competence. In project-based learning (Bereiter, 2002), students learn "to do" through successive approximations. A learner tries it out (whatever the it is), looks at the outcome, tries it again, and so on. In his discussion of the learning that occurs in the process of constructing hypertext, Bereiter contrasted emergent and presentational modes. An emergent mode is seen as having more learning opportunity than a presentational mode. By analogy, a teacher shifts from a focus on the project-product parameters to a focus on the inquiry strategies deployed during the students' "knowledge building" (p. 75) to capitalize on the embedded literacy lessons. Bereiter's binary between building and telling (emergent and presentational) as applied to hypertext resonates with the similar use of product-process bina-ries in critical literacy (e.g., deconstructed differences in race, gender, or sexual orientation).

The teacher needs to shift focus to the learners' discourse while they are engaged in project-product completion. Completing a project is certainly important, especially from the students' perspective. From a literacy learning perspective, it is the language that is used in the production that is a focal point. Talk and texts *about* the construction (the metaproject discourses) are fairly distinct from the object itself. Separation between the actual product and talk about the product is more subtle in a language arts classroom, where the project-product and the metadiscourse (talk about the production) are both linguistic endeavors. Focus on the accuracy of the requirements will more likely be perceived as authority-based imposition, whereas the process texts (talk, writing, enactments) are the data with which to guide instruction. For example, presenting a group with an analysis of their language collected while they were engaged in a project of building a canoe can lead the group to opportunities for learning.

The reflexive use of language as data to influence subsequent iterations of a process is tricky for teachers. Feedback loops should not and cannot come from didactic or curricular intents. Yet teachers can experience a "covered the required content" windfall through their redirection of process discourses. One way around this dilemma is to use real audiences outside the immedi-ate production context. A metaphor for this intent is *boundary breaking.* The intent is to move the product (and the intention that drives the production) away from a focus on teachers and schools and toward real audiences that the students believe count, or wish to influence (peers, politicians, policy makers, community leaders, administrators, families, marginalized groups). By enact-ing and reifying an outside audience, the teacher provides the students with a rationale (other than grades or school) to shift their attention to the product (i.e., the student identity that is embedded in the eventual product). At the same time, the teacher maintains a focus on the students' metastrategies that are deployed during the emergent processes to take advantage of the opportu-nities for teaching that emerge.

In a study of elementary and middle school students, Leland and col-leagues (2003) engaged the students in critiquing "the difficult things that happen in the world around them." Yet the class project stayed inside the classroom. In contrast, Johnson and Freedman (2005) provided several examples of service learning initiatives that took the critical awareness that was developed in the classroom out into the community. It is not our inten-tion to suggest that the results of all project-based learning must leave the classroom; rather, it is a factor that might be considered for the students' interest and valuation of the work they do.

REFLEXIVE ANALYSIS OF TEXT

In the response to literature approaches to critical literacy, literature is often used as a springboard to students' discussions that relate conflicts in a story to their lives. Bleich's (1986) relatively early resistance to the new critics text-based analysis proposed a subjective criticism that centered on readers' emotional connections to the text that were based on their own experiences. Rosenblatt's (1978, 1995) reader response is also a framework for this individual, emotion-based interaction with a text. For McLaughlin and DeVoogd (2004), Rosenblatt's theory is used as a prototype for a critical stance in reading. Readers are brought to focus on power, complexity, perspectives, and adaptations as their teachers direct them to alternative sources. For adolescents who engage with novels as part of their academic literacies work, Johnson and Freedman (2005) suggested that critical literacy is "resistant reading by teachers and students working together to discover language patterns that promote particular ideas about power and oppression based on race, class, gender, or a combination of these three" (p. 11). Accordingly, students are cultured in a resistant stance. Their treatment of multiple theories of response requires that students embody a stance to critique.

Leland et al. (2003) suggested that "a critical literacy perspective encourages readers to use language as a tool for interrogating and critiquing the difficult things that happen in the world around them" (p. 7). With teacher-selected text sets, the range of issues and students' reactions are perhaps circumscribed in ways that might not be to some middle school and secondary students' tolerance. In analyzing and using discussion as text, Rogers (2004) described the use of CDA for conceptualizing critical literacy. Ostrow (2003) recommended that such critical stances be deployed on all media. For literature, classroom discourses, and media, in general, a critical approach directs students to an examination of these texts. Who determines which stances are the permissible ones?

Critical literacy that focuses on text-based reading strategies also uses back reading, or subversive interpretations, to uncover subtexts in the author's writing. A systematic approach to this reading against the grain can be found in Gee's (1999) discourse analysis methods. In studies that deploy critical discourse analysis, the interrogation of texts from personal, political, and sociological perspectives often breaks the physical and psychological borders that frame the project activities as academic work. Yet there is little available description of how teachers or students orient themselves toward critique.

For critical theorists who use literature, the story acts as a catalyst that subsequently results in activism. Breaking the borders from this perspective means that the critical literacy work enters the larger community and gains a larger audience for its outcomes. Yet critical discourse analysis of the type that informs critical literacy must emanate from a stance. As we previously pointed out, criticism emanates from a multitude of stances. Individuals' deployment of a particular stance may be seen as a strategy. Spivak (1993) referred to this practice as strategic essentialism, or the temporary, purposeful adoption of an identity to do critical work with language products. To engage in criticism, the critic must embody a standpoint. Students who are led to deconstruct texts through their critical examination of them should also be made aware that their critical analysis comes from text practices that are premised on a way of seeing, understanding, and responding to the world as it is represented in the discourse under examination. To what extent students actually label (or should label) their stances is not clear. Yet grounding the identity of self-as-critic is establishing yet another text that is related to other texts. This is the important point in the identity construction through critical literacy approaches with adolescents.

Stein (2001) described a project in multilingual storytelling practices with 12 16-year-old students in Johannesburg. She noted that what began as a project exploring multilingual resources with English as a second language students who were focused on storytelling practices "unexpectedly turned into an important project in the re-appropriation and transformation of textual, cultural, and linguistic forms" (p. 151). The chances of such redirection and personal transfer are enhanced when students examine their own role in the research findings. Vignettes and first-person accounts attest to the fact that adolescents are not only capable of but eager to participate in critical discussions about texts, both narrative and expository (Alvermann et al., 1999). We understand the predilection of youth for criticism as not different from our own, though perhaps more constrained by our permissions.

MEDIA LITERACIES

The connection between technology and adolescent literacy is ubiquitous, if not isomorphic. Media-based literacies enable the use of popular culture texts. Media that resonate with adolescents are readily available. Availability promotes agency. What individuals value can easily be imported into classrooms. Technology has provided youth with new forms of literacy that they have championed, mastered, and, at times, used against their teachers. In fact, there are now more outlets with Internet writing spaces than ever before. With the appearance of MySpace.com, YouTube.com, and Internet poetry sites, there are limitless opportunities for publication. More traditional approaches to literacy have followed a more canonical mainstream approach of draft, submit to authority, revise, resubmit. The use of multimedia literacies enables multiple constructions of personal identities. Students (indeed, all of us) can construct themselves in variable modes. Traditional literacies have valued rigor, accuracy, and verifiability, however.

Dickinson (2001) pointed out that students are repeatedly trained to acquire information for their school-based texts from commercially sponsored Web sites. This would suggest a quid pro quo. Students get the information they need. Advertisers get the exposure they need. Yet we may not be teaching the critical approaches needed to resist this "marriage between literacy advertising" (Dickinson, 2001, p. 3). If students are taught to analyze critically the corporate persuasion that is visually delivered, will corporate sponsorship be maintained? Or does that effort simply up the ante for advertisers? When advertising is a constant presence, it eventually recedes to meaninglessness, with a subtextual effect.

Myers and Beach (2001) illustrated the productive use of several media platforms that students use as authoring tools. To support their claim that hypermedia promotes critical literacy, they propose immersing, identifying, contextualizing, representing, critiquing, and transforming. These strategies are simultaneous and mutually constitutive. Myers and Beach also suggested that the use of hypermedia challenges the more traditional pedagogies that aim to produce a single, coherent version of a text. They call for more divergent pedagogies of possibilities for texts. Yet the effect of hyperlinking is not all to the good. "Students may be so mesmerized or overwhelmed by navigating the many options and paths in these texts that they may focus more on structural cues for activating links that on critically responding to texts" (Myers & Beach, 2001, p. 543). We see this competence as one that is paramount and one that is easily incorporated into critical analysis of the structures of multimedia literacies.

Albright, Purohit, and Walsh (2002) made a case for the reformulation of readers' responses to narratives that usually occur in classroom literature circles (Daniel, 2002) when analogous responses to literature occur in chat rooms. While the language features vary from more traditional discourses of classroom-based literature circles, Albright and colleagues (2002) pointed out that the strategies of reader response that occur in classrooms also occur in chat rooms. Albright et al.'s example is a reminder of the transmediation that occurs across different texts. What is acquired in a chat room as a strategy can then be deployed in other media contexts such as a standardized test of reading ability. In fact, proponents of new literacies argue that the measured illiteracy of, for example, urban youth is more a product of sociocultural factors that have been attached to literacy than the lack of intellectual capabilities of the students. Much research sets out to document the literacies of various groups of marginalized youth (Moje, 2000; O'Brien, 1998). From a new literacies perspective, these youth are literate, just not in the ways that count in schools. Since literate operations are strategic, the learning strategies that have been acquired through interaction in popular culture texts should transfer to the more canonical texts of institutional literacies. To that end, Morrell (2002) suggested that learning literacy strategies can be accomplished with hip-hop culture texts, through popular films, and with television and media. Given our current investments in media literacies, we would add that these *should* be taught.

WHAT DO THESE THEMES MEAN TO US?

The first implication from this review is that our findings are not definitive; they are descriptive. Our discourse analysis of definitions, influences, and intents was a recursive process that continually returned to the critical theory that frames critical literacy work. Analyzing the literature in this manner allowed for an understanding of the manners in which critical theory has been applied to literacy education of adolescents. If the themes that we have formulated are to be useful, it will be in their interpolated relationship with each other; that is, the patterns that we teased from our review of critical literacy with adolescents are mutually interdependent. In fact, one way we participated in testing out the economy of our model was to play the categories against each other. For example, not all project-based learning in literacy for adolescents is critically conceived. If the other five characteristics are included with the intent to engage in projects that lead to literacy learning, it is reasonable that these projects would be more critically inclined. Projects that consider students' identities, offer student choice, and potentially lead to student empowerment would be characteristics of a critical literacy project. If a project engages students with popular culture texts, resists censorship, and reverses power dynamics between teachers and students, it is more likely a critical literacy piece. Furthermore, if the project reflexively analyzes media, reads for the subtexts, and returns those interpretations to the context, it is more likely critical. If the project works within technological approaches to literacy and involves students in the production of fast literacies for public consumption beyond the classroom, it is more likely critical literacy. If the same analysis began with the intent to focus on student identity, that factor could also be played against the other five so that the assumption of identities would more likely be the work of critical literacy.

Our aim for this chapter was to continue to engage the field of adolescent literacy in praxis. Our analysis focused on how critical theory influences practice. In turn, our analysis of practices needs to be turned back onto the theory. We accomplished this in a sense when we talked about dilemmas. Perhaps critical theory as it applies to literacy education needs to be revisited to address the real-world struggles of enacting the theory in today's schools.

REFERENCES

Albright, J. (2001). The logic of our failures in literacy practices and teaching. *Journal of Adolescent and Adult Literacy, 44*(7), 644–658.

Albright, J., Purohit, K., & Walsh, C. (2002). Louise Rosenblatt seeks QtAznBoi@aol.com for LTR: Using chat rooms in interdisciplinary middle school classrooms. *Journal of Adolescent and Adult Literacy, 45*(8), 692–705.

Alvermann, D. E., & Hagood, M.C. (2000). Fandom and critical media literacy (re/mediating adolescent literacies). *Journal of Adolescent and Adult Literacy, 43*(5), 436–446.

Alvermann, D. E., Hagood, M. C., & Williams, K. B. (2001, June). Image, language, and sound: Making meaning with popular culture texts. *Reading Online, 4*(11). Retrieved October 1, 2006, from http://www.readingonline.org/newliteracies/lit_index. asp?HREF=/newliteracies/action/alvermann/index.html

Alvermann, D. E., Moon, J. S., & Hagood, M. C. (1999). *Popular culture in the classroom: Teaching and researching critical media literacy.* Newark, DE: International Reading Association.

Ashcraft, C. (2003). Adolescent ambiguities in *American Pie:* Popular culture as a resource for sex education. *Youth and Society, 35*(1), 37–70.

Atwell, N. (1987). *In the middle.* Portsmouth, NH: Heinemann.

Bereiter, C. (2002). Emergent versus presentational hypertext. In R. Bromme & E. Stahl (Eds.), *Writing hypertext and learning: Conceptual and empirical approaches* (pp. 73–78). Oxford: Elsevier.

Bleich, D. (1986). *Subjective criticism.* Baltimore: Johns Hopkins University Press.

Bloor, E. (1997). *Tangerine.* New York: Scholastic.

Bly, R. (1990). *Iron John: A book about men.* New York: Addison-Wesley.

Brozo, W. (2002). *To be a boy, to be a reader: Engaging teen and preteen boys in active literacy.* Newark, DE: International Reading Association.

Daniel, H. (2002). *Literature circles: Voice and choice in book clubs and reading groups.* Portland, ME: Stenhouse.

Dickinson, S. C. (2001). *Taking care of business: The repercussions of commodified electronic literacy.* Paper presented at the meeting of the Conference on College Composition and Communication, Denver, CO, March, 2001. (ERIC Document Reproduction Service No. ED451538)

Fairclough, N. (1995). *Critical discourse analysis: The critical study of language.* New York: Longman.

Felman, S. (1997). Psychoanalysis and education: Teaching terminable and interminable. In S. Todd (Ed.), *Teaching desire: perspectives on pedagogy, culture and the unsaid* (pp. 17–44). New York: Routledge.

Gee, J. P. (1996). *Social linguistics and literacies* (2nd ed.). London: Falmer.

Gee, J. P. (1999). *An introduction to discourse analysis.* New York: Routledge.

Graves, D. (1983). *Writing: Teachers and children at work.* Portsmouth, NH: Heinemann.

Habermas, J. (1973). *Theory and practice* (J. Viertel, Trans.). Boston: Beacon Press.

Hagood, M. C. (2002). Critical literacy for whom? *Reading Research and Instruction, 41*(3), 247–266.

Harman, D. (1985). *Turning illiteracy around: An agenda for national action.* New York: Business Council for Effective Literacy.

Johnson, H., & Freedman, L. (2005). *Developing critical awareness at the middle level: Using texts as tools for critique and pleasure.* Newark, DE: International Reading Association.

King, J. R. (in press). What can he want? Masculinity, desire, and teaching young children In W. Martino & M. Keleher (Eds.), *Masculinities and schooling.* Binghamton, NY: Haworth Press.

Lankshear, C., & Knobel, M. (2002). Do we have your attention? New literacies, digital technologies, and the education of adolescents. In D. Alvermann (Ed.), *Adolescents and literacies in a digital world* (pp. 19–39). New York: Peter Lang.

Leland, C. H., Harste, J. C., Davis, A., Haas, C., McDaniel, K., Parsons, M., et al. (2003). "It made me hurt inside": Exploring tough social issues through critical literacy. *Journal of Reading Education, 28*(2), 7–15.

Lingard, B., & Douglas, P. (1999). Programmes for boys in schools. In B. Lingard & P. Douglas (Eds.), *Men engaging feminisms: Pro-feminism, backlashes and schooling* (pp. 131–155). Buckingham, UK: Open University Press.

McLaughlin, M., & DeVoogd, G. (2004). Critical literacy as comprehension: Expanding reader response. *Journal of Adolescent and Adult Literacy, 48*(1), 52–62.

Moje, E. (2000). *All the stories that we have: Adolescents' insights about literacy and learning in secondary school.* Newark, DE: International Reading Association.

Moje, E. B., Young, J. P., Readence, J. E., & Moore, D. W. (2000). Reinventing adolescent literacy for new times: Perennial and millennial issues. *Journal of Adolescent and Adult Literacy, 43*(5), 400–410.

Morrell, E. (2002, September). Toward a critical pedagogy of popular culture: Literacy development among urban youth. *Journal of Adolescent and Adult Literacy, 46,* 72–77.

Myers, J., & Beach, R. (2001). Hypermedia authoring as critical literacy. *Journal of Adolescent and Adult Literacy, 44*(6), 538–546.

O'Brien, D. (1998). Multiple literacies in a high-school program for "at-risk" adolescents. In D. Alvermann, K. Hinchman, D. Moore, S. Phelps, & D. Waff (Eds.), *Reconceptualizing the literacies in adolescents' lives* (pp. 27–50). Mahwah, NJ: Lawrence Erlbaum Associates.

Ostrow, J. (2003). A letter to a niece: Critical media literacy, one child at a time. *Voices from the Middle, 10*(3), 23–27.

Rogers, R. (2004). *An introduction to critical discourse analysis in education.* Mahwah, NJ: Lawrence Erlbaum Associates.

Rosenblatt, L. M. (1978). *The reader, the text, the poem: The transactional theory of the literary work.* Carbondale: Southern Illinois University Press.

Rosenblatt, L. M. (1995). *Literature as exploration.* New York: Modern Language Association. (Original published 1938)

Spivak, G. (1993). *Outside in the teaching machine.* New York: Routledge.

Stein, P. (2001). Classrooms as sites of textual, cultural, and linguistic reappropriation. In B. Comber & A. Simpson (Eds.), *Negotiating critical literacies in classrooms* (pp. 151–169). Mahwah, NJ: Lawrence Erlbaum Associates.

Vacca, R., & Vacca, J. (2002). *Content reading: Literacy and learning across the curriculum.* Boston: Allyn and Bacon.

Walkerdine, V. (1991). *Schoolgirl fictions.* London: Verso.

Wigginton, E. (1986). Sometimes a shining moment: The Foxfire experience: Twenty years teaching in a high school classroom. Garden City, NY: Anchor Books.

Wodak, R., & Meyer, M. (2000). *Methods of critical discourse analysis.* Newbury Park, CA: Sage.

Young, J. P. (2000). Boy talk: Critical literacy and masculinities. *Reading Research Quarterly, 35*(3), 312–337.

Young, J. P. (2001). Displaying practices of masculinity: Critical literacy and social contexts. *Journal of Adolescent and Adult Literacy, 45*(1), 4–14.

Young, J. P., & Brozo, W. G. (2001). Boys will be boys, or will they? Literacy and masculinities. *Reading Research Quarterly, 36*(3), 316–325.

Chapter Twelve

I USED TO TREAT ALL THE BOYS AND GIRLS THE SAME: GENDER AND LITERACY

Heather Blair

As a classroom teacher, I used to believe that we should treat all our children the same. I knew that the boys and girls sometimes responded differently to literature, games, and activities in the classroom, but it never crossed my mind that their differences were something that required significant attention. This chapter is a reflection on my teaching in rural and urban coeducational classes from 4th to 9th grade. I am also writing this chapter from my perspective as a researcher conducting observational and longitudinal research on literacy inside and outside of school in a coed, 8th-grade classroom. I have conducted research on classrooms that included all girls or all boys and on single-gender middle years programs. Most recently, I have studied a group of early adolescent boys over a five-year period. This chapter will also include what other researchers have written about gender and literacy.

It was the girls in the single-gender classroom over a decade ago who first made me conscious of the powerful role of gender in classrooms. In the context of a single-gender program, gender becomes extremely salient. In this study of children's practices, the teachers and I became critically aware of the gender realities of classrooms, the gendered (stereotypical by gender) nature of literacy, and the many complexities of literacy. I hope that this chapter will bring awareness of differences, realities, myths, and ways of thinking about addressing the complexities of boys' and girls' literacy practices that I never realized when I taught adolescent youth.

Andrew is one of those boys who disrupted every stereotype about boys not wanting to read and write. When I first met him in 3rd grade, he was a voracious reader and loved to write. He wrote a 500-word story in 4th grade with chapters, a prologue, and a drawing system that accompanied each page. His story, which chronicled a monster teleported from place to place in the year 3005, was full of action, adventure, mythical characters, and intrigue. He drew on his knowledge from video games, picture and chapter books, toys, movies, and his everyday world. As was typical of Andrew, he did it to fulfill his teacher's curricular expectations, which he far exceeded, yet at the same time, he integrated his understanding of popular culture into his academic work. He orchestrated multiple worlds in this way in his fictional writing, and although the story lines puzzled his female teacher, the writing quality was rewarded by good grades. He knew how to derive some fun from this exercise, while he met his teacher's expectations.

At the same time, Andrew moved very fluidly in a boy's world. He played soccer, took swimming lessons, traded Yu-Gi-Oh! cards, and engaged with his friends in numerous games on his computer at home. Even at this age, he was very adept on a computer; had games he loved, such as Baldur's Gate II and Ancient Empires; and believed that he was learning many strategies that he could apply to real life. Andrew taught me much about a boy's world and what it means to be literate in multiple ways in the digital age.

Tanis also taught me a great deal about what it is like to be an early-adolescent girl in an inner-city community who is also literate in multiple ways and loves to write. Like Andrew, Tanis also did not fit into the stereotype of girls' literacy practices and products and what they like to read or write. As a child of mixed-race parentage, she had had many experiences in a multicultural world, she knew what it was like to be poor and discriminated against, and she wove these life experiences into her writing. Tanis had ample ideas, trusted her own writing decisions, and reflected on her own work. She admired other writers and read daily for enjoyment. She had a vivid imagination, and her fictional reading could be traced in her writing.

Contrary to what some say about girls' writing, Tanis's stories were often action-packed murder mysteries that contained a great deal of violence. The main characters were all young women, and each had some act of violence inflicted on her. Interestingly, these female characters all reacted to the violence with violence. Tanis believed in the importance of a good ending to a story and liked to leave the reader wondering what happened to a character. She also wrote poetry about love, friendship, and world issues.

Tanis was also an avid reader, but she did not have the same proclivity for digital texts that Andrew had. That is not to say that she was any more or less literate than Andrew; they were just different. They remind me that we need to be very cognizant that difference is not constructed as a deficit or as one display of literacy that is better or worse than another. These differences do not imply potential failure on anyone's part, unless teachers and parents allow biases and limited understandings to construct them as such.

Diversity, democracy, and equity are issues addressed in schools, yet issues of gender continue to be marginalized. For example, an equality framework has prevailed in much of the educational thinking that upholds the belief that same means equal. We also know that men and women, boys and girls, do not experience their worlds in the same ways. It is important to interrogate these issues and continue to ask questions such as, How do we understand the gendered experiences of our children? What are we doing to rethink what we do as teachers or parents in terms of these differences?

I hope that this chapter and the discussion here challenges the reader to examine issues of gender, the construction of gendered identities, the gendered aspects of literacy, and the spaces in schools and curricula for gender specificity and gender neutrality. It is important to listen to all boys and girls to understand how they are unique and what commonalities they share as literate youth. The late Myra Sadker (Sadker & Sadker, 1994), an advocate of improving education for girls, said,

> If the cure for breast cancer is forming in the mind of one of our daughters, it is far less likely to become a reality than if it is forming in the mind of one of our sons. Until this changes, everyone loses. (p. 14)

Concerns about equity apply to all subjects across school curricula and in our homes and to the potential for all children, boys and girls, to reach their potential.

WHAT IS GENDER, AND WHY DOES IT MATTER?

Gender is not just a biological entity; it is socially constructed from a very young age. Watch preschool-aged children, and think about the genderedness of their play. How do a group of same-gender children play together, and how do they interact across genders? Gender, for the most part, is not something that we do alone; we construct our gender in relation to those around us. Thus it helps to have an other from whom we can be different.[1] All children come with multiple identities; they are impacted by race, class, ethnicity, culture, language, position, and lived experiences, and within the subgroups of boys or girls, they are not all the same.

Researchers from numerous disciplines have contributed to our understanding of these issues of gender. Anthropologists, particularly those involved in linguistic and educational anthropology, have done foundational work in gender, language, and power that informs our thinking. Researchers such as Tannen (1991) have helped to delineate how we maintain power differentials through talk and how the child is socialized into a gendered being. She discussed differences in discourse and gender privileging and documented how men and boys often gain and maintain control of talk in mixed-gender groups.

Others taking up Tannen's ideas have suggested that language is one of the contributing factors to some girls' failing to fulfill their potential in school.

Educational anthropologists, such as Mehan (1979) and Fine and Zane (1989), described how the structure of schools and classroom talk differentiates between children. Fine and Zane reminded readers of how insidious it is that "public schools are marbled by social class, race and ethnicity, and gender, yet they are laminated in denial, represented as if race, class and gender neutral" (p. 24). They found that girls were silenced in classrooms. Mehan (1979) made the point that "to be successful in the classroom students must not only master academic subject matter, but also learn the appropriate form in which to cast their academic knowledge. Classroom competence thus involves matters of form as well as content" (p. 49). Are there particular ways to demonstrate knowledge for different subjects, and if so, what are they? What, for example, are the appropriate forms to cast literacy knowledge? Do boys and girls represent their understandings differently, and how are they interpreted?

Psychologists have concerned themselves with gender. The self-esteem and success of teenage girls in schools was a topic under scrutiny during the 1980s and 1990s. Researchers discussed how, as girls move from the elementary grades into junior high and high school, they seem to lose confidence in themselves as scholars. The American Association of University Women's (1992) research report "How Schools Shortchange Girls" reinforced this finding:

> On average, 69 percent of elementary school boys and 60 percent of elementary school girls reported that they were "happy the way I am"; among high school students, the percentages were 46 percent for boys, and only 29 percent for girls. (p. 12)

Clearly students' attitudes change during the middle years, and this time is particularly important for girls.

More recently, there has been discussion of the limited repertoires of ways to be a boy in our schools and the problems of identity that this may bring. Pollack (1998) suggested that many boys are in crisis, and although they may appear tough on the outside, they may remain lonely and confused on the inside. Others have critiqued the limited ways that boys are allowed to display their masculinities in schools and society today and have suggested that we need to open avenues to cast new ways to be a boy. It becomes obvious from the range of disparities among educational outcomes that the gendered experience is different for boys and girls and has real consequences. Girls and boys not only succeed differently, but also perceive their success differently.

In talking about Discourse, Gee (2001) provided a framework to think about what all these components of who we are mean in terms of literacy configurations. He defined *Discourse* as ways of being in the world as "ways of talking, listening, writing, reading, acting, interacting, believing, valuing, and feeling" (p. 719). Given this perspective, Discourse is a key overarching construct in examining gender and literacy.

GENDER AS DISCOURSE IN THE CLASSROOM

The ways of being a girl in the world are evident in classrooms. The girls in my 8th-grade class were continually constructing their gender identities as they chose their attire, adornments, hairstyles, and cosmetics. It was not an accident that they carried themselves in the manner that they did and used particular gestures and facial expressions. The way they talked, to whom they talked, how much private and public talk they took part in, the terms they used, the topics of their talk, when and how they interrupted the talk of others—these were all part of their construction of gender.

The ways of being a boy in the world are very different from those of being a girl. In a study of early adolescents, Cherland (1994) found that

> only three or four of the 21 sixth-grade boys dressed carefully. In doing so, they established their gender by appropriating a "look" for boys that they had seen advertised on television and on sale at the mall. But the boys who did not put any effort into their dress were also proclaiming a gendered message. Their dress said, "I don't care what I look like because appearance isn't important for me. I am free to be comfortable and attend to other things." While this was an acceptable fashion statement for a boy to make, it was not acceptable for a girl, and only one of the sixth grade girls occasionally neglected her appearance. (p. 35)

Others have recorded the stereotypical image of a boy as rough and tough to be considered masculine. Then there are those boys who do not so easily fit into the typical boy-gendered identity. Think of the small boys and the more effeminate boys in classrooms. What does it mean for them if there is one very strict way to be accepted as a boy in school? If it is so important to be gendered to be accepted and to be gendered in a particular way to fit in, what happens to the kids who are not displaying typical notions of gender? The suicide rates of gay and lesbian adolescents are about 10 times the rate of other adolescents. Obviously, nontraditional gender roles are hard to live out in classrooms. This is an important reminder.

In reality, we all "do gender" every day, and this is something that we need to understand to determine whether gender identities, gendered roles, the differentiation of genders, and the discourse of girls and boys are all part of the inequities in classrooms and schools. Why is it so important to fit into one category or the other? Why has this dichotomy been established? How are adults contributing to this in interactions with children? It is time to think seriously about how some of the tightly constructed categories might be opened up and how children can be allowed the space to be themselves in the world to take on new ways of being in positive and helpful ways. Discussing the permeability of these borders with children could be helpful. It is possible to embrace difference and let children know that they do not have to behave in stereotypical ways to be accepted.

INTERSECTIONS OF GENDER AND LITERACY

Many definitions of literacy have been discussed in the earlier chapters of this book, and I will highlight a few that connect to issues of gender. Many terms are used for literacy: *media literacy, technological literacy, computer literacy, digital literacy, cultural literacy,* the *new literacies, visual literacy, multimodal literacy,* and *critical literacy,* to name a few. Most researchers acknowledge that these frames all represent one component of this illusive entity called literacy. There are multiple definitions of literacy and multiple paths to literacy. Most literacy researchers today prefer to think of these literacies as some complex combination of these domains that varies with context: literacy as a mix of visual, print, and other communication systems, in particular, cultural and contextual situations.

One of the major tenets of this expanded view is that literacy is not "a single essentialist thing with predictable consequences for individual and social development. Instead there are multiple literacies that vary with time and place and are embedded in specific cultural practices" (Street, 1997, p. 48). It then follows that if the sociocultural practices of boys and girls differ, so too do their literacies vary.

From the research over the past decade, it is clear that there are many ways that literacy is gendered. Boys and girls display differences in their talk, writing preferences and practices, and reading practices and preferences. Males and females have distinct hidden literacies and unique relationships with popular culture, and these different genders interact differently with digital texts. Boys and girls may experience visual representation in different ways as well, although this is less well documented.

Genderlects: Boy Talk and Girl Talk

I use the term *genderlects* (Blair, 2000) to delineate a variety of talk within any language that is distinct to a gendered group, similarly to how a dialect is specific to a regional or cultural group. This is the kind of talk in which boys and girls engage that is representative of their gender, and, at the same time, their talk contributes to the construction and maintenance of their gendered identities. "Boy talk" and "girl talk" include both the topics of talk (what they talk about) and the tools of talk (the way they talk) that can be specific to their gender or to the group to which they feel they belong. Boy talk and girl talk can also impact classroom discourse dynamics and contribute to who gets heard in the classroom.

Genderlects are like dialects and have their own set of social rules: rules for what, when, and how we talk; when it is right to talk or not talk; what silence is; and who gets the floor to speak. These are key components of how students see themselves as gendered male or female, boy or girl. Boy talk and girl talk are used to establish and maintain relations among members of a group and between groups. These power differentials are obvious in classrooms. For example, in one 8th-grade classroom that I observed, it became evident early in the school year that the gendered dynamics of talk were established clearly: those who spoke first and the loudest, interrupted the most, made side comments to classmates, or mocked previous ideas were most often boys. This public talk to establish status was a tool that the boys had learned; they used it, and it worked to maintain their dominance in the classroom talk.

Boy talk in this classroom also included numerous homophobic references. This draws attention to the need to understand the complexities of the constructions of masculinities that these particular adolescent boys experienced and the prevalence of the image of an able-bodied, white, heterosexual guy as the norm. There was little room for any other interpretation of ways to be a boy, and name-calling worked as a reminder. It also eroded the classroom cohesion, silenced the voices of many of the girls, and disrupted the comfort of the quieter and more effeminate boys. Talk remains a very important component of classroom participation, and if this access to talk is closed for some, there can be a number of ramifications for the ways that youth get to develop their literacy and demonstrate their learning.

Genderprints: Boys' and Girls' Writing Preferences and Practices

Numerous authors, such as Newkirk (2000), Smith and Wilhelm (2002), and Barbieri (1995), argued that gender and literacy are tightly interwoven and that boys and girls are differently literate. This has been more clearly defined for young children, and the essentials of these differences and the congruency of findings have not been fully explored with adolescents. Barrs (2000) suggested that we need to understand the respective discourse and genre strengths of adolescents. In her estimation, boys' stories have more pace and action than girls', whereas the girls write more about social and moral issues. She suggested that girls are more thoughtful about keeping their readers involved. In my own study of early-adolescent girls' writing (Blair, 1998), I found that the girls I observed liked to write about their feelings, fears, angers, and difficulties in their lives. The multiple realities of their lives as girls are evident in their written texts. Their lives as young women in a multiracial, working-class neighborhood with numerous media influences were continually reflected in their texts. These girls wrote primarily in the genres they liked to read about topics such as friendship, romance, and love; life and death; and social issues such as family violence.

According to Newkirk (2000), research during in the 1990s outlined numerous differences that framed boys as lacking particular traits in their writing that are expected in schools and found in girls' writing. Newkirk suggested that these should not be viewed as deficits for boys; rather, he recommended that researchers and teachers look further at how boys are actually using action and plot development in their stories to engage readers. He urged teachers and parents not to equate boys' use of violence in their writing with an intention to be vicious, and he maintained that the ways in which boys mediate this violence with humor and a kind of detachment show that they are dealing with these incongruencies. One end result for the boys is camaraderie and relationship building with their friends. Boys are indexing their multiple worlds, virtual and real, and, as Andrew taught me, bringing these complexities to their stories. The fact that they are different from girls and perhaps more connected to their out-of-school literacies does not make them less literate.

Writing is essentially about audience for both adolescent boys and girls. I have found that some girls are reluctant to share their work when the audience includes boys because they fear ridicule from the boys. Their written discourse is a private or semiprivate event, and, in contrast to oral discourse, if not made public, they had less chance of being pressured by boys about what they had to say. The boys in my study (Blair & Sanford, 2004) also censored their writing because they knew that their teachers were their primary audience and might disapprove. Their secondary audience was their friends, and they knew that they would find approval. They took ideas, characters, plots, strategies, actions, and resolutions into their school writing from what they read, played, and experienced outside of school. They enjoyed these adventure and fantasy worlds among themselves and did not expect the same of girls or teachers. They then morphed their written texts to make them more acceptable to teachers in their desire to get a decent grade.

Boy Books and Girls Books: Reading and Representing

The genderedness of reading practices has been talked about quite extensively. It has been suggested that there are boy books and girl books, and that there is a need to provide both boys and girls with appropriate choices of fiction. This implies that boys tend to like more action and adventure, whereas girls like stories about relationships, friendship, and love. Although not everyone agrees on the value of these books, it is generally thought that as well as giving youth the opportunity to select the kind of books they prefer, there is a need to expose them to quality literature that they might not necessarily select. Discussions with adolescents about the qualities and gendered perspectives of the stories can be an opening point for explorations of how each gender is represented or misrepresented.

There is some thought that girls are more versatile in their reading than boys. One of the girls in my study, when asked about girls and boys reading books with male or female protagonists, thought that girls read more of both, whereas boys preferred male characters. She suggested that girls would wear both jeans and skirts, but boys would wear only jeans. Therefore girls are gaining a broader understanding than boys not only of literature, but also of the lives depicted in literature. Classrooms should offer a variety of choices.

All fiction also needs to be analyzed critically with young people to discuss the complications and critique the notion of simple dichotomies. All children's experiences with books need to be thoughtful. Literature should provide them with opportunities to empathize, enjoy, and connect to others, taking into consideration their proclivities, interests, and comfort.

Nonfiction has been much overlooked in the discussions of gender. Boys tend to like nonfiction and are drawn to it in libraries and classrooms. They have nonfiction selections in their desks and book bags and pore over them with their friends. This kind of reading to take away information and ideas has a certain appeal to adolescent boys that may very well serve them in high school and college. There does not seem to be the same quality of nonfiction books or attraction to it for adolescent girls, with the exception of magazines. Given the interests and strengths of youth from each gender, there needs to be a balance of fiction and nonfiction in classrooms so that both boys and girls can find their interests represented.

NONCURRICULAR LITERACIES

Research on girls' literacy practices has brought to light a range of underground or private literacies inside and outside of school that are not considered part of school curricula. These may include note writing, diary writing, graffiti writing, magazine reading, and the writing of teen zines (self-published alternative magazines). Girls engage in these underground literacies with same-aged peers as a way of developing and bonding friendships. For example, when a note is written in a classroom and passed from girl to girl to its final destination, they know who it is written to, and the informal code of privacy is in place. Girls simply do not read a note intended for someone else in their social circle; it is a way of cementing trust and relationship. It is also a way to resist classroom rules and adult authority because note passing is forbidden.

Boys' underground literacies include their engagements with video, computer, card, and figurine games. In my research with Kathy Sanford (Blair &

Sanford, 2004, in press), we documented the ways that boys enthusiastically engage in these literacies, including gaming and digital literacies, and suggested that these findings show that many boys are enthusiastically engaged in some gaming activities, and many are able to sustain their interest for extended periods of time in each game or level of the game. Even the boys whom their teachers believed could not maintain focus on a topic were able and willing to spend numerous consecutive hours playing one game, leaving it, and coming back the next day immediately to resume their focus. They kept memory records of their own progress as well as the progress of each opponent, either virtual or real. When they played with their Yu-Gi-Oh! cards, for example, they counted up and subtracted points in the thousands in their heads as they proceeded through the game. They read the symbols on the cards, knew the histories of each of the characters, and knew what each was capable of doing. They were able to remember and explain the many intricate rules of the game that they had learned by reading magazines, watching others play, trading cards, and sharing understandings among themselves. Street (2005) reminded us that in examining boys' literacies, it is essential to build on the richness and complexity of their prior knowledge and consider these out-of-school literacies not as deficits, but as connected to their sense of self and their ways of knowing and engaging in the world.

The literacy events and practices in which boys and girls participate both inside and outside of school must be examined with gender in mind. This examination should recognize that there is a wide range of literacy practices that are strengths for these children. Boys and girls should be encouraged to explore new literacy practices.

DIGITAL LITERACIES

The new literacies in this digital age are affecting children in very powerful and nuanced ways. With these shifts in technology and media, the meaning of literacy is rapidly evolving. It appears that boys are taking these up more quickly and in more depth than girls. The boys in the Blair and Sanford (in press) study embraced a great number of digital texts in a variety of forms. Their digital text preferences were similar to their interests in literature and fell into several categories or genres, with action, adventure, sports, racing, science fiction, and fantasy at the forefront. These boys' life interests tended to align with their game interests, as was evident when more rural than urban boys identified sports, car, and racing games as their favorites. These were boys who had more access to motorized and all-terrain vehicles than city boys and tended to play in all their small-town sporting events.

The boys in this five-year study were involved in playing various generations of these games for many years. They were not newly literate in these genres.

They learned to read and play them shortly after they learned to read more conventional texts in 1st or 2nd grade, and they grew out of some games and moved on to new ones. Their favorite digital texts, like their literacy practices, were continually changing.

Girls, on the other hand, appear to be lagging behind. In *Tech-Savvy: Educating Girls in the New Computer Age*, the American Association of University Women (2000) reported that girls have reservations about computer culture and are not using computers as much at home or taking advanced computer courses at school. In this report, girls asserted that they can use computers, but do not want to do so. The association concluded that girls are not keeping up with boys on today's standards of computer literacy and posed the question of what this may mean for the future. This is a very serious concern as the world and workforce become more dependent on these literacies every day. Where will this leave girls if they remain on the impoverished side of the digital divide? It is not possible to think about these digital literacies without considering the economic possibilities.

It is essential that both girls and boys be given access to computer technologies that will enhance their futures and opportunities to consider these new visual and technical literacies through a critical lens. All children need to be well versed in the power of the Internet to inform, persuade, and misinform. They need to acquire the savvy not only to use, but also to critique it.

These new literacy practices have impacted learning in classrooms, and researchers need to explore how students read these visual texts. They should explore more than just the question of whether one type of digital text is more attractive to one group or another, but also how students are taking up the writing of these digital genres. It has been suggested that as new technologies and digitized formats continue to replace books, magazines, and newspapers as the most efficient and up-to-date ways to communicate and share knowledge, those who use these technologies will have the upper hand in knowledge exchange and participation in a global economy.

Although they were very well versed in reading and manipulating digital text, the early-adolescent boys in our study were not yet constructing or writing their own digital Web sites or computer games. A few had built a simple Web page as a class project, and one boy had created a Web page at home with downloaded software. They were, however, gaining a fair degree of knowledge and/or speculating about these digital formats, how the effects were created, and what is possible. In response to a question on how games are designed, one boy explained,

Basically there's a 3-D format, and it's a black screen or sometimes a white screen, and if they were going to make a pen, then they'd have the tip here; they'd put a little dot there, a dot there, a dot there, a dot there and they'd have lines; then they add texture, color, etc., until it was a good full image. Basically it's a lot like that. Sometimes they use 3-D models, add light onto them, and then scan them into the computer, then go from there; add things, take away things, like that. (Personal interview, April 18, 2003)

It appeared to us as we spoke with boys that they were acquiring conceptual knowledge and that as they gained more technical expertise and opportunity, they would begin to build, write, and compose in the digital world. In discussing the technological savvy of Artemis Fowl (the starring character in a popular adolescent fiction series), one boy clearly explained how Artemis could capture images on his digital camera, download a file to his laptop, and e-mail the data from anywhere in the world to his server at his home in Ireland, and then have access to it from wherever he was. Although this boy had never done this himself, he completely understood and was at ease in explaining the process in detail.

Microsoft Network provides an instant messaging system that has become a preferred communication tool for adolescents. Girls see it as an important place to connect with their friends; it is inexpensive, and they can text message concurrently with other tasks such as doing homework. The conversations are immediate, short, and snappy and do not require a great deal of effort. These instant messaging platforms may be replacing telephone conversations among teens as they exchange events of the day or week and pass on important notices. This genre appears to have been taken up by both boys and girls of this age and often in cross-gendered groups. The compacted and invented text gives them a genre of their own.

GENDER AND LITERACY ASSESSMENT

Although assessment has been addressed in a previous chapter, the ways in which boys' and girls' literacy practices and products are assessed need careful reconsideration in terms of gender implications. Street (2005) suggested that traditional standardized tests cannot actually measure with any degree of accuracy the extent of the child's learning, nor can they assess what learning is not being examined or recognized. Large-scale standardized tests can provide a basis from which to compare a narrow range of literacy activities—for example, reading for comprehension, writing to substantiate a perspective—but they do not begin to assess the wide range of literacy practices or recognize gender or cultural differences. These large-scale tests have in some cases shown that girls are faring better on reading and writing than boys.

This raises questions: How might test items favor one gender or another? What can standardized measures actually reveal about the literacy learning of boys and girls, taking into account race or social-class realities? These are important considerations because what is tested is often what is valued and taught. Therefore an examination of tests is crucial. There is clear evidence to support the premise that not all girls are faring well in school and not all boys are doing poorly. A great deal has yet to be known to fully understand this topic.

Newkirk (2000) suggested that boys see school definitions of literacy as excluding their preferences and that in-school literacies are girlish. This perception may account for some of their disengagement and differences in performance scores. Girls, on the other hand, are generally thought to be more compliant when it comes to performing school tasks, more willing to follow adult directions, and better at "doing school." This does not mean that one group is more capable than the other; rather, they may just demonstrate their learning differently.

Differential achievements are just one small piece of a much bigger puzzle. Close examinations are needed, and caution must be used not to misread gender differences. It is necessary to understand the literacies of both boys and girls and to work to ensure that all children do well; it is not enough for one group to do well at the expense of the other.

CONCLUSION

It is important not to essentialize notions of gender by putting children into rigid categories of what it is supposed to be like to be a girl or a boy. Gender is a social construction and not a biological distinction, and these social constructions come in many forms. By reducing discussions of gender and literacy to simplistic binaries, such as those reported in large-scale comparative reports, there is a tendency to perpetuate the myths created through generalizations. In addition, identifying achievement differences between boys and girls does not imply that one group has more ability in an area than the other. The diversity of masculinities and femininities and issues of race and class need to be interwoven throughout discussions of boys and girls and their literacy learning and success. There is clear evidence to suggest that schools in low socioeconomic areas have lower test scores on literacy measures than schools in areas of affluence and advantage.

It is important to challenge past definitions and work toward shaping future definitions and create purposes for literacy that are open and accessible to all students. As readers and texts change in ways that appear to be particular to boys or girls, all children must be included in all kinds of literacy practices, while being challenged at the same time. Many boys are teaching themselves to read the new digital literacies and may be gaining more experience in a range of modes of representation: print, video, and graphic images in multimodal ways; visual and verbal; spoken and written; narrative; and display. It is important to figure out the essentials from this array that will also be useful for girls. These multimodal literacies will need to be accessible to all children in the future.

Researchers need to explore further the literate lives of adolescents to enable connections to children's experiences in both in- and out-of-school literacies. The literacies of young people are intricately connected to popular culture, and these new forms of literacies and the cultures that accompany them need to be recognized. Teachers and parents are in a cultural lag when it comes to the new literacies and have a great deal to learn to catch up to young people. Adults can learn a lot from adolescents and need to be open to learning and asking youth to teach them.

There is a role for quality adolescent literature in middle school and high school classrooms. All youth can benefit from the experience of enjoying a story, finding themselves in the shoes of another person, and living through other people's possibilities. They also need to be able to read to acquire information and take away ideas from a nonfiction text. Good books can take readers into many experiences that they might not otherwise have in their lives and draw on their understandings of others—including books that might be considered boy books or girl books. Empathy and compassion can be evoked in a fictionalized account of someone else's lived experiences. Adventure may lead to problem-solving, and fantasy may take the reader to a place of exploring the unknown simply for the intrigue. These are experiences that are important for all children. More adolescent literature from a range of perspectives, positions, and cultures with more varied roles across all genres is needed. There is much to accomplish in moving past gender stereotypes. Both boys and girls can learn from a further understanding of each other's experiences in literature by coming to understand experiences other than their own.

All writers write best from the place they know best, and this is also true of adolescent boys and girls when they write. It is important to give young people an opportunity to write from their places of strength and explore new possibilities. If boys have fun in their expressive writing, have a penchant for action, and can use this cultural material to become better writers, this is an asset. Girls' writing preferences, which originate from their hearts and feelings, also need to be explored, valued, and extended. Rewriting a story in an unfamiliar genre from a different gender perspective could give them an opportunity to examine other ways of being.

In a world that is rapidly evolving, with new literacies emerging almost daily, today's adolescents will need to adapt and innovate to deal with these changes. At this time in their lives, young people need opportunities to explore new literacies across their various identities as students, game players, bloggers, and so on, without some being privileged over others. They need the chance to demonstrate their literacy learning in fair and equitable ways. They need to understand that there are many ways to be a girl or a boy in school and still be successful and accepted. Young people need to realize that they will encounter many complexities in life ahead and will need to move beyond dichotomies. It is essential to model possibilities and support young people in their growing understandings.

NOTE

1. At this point, I must clarify that although I am referring here to two principal gender constructions, boys and girls, these categories are not necessarily mutually exclusive. There are children who do not tidily fit into one group or the other, but that is a discussion for another chapter.

REFERENCES

American Association of University Women. (1992). *How schools shortchange girls.* Washington, DC: Author.

American Association of University Women. (2000). *Tech-savvy: Educating girls in the new computer age.* Washington, DC: Author.

Barbieri, M. (1995). *Sounds of the heart: Learning to listen to girls.* Portsmouth, NH: Heinemann.

Barrs, M. (2000). Gendered literacy? *Language Arts, 7,* 287–293.

Blair, H. (1998). They left their genderprints: The voice of girls in text. *Language Arts, 5,* 11–18.

Blair, H. (2000). Genderlects: Girl talk in a middle years language arts classroom. *Language Arts, 77,* 315–323.

Blair, H., & Sanford, K. (2004). Morphing literacy: Boys reshaping their school-based literacy practices. *Language Arts, 81,* 452–460.

Blair, H., & Sanford, K. (in press). Game Boys: Where is the literacy? In K. Sanford & R. Hammett (Eds.), *Boys, girls, and the myths of literacies and learning.* Toronto, ON: Canadian Scholars Press.

Cherland, M. R. (1994). *Private practices: Girls reading fiction and constructing identity.* Bristol, PA: Taylor and Francis.

Fine, M., & Zane, N. (1989). Bein' wrapped too tight: When low income women drop out of high school. In L. Weis, E. Farrar, & H. Petrie (Eds.), *Dropouts in schools: Issues, dilemmas, and solutions* (pp. 23–53). Albany: State University of New York Press.

Gee, J. (2001). Reading as situated language: A sociocognitive perspective. *Journal of Adolescent and Adult Literacy, 44,* 714–725.

Mehan, H. (1979). *Learning lessons: Social organization in the classroom.* Cambridge, MA: Harvard University Press.

Newkirk, T. (2000). Misreading masculinities: Speculations on the great gender gap in writing. *Language Arts, 77,* 294–300.

Pollack, W. (1998). *Real boys: Rescuing our sons from the myths of boyhood.* New York: Henry Holt.

Sadker, M., & Sadker, D. (1994). *Failing at fairness: How America's schools cheat girls.* Toronto, ON: Maxwell Macmillan International.

Smith, M., & Wilhelm, J. (2002). *Reading don't fix no Chevys: Literacy in the lives of young men.* Portsmouth, NH: Heinemann.

Street, B. (1997). The implications of the new literacy studies for literacy education. *English in Education, 31,* 45–59.

Street, B. (2005). Recent applications of new literacy studies in educational contexts. *Research on the Teaching of English, 39,* 417–423.

Tannen, D. (1991). *You just don't understand: Women and men in conversation.* New York: Ballantine Books.

Part Three

ADOLESCENT LITERACY BEYOND THE CLASSROOM

Chapter Thirteen

DIGITAL LITERACIES

Cynthia Lewis, Kevin Leander, and Xiqiao Wang

In a recently published newspaper article on the use of so-called text speak or Web language, 9th-grade English teacher Lindsey Martin bemoaned how the Internet was "destroying [her students'] grammar skills," stating, "Students cannot spell, they don't capitalize proper nouns and they have no idea how to use commas or semi-colons" (Sarrio, 2007). Ms. Martins's complaint was supported by other teachers in the article. Similar statements about the Internet's negative influence on literacy are echoed across elementary and secondary school classrooms in the United States and beyond. Young people are changing the face of literacy through their online reading and writing practices. Questions about the nature of literacy—what counts as literacy? What counts as a text? Whose literacies are most legitimate?—have always been hotly contested, but new literacies have interrupted all our dependable theories about literacy practices and texts, leaving those of us who teach and study reading and writing in a quandary.

What stance should educators take on these new literacy practices and their relationship to the literacies traditionally developed in school? However educators choose to answer this question, the answers must be informed by an understanding of the actual literacy practices of young people. As teachers and researchers, we must face our own anxieties that youth often are ahead of us as writers and readers of online texts. Moreover, a key challenge in achieving a deep understanding of youth literacies is to move past the surface features of texts. For although texts do tell something, they also are often stubborn at hiding how they were made, and for whom, and toward what ends, and in what circumstances. In short, once they arrive on the scene of classrooms, texts tell little about how they have been used within complex social practices. This ability of texts (as surfaces) to hide their own social uses and social lives seems to be all the more true with digital texts.

Literacy researchers and educators have dealt with these developments by trying to understand more about what young people do when they read and write online, attempting to learn more about digital literacies as social practices. Given a decade or so of such empirical research, much has been learned about online reading and writing practices.

In this chapter, we will discuss three significant changes in literacy practices that have implications for the teaching and learning of English and language arts in digitally mediated times. To do so, we will use examples from our own and others' research on the uses of Internet communication technologies among young people. We argue that literacy educators need to consider these new dimensions of practice in rethinking teaching and learning literacy in digitally mediated times. Technological tools cannot simply be imported into classrooms because doing so would change the objectives and motives of the activity, the roles of the young people engaging in that activity, and the group norms associated with it. One of the reasons that youth use online literacies productively is that they are very clear about these aspects of the activity. This heightened awareness leads to strategic and analytic uses of literacy outside of school. Although we believe that it would be misguided to try to replicate in school the digital literacy tools and practices that young people select to participate in outside of school, we do believe that a better understanding of the changing dimensions of literacy practice based on our own and others' studies of young people engaged in online literacies will help educators reconceptualize the teaching of reading and writing around these new dimensions of practice.

ADDRESSIVITY AND VOICE

Writers in digital environments frequently address and are addressed by multiple audiences simultaneously, and consequently, discerning expectations and social codes can be complicated. Instant messaging (IM) is a case in point. IM is a form of computer-mediated communication (CMC) that allows two or more participants to create a synchronous written conversation. IM users each have one or more lists of buddies, or frequent contacts, some of whom they regularly talk to online, and others they talk to more occasionally. The list allows users to track whether their buddies are on- or offline at any given time and talk to those who are online. In 2005, 65 percent of American teens, and 75 percent of American teens who were online, used IM, most on a daily basis. To manage the complexity of IM communication, users have to draw on the intertextual chains (New London Group, 2000) that exist through the textual history of each exchange and the larger textual network. One of the participants in a study of young people's uses of IM (Lewis & Fabos, 2005) demonstrated her lived understanding of these intertextual chains in her ability to shift her voice and stance almost instantaneously. She would shift from sympathetic friend to casual acquaintance to flirty teen, depending on the tone and stance of her buddies, with whom she sometimes carried on conversations all at once. Although face-to-face interaction and writing offline also involves addressivity, the need to fluidly shift stances from audience to audience is unique to the dyadic yet nearly simultaneous nature of online communication.

Addressivity online often involves performing an identity that appears to be required for a particular exchange. This identity can be entirely fictional but still dependent on a careful reading of the situation, including the audience, tone, and purpose. For example, one of the young people in Thomas's (2004) study reported making conscious linguistic choices to perform alternative identities online and playfully trick her friends. Instead of gender swapping in their role-playing, however, most of these young people chose avatars that represented idealized notions of being female through their talk about appearance and the body. Similarly, in the IM study mentioned earlier, one of these young people chose to pose as blonde haired and blue eyed, in keeping with her vision of what it means to be the idealized female. These are examples of young girls being influenced by stereotypical notions of femininity. Addressivity, in this case, is not directly related to particular audiences, but to particular cultural expectations. Although such expectations and performances of gender are not limited to life online, answering the address is almost effortless in online spaces given the potential for anonymity and the relative ease of posing or disguising oneself.

Youth's performance of identities in digital environments often involves addressing a massive audience of readers and viewers through the creative use of resources from multiple media. Consider, for example, the new Internet phenomenon, YouTube.com, a tool that mediates and promotes youth's understanding, experimenting, and making of their identities, beliefs, and attitudes toward a wide range of social issues. YouTube.com is a so-called consumer media company that offers free hosting for videos. With "Broadcast Yourself" as its slogan, YouTube.com is designed to enable simple, fast, and free sharing and viewing of videos online. Among the more than 12 million videos uploaded each day, many are personal, original productions, such as home movies, video blogs, and amateur film works. It is a tool for social networking as well as a user-generated database containing a wide range of information related to users' backgrounds and motivations. Through YouTube.com and other digital tools, youth experiment with issues relevant to their identity making and develop beliefs and attitudes toward sexuality, morality, legality, and political engagement.

Young people experimenting with materials drawn from their routine lives and from the remixing of images from various media often form very complex rearrangements of a wide array of old and new symbols and meanings. One example of remixing that has been widely circulated on the Internet is a short video consisting of edited news footage of President George W. Bush and British prime minister Tony Blair appearing to gaze adoringly at one another as they sing "Endless Love." This remix of news footage with the hit duet originally sung by Lionel Richie and Diana Ross makes a powerful political statement. Similarly, in their video blogs, youth combine a variety of genres, forms of communication, and discourses to accomplish particular effects, such as parody, humor, or social commentary.

Video-sharing sites can be good sites for investigating how youth learn to create and share their productions and how they accomplish participation and social acceptance in a community mediated through a specific technology. Finding acceptance within this community demands that users address the expectations and social codes of the community, display their knowledge of images and footages that are most *de rigeur*, and remix and parody for others in the know about the content. The user is thus a knowledgeable receiver of digital media, someone who understands the intertextual references and parodies, and, often, a dynamically resourceful producer of digital media, someone who alters the content or remixes elements of the production to make his or her own statement.

Voice in online writing is closely connected to addressivity. The fluid shifting of tone and stance that has emerged out of the need to address different audiences and discourses almost simultaneously has called into question what it means to have an authentic or personal voice as a writer. Envisioning voice as authentic or personal privileges stability across texts, rather than the dynamic, fluid concept of voice exhibited by online writers as they enact identities that depend on a running analysis of complicated online and offline contexts. Thiel (2005) studied adolescent girls' uses of IM and found that her participants presented themselves differently as they shifted from conversation to conversation with different buddies. For example, one of her participants presented herself as tempted by physical relationships with boys when talking with a girlfriend; however, a short time later, she presented herself as serious about religion and school when exchanging IMs with a boyfriend.

The technology of Internet communication is conducive to these shifts in identity. A case in point is the IM study by Lewis and Fabos (2005) mentioned earlier, in which the participant shifted seamlessly between being a sympathetic friend, casual acquaintance, and flirty teen, depending on the nature of her relationship with each of her conversational partners. IM uses windows to display each evolving conversation between an IM writer and his or her buddy. A new window pops up with each new buddy who enters a conversation. The IM writer usually attempts to converse with each buddy as windows continue to pop up, sometimes at rapid speeds. If the writer's relationship is different with each buddy, as is often the case, then the tone and purpose of the conversation is also different. These shifts in tone—and often in self-representation, as already described—are enhanced by the technology of multiple windows. Other Internet communication technologies also add to the shifting voices that writers take up in such environments. For example, IM technologies allow users to stream in video as well as use different fonts, emoticons (symbols, such as smiley faces, to express emotions), and colors to express one's voice as a writer. Again, because conversations take place almost simultaneously, with writers jumping from window to window to sustain conversational exchanges with many buddies, it is important for users to develop dexterity in terms of writing voice or tone.

Black's (2007) study of a fan fiction writer who was an English language learner showed how the writer's sense of audience was very much connected to the voice that she took up in her writing of fan fiction. Fan fiction is fiction that is written by fans of a particular print or media series (such as *Star Trek*) or icon (such as Captain Kirk). Fan fiction includes some of the characters, settings, and plots of the original fiction, but builds on, substitutes, or otherwise alters the original works. The fan fiction writer in Black's study shifted her voice in her fan fiction about a character in a Japanese animation when she included an author's note that had both a public and personal voice, addressing specific readers with whom she had corresponded before as well as the larger group of readers affiliated with that particular fan fiction.

The hybrid nature of textuality in Internet communication also contributes to a dynamic view of voice. Often, Internet communication demands that the textuality of writing be used to perform the textual qualities of speech. This blending of spoken and written textuality results in hybrid language forms to represent the casual, insider exchanges of informal speech through written textual features. To achieve a speech-like quality, electronic writers use syntax, vocabulary, and grammar more common in speech and abbreviations to make for quick, speech-like exchanges and communicate paralinguistic features of face-to-face communication contexts.

This dynamic textual voice is significant as it relates to the kinds of social identities afforded through its use. As Thomas (2004) pointed out, "In the online context ... to write is to exist.... Writing is an essential component for performing identity" (p. 366). One of the young people in Thomas's study, Violetta, explained the strategies that she used to create interaction through textuality (e.g., exclamation points, references to actions and facial expressions). Thomas made the link to identity performance:

> What is rarely reported is that the linguistic variations of cybertalk are directly related to identity performance. Violetta revealed that her words had to look just so, and that she would vary her style of speech according to the persona she was performing. (p. 367)

The girls in the IM study by Lewis and Fabos (2005) mentioned earlier enacted identities through language that had to sound and look semiotically like speech but be accomplished through writing. One of the girls, Sam, wrote her way into the textual worlds of a new group to which she wanted to belong by hearing the cadences of their inside jokes and trying to sound right in her writing to that group. In interviews, Sam explicitly referred to her efforts to "talk like they do" when she posed as the friend of someone who accidentally got onto Sam's own buddy list. She emulated the voice of this person to maintain the connection. "I'll use the same exclamations where she uses them and I'll try to talk like they do," Sam told us. In adapting the tone and content of the anonymous correspondent's message, Sam had to analyze how the girl's tone worked and how it accomplished its purposes. Besides adapting her tone, Sam was also careful to adjust her subject matter according to her particular audience.

In this way, IM writers produce the sound of speech. According to another of the IMers we studied, however, this virtual speech takes on a life of its own, with adept IM writers using the disembodied textuality of writing to "sound smart and sophisticated" in ways that go beyond face-to-face. The virtual, it seems, may idealize the real, becoming the way that so-called real speech ought to sound, thus further interrupting any facile distinctions between the virtual and the real or between voice and self. Having a voice online involves performing multivocal textual repertoires with speed and flexibility. Online readers and writers are involved in the generative act of using texts in new ways by reconfiguring messages, cutting and pasting, parodying, and creating textual forms to fit their social needs.

SOCIALITY

In digital environments, writing is used far more often for the purpose of sustaining social relationships and friendships, but also for maintaining professional networks and creating learning opportunities. Some label today's students as a Net-centric generation that has different expectations about social relations. Being raised in the "always on" world of interactive media, the Internet, digital messaging technologies, and online social networking environments, today's students value their ability to use the Web to create a self-paced, customized, on-demand learning path that includes multiple forms of interactive, social, and self-publishing media tools.

Short message service (SMS) mobile technologies, such as text messaging, have become a popular medium for casual online interaction in countries where technological means exist. SMS is a service available on most digital mobile phones that permits the exchange of concise, text-based messages between mobile phones. Considered by youth to be convenient, less expensive, and faster alternatives to traditional technologies, mobile technologies are popular with adolescents as they enable them to make time-shifted communications across geographical and national boundaries, make plans, and maintain contact with family and friends.

Young people's close engagement with social networking environments has also transformed their way of forming relationships, building complex communities, sharing musings and opinions, and discovering and using new information. MySpace.com and Facebook.com provide such an environment through interactive Web sites that include personal profiles, blogs, photos, music, and videos submitted by users for the purposes of networking with others who share their interests or social affiliations. These social networking Web sites affect all facets of students' campus experiences, ranging from forming social clubs and study groups, communicating with friends, keeping track of campus news, dating, or even researching roommates. It is possible to imagine a partnership between formal education and these social networking environments to facilitate collaboration and creation of multimedia projects. Some faculty members suggest that Facebook.com can be a medium for faculty, staff, and even administrators to create an easy networking space that leads to positive interaction with students.

Wikis are collaborative digital writing spaces that allow multiple authors to edit and revise the same document simultaneously. Always works in progress, wikis assume equal responsibilities among all users and represent individual as well as group perspectives. Since they both store and manage knowledge, wikis can be used in the classroom for collaborative writing projects such as group research reports or class newspapers. The fact that texts can be revised or removed without consultation requires students to grapple with ways of achieving agreement and resolving difference, leading to productive critical reading (Beach, Anson, Breuch, & Swiss, in press).

Blogging is another powerful digital writing tool that can serve as a useful platform to collect, organize, and share personal writing. As a form of journal writing, blogs value personal and dialogic expressions that are "spontaneous, subjective, exploratory, and even contradictory" (Beach et al., in press). The commenting feature helps to create conversational exchange, and critique presents opportunities for students to express opinions and creates a community based on shared interests (Watrall & Ellison, 2006). Writing in such a community creates a sense of audience and purpose that is grounded in an enhanced understanding of different perspectives and content. Juxtaposition of inquiries, arguments, and investigations through links creates a site to examine not only consensus, but also dissonance. Such a conversation is also extended in both temporal and physical spaces. A common class blog can serve as a continuously updating teaching resource center of class materials.

In engaging these technologies, youth carry out complicated dances of online and offline relationships. They are situated *at once* within the technosocial space of the Internet and the socially embodied space offline. A few recent network phenomena have gained fast and tremendous popularity because of their capacity to accommodate this dance of online and offline social networking. First created as a campus face book within Harvard University in 2004, Facebook.com has quickly grown to be serving college, high school, university, and other network-based communities. As of December 2005, it had the largest number of registered users among college-focused sites (at over 7.5 million U.S. college student accounts created, with an additional 20,000 new accounts being created daily). MySpace.com currently ranks the fourth most popular English Web site, reporting 106 million accounts as of September 8, 2006, and reportedly attracting new registrations at a rate of 230,000 per day.

Users construct their online identities by using the multimedia affordances of such social networking technologies to perform their identities. A MySpace.com or Facebook.com user can update a profile that consists of a picture, brief biographical information, a list of favorite books and music, and an inspirational quote; one can post and import notes (blogs), photos, people tags, and comments; one can share with friends updated, personalized news stories through the News Feed and Mini Feed features; a user's status can be identified (at home, in exam, in dorm, etc.). Social interactions are enabled as individuals search for classmates, colleagues, and friends. Students form their own communities by adding and inviting friends to join existing or newly formed groups or can "poke" someone online (a way to say hi to someone that is not a mutually accepted friend) to make a new friend. Through postings, uploads, inside e-mails, and forums, students carry on conversations, share audio and video files, and catch up with each other. Young people who regularly use social networking Web sites can also use these digital environments to realize offline social functions such as creating social events, sending out invitations, and making announcements about upcoming social events. Although they usually use such technologies to maintain existing social relations, they can extend their social network by taking advantage of the mobile and media services. For example, MySpace.com hosts films, songs, and other works from various musicians, filmmakers, and comedians. Also, MySpace.com is currently working with American mobile phone provider Helio to develop MySpace Mobile, a service enabling one to use a cell phone to access and edit one's profile, communicate with other members, and view others' profiles. This process, already popular in Japan, is called *moblogging*.

In their article on the past and future of Internet research, Leander and McKim (2003) destabalized the offline/online binary that underlies much research on adolescents' uses of digital media and argued for methodologies that trace technosocial-embodied networks across contexts and bounded notions of time and space. Merchant's (2001) study of girls' participation in Internet chatrooms made the further point that while buddies actually chat online, providing advice and support to offline friends, they often converse online about things that they would find difficult to take up in face-to-face conversation. He illustrated this point with a conversation between a boy and a girl in which the girl advised the boy that he was "crowding" the girl he fancied, something that would be difficult to say in person. Writers in the IM environment are constituted in voices, their own and others, that merge and overlap within and across contexts as the writing self is addressed by and answerable to others.

In a large-scale study conducted by researchers in the United Kingdom, Livingstone and Bober (2004) investigated uses of the Internet among young people (ages 9–19) to find out how the Internet is shaping family life, peer cultures, and learning. These researchers found that one-third of the young people chatting with friends online, more often than not local friends, found this to be at least as satisfying as talking face-to-face. Many of these youth used Internet communication to engage in identity play involving some pretense about themselves (their age, appearance, etc.). Rather than thinking of offline and online spaces as separate social worlds, researchers have found that these spaces intersect and overlap. In fact, the maintenance of offline relationships is a documented feature of online communication (Leander & McKim, 2003). For many people, writing online is used so often for the purpose of sustaining social relationships that its ordinariness is taken for granted as a part of the fabric of daily social life (Wellman, 2004).

Leander and McKim (2003) suggested that examining how digital texts travel or circulate can lead to insights about the kinds of practices and relationships a particular technology affords. Being social online often means monitoring where friends are in online space. A simple and ubiquitous way of accomplishing this goal is through the commonly asked question, Who else are you talking to?, resulting in chat buddies having indirect exchanges with a wider range of people through other buddies (e.g., "Tell her …"). This simple question allowed the question asker to have some degree of knowledge about and control over the movements and conversations of buddies outside of the immediate dyad.

In the IM mentioned earlier (Lewis & Fabos, 2005), conversations easily became part of other conversations within a given IM session. Participants routinely cut and pasted elements of one conversation and shared them with another buddy—often without disclosing their actions with the first buddy, who may have done the same with someone else. Several of the girls also tried surreptitiously to discover who was currently talking to whom and what they happened to be talking about by IM inquiries to friends and asking them to report back. For example, one of the girls would report to her girlfriends to tell them about her conversations with boys, sometimes cutting and pasting the most important parts for her girlfriends' pleasure.

Being a competent participant in these patterns of circulation requires quick, in-process thinking. It requires that users swiftly assess the nature of the circulating text, the purpose or agenda that led to its circulation, the audiences involved, the allegiances it may foster or damage, and so forth. Participants perform identities in relation to these circulating texts. These patterns of circulation function to reinforce social connections, creating bonds between particular users, sometimes at the expense of others, adding intrigue to the IM experience.

In her book on young people's uses of new media, Livingstone (2002) pointed out that Internet spaces are more often "based on bricolage or juxtaposition" (p. 3). As already discussed, Internet sites blend and remix old and new images, sounds, and words to achieve particular effects. This kind of creativity, much valued in Internet spaces, is a representational style keyed to new ways of being and thinking (Lankshear & Knobel, 2003). I would argue that these new ways of being and thinking are related to new practices of sociality, which depend on a cut-and-paste, remixed style for production and exchange.

SPACE AND TIME

One common yet difficult to understand aspect of emerging digital literacy practices is how they transform experiences of space and time. Even from the advent of the early public Internet, there was a sense that experiences of space and time might shift with a resource that crossed national and cultural borders and moved information and communication at such speeds. Some spatiotemporal changes influenced by the Internet may not have been predicted in advance, however. For citizens of small countries such as Trinidad, for instance, we might have predicted that practices of national identity online would have been swamped by the overwhelming practices of more powerful nations, cultures, and corporations. As documented in the work of Miller and Slater (2000), however, despite the manner in which Trinidadians are spread across the globe and do not all share a common physical geography, and despite the ways in which powerful forms of globally circulating popular culture may be seen as a threat to local cultures, Trindadians use the Internet to practice and reinforce their national identities, and they consume the Internet as a source of national pride and national identification. For example, the home pages of Trinidadians are often replete with core nationalistic symbols such as flags, crests, maps, and national statistics. Web pages, online chat, and news groups are also used to practice cultural identities through language play (*lyming*), Trini-style jokes, and even explanations for outsiders to help them learn about Trinidadian culture.

Trinidadians—including those physically located within the country as well as those who are digitally connected, living thousands of miles abroad—celebrate national identification in ways that run counter to the threats posed by some early theorists of the Internet and global cultural shift. One primary threat, for example, was that nation-states, regions, or other geographical-political places might lose their local identities and have them substituted with global forms of cultural identification (e.g., Castells, 1996). Currently, the picture is much more complex than this, as we see the Internet being used to reinforce national and community identities, even as it is used to spread global cultural practices, forms, and identities.

Lam (2004) developed case studies of Chinese immigrant youth, analyzing their school-based and online literacy practices. This work was, at least in part, motivated by seeing different social-spatial arrangements among Chinese immigrant youth online than are possible in school. For instance, while these youth often experienced de facto segregation in school as well as social disparagement for their accented speech, in online environments, such as the Hong Kong Chat Room, they practiced a very large degree of freedom to shift between English and romanized Cantonese. This blend of language use and social alignments created a social space that allowed much more free play of identity and literacy development than did school contexts for these students.

The mismatch between how youth experience space and time in school and out of school in online contexts is evident in a broad range of literacy practices and even confuses some of the received views of divisions between such practices, including orality in contrast to literacy. As discussed earlier in the section on addressivity and voice, using writing to talk in real time (IM/chat) challenges the oral/literate divide as well as assumptions about context being less important in writing than in talk. As Merchant (2001) argued, "traditional distinctions between speech as synchronous face-to-face communication in a shared location and writing as a means of communicating through time and space are challenged by new technology" (p. 299).

Jones (2005) discussed how digital literacies become overly "schooled" in his discussion of Hong Kong classrooms. Schooling can be understood as the control of space and time from a particular mind-set and group of schooled practices. To understand this mind-set and associated practices, it is necessary to look beyond the obvious walled divisions of classrooms and the separation of the school day into 50- or 55-minute periods. Jones contrasted the school's perspective as essentially monochronic (treating time as linear and tangible, and divisible), in contrast to the students' perspectives, as informed by digital culture, as essentially polychromic (seeing time as more fluid, layered, and simultaneous). In the monochromic orientation, one action occupies time to the exclusion of all other actions, an approach to activity that would be quite foreign to many cultural contexts, including much of the modern workplace (Gee et al., 1996).

Jones's (2005) findings in Hong Kong closely parallel those of another study, which analyzed the practices of girls in a private school where a wireless network had been installed and the girls carried laptops with them from class to class and to home at night (Leander, 2007). Despite a very large investment by the school and parents into the laptop program, Leander found that the following principles of space and time overwhelmingly described how the laptops were used in the school:

> Defined plans precede resources and activity; students and teachers know what they need or are seeking in advance.
> Sequential activity is dominant, and everyone follows the same sequential path.
> Asynchronous communication is primary to synchronous communication (e.g., e-mail or Web searching is more "schooled" than instant messaging).
> A single space is dominant (and under surveillance) for each task; "task" is mono-spatial, and "off-task" is partially defined as departure into another social space.
> Public social spaces, including the Internet, must be bracketed for student use; school needs to produce kindergartens of public spaces for students to understand them, learn within them, and be safe within them.
> Material print texts and print spaces (the built environment) are primary and are authorized, while virtual texts are unauthorized and supplemental.
> The Internet is primarily a tool for information rather than a tool for communication. Information and communication technologies (ICTs) are primarily ITs in school.

Given this background, it may come as no surprise that the most prevalent literacy practices in using the laptops at the school included the following:

> writing process pedagogies
> students' note taking
> an online newsletter for the school community, produced by the central office
> distributing assignments and submitting work
> keeping absent students up to date
> quick searches for online information

With the exception of the last two practices, the most common uses of the laptops either did not require a wireless network or were simply online versions of former print technologies and distributions (e.g., the school newsletter).

In rethinking schooling and its relation to digital literacies, it may be necessary to place less emphasis on the introduction of new tools and networks and reconsider how online practices challenge very familiar and well-schooled experiences of space and time. In online contexts, plans often develop within activities, and people seek out materials they need in the very course of their action. Moving across multiple, simultaneous activities is also often considered normative, as evidenced in the earlier section on IM. As such, synchronous communication or other simultaneous activity involves monitoring and responding to fluctuating demands of different activities as they emerge over time, rather than merely planning in advance. A single social space is often not considered dominant. Hence digital environments are often developed to increase the movements of participants across different fields of action and communication, rather than keeping everyone on a single, stable task. Another key difference is that information seeking and communication are highly integrated in many digital practices. Whereas in school, information seeking is often set apart as a special activity of "research," in online practices, the social space and time of research is often highly integrated into the space and time of communication as a relatively seamless movement.

Because much of the conversation around space and time and digital literacy practices can become quickly abstract, in the following example, we take you briefly into one youth's play of a massively multiplayer online role player game. We use this example from research (Leander & Lovvorn, 2006) especially to make evident how gamers often experience a macro view, or big picture, of their current activity, while simultaneously experiencing a micro, or small picture, view. This dual view stands in stark contrast to that of school, where students often are only aware of the small picture and are not clear on its relation to top-level goals.

In this case, we focus on 13-year-old Brian's use of a skills screen and experience points (XPs) in the game Star Wars Galaxies: An Empire Divided (Lucasarts and Sony Online Entertainment, 2003). The skills screen and XPs were not merely passively present in local activity, or referred to as "summaries" following activity, but were made to circulate constantly in the midst of the real-time play in such a way as to facilitate an "active, critical learning principle" (Barton et al., 1999).

During the course of his first three weeks of play, Brian became increasingly involved in monitoring XPs, skill acquisition, and title or profession acquisition. *Profession* in the game, as described in the guide packed with it, refers to a "collection of skills and titles." In creating Tiumbe, his game character, or avatar, Brian initially selected the profession of brawler, but after a few days of game play, he began to direct his effort to what is termed a *hybrid profession,* or one requiring the player to attain the titles of Master Marksman and Master Scout. (The game guide lists 25 different possible elite professions and hybrid professions for game players to pursue.) Skills screens consist of 16 boxes, distributed in four columns, each one of which describes a skill that one needs to complete en route to the chosen profession. When a particular skill is completed, the color of the box listing that skill changes on the chart. To become a Master Scout, a player needs to fill in four skill levels in exploration, trapping, hunting, and survival. In his third week of game play, Brian's skills screen told him that he had yet to demonstrate skills in Survival IV: Special Techniques, Hunting III: Trandoshan Methodology, and four other skill sets (10 of the 16 skills completed). Thus the skills screen serves a dynamic model of identity-in-the-making.

In Brian's play, and in particular, during the hunting episodes, he repeatedly shifted his perspective between the immediacy of Tiumbe in the scene of action (typically, a hunt) and the hypermediated perspective given by the skills screens for Master Scout and Master Marksman. The skills screens functioned as a record of Brian's history in the game that was called up into the present. Brian's after-hunt talk—what Barton et al. (1999) would call his "metalevel thinking"—included his thinking aloud for the observing researcher and his chat with hunting partners. These conversations were dominated by self-evaluation concerning how many XPs he had just earned, and of which type.

On the skills screen, the past actions of Brian translated into XPs and then retranslated into skills—mobilized, organized on a chart, and indexed as a particular form of becoming. The game, in this manner, was recruiting Brian not just as a generic player of Star Wars Galaxies, but as a player building a particular, organized set of experiences, distributed and yet coherently organized with representations. The skills screens were also a form of prolepsis (Wertsch & Stone, 1985) or projected identity, a particular account about who Brian might become in the future in relation to his avatar. These screens presented a tidy and colorful version of a hybrid actual and potential life timeline and could be pulled up instantly with the Control + S keys.

The skills screens influenced Brian's activity in a number of ways. For instance, on one occasion, Brian was hunting (through his character Tiumbe) with a friend, Ben. Brian explained that he was hunting that day with a pistol, rather than a more appropriate rifle, because he was trying to get more pistol experience points. In this case and many others, Brian's decisions about particular weapons or traps to use, or game to hunt, were guided by the skills screen and not by what might be considered to be practical, commonsensical, or a most efficient means in locally embodied activity; rather, the skills screen, and its own particular sensibility for advancement, structured goals and subgoals that influenced Brian to shape his experiences in particular ways that would "give good experience," where *good* was defined as filling in particular slots for future goals.

FINAL THOUGHTS

In the research we have conducted and in our reading of others' research, the three changing dimensions of practice described in this chapter—audience-voice, sociality, and space-time—are central to adolescents' uses of digital literacies. We would argue that these changing practices are more fundamental to reading and writing online than any change in tools (journal to blog) or conventions such as those that the teacher at the start of this chapter holds dear.

If educators hope to make school literacy more engaging for students and more meaningful to their present and future lives in a digitally mediated world, then they need to understand the shifts in practices and belief systems that have taken place and consider how these shifts should inform the teaching of reading and writing. The research we reviewed for this chapter can better inform these shifts in practice and the fears associated with them. The process of researching digital literacies today is much like the beginnings of writing research some 50 years ago. We are, in many ways, witnessing the making of a discipline (which is, of course, interdisciplinary at its core). As such, it will involve reenvisioning what will count as literacy in digitally mediated times and how new conceptions should shape the teaching and learning of literacy in schools.

REFERENCES

Baumer, S. (2006). Informal learning and social development of American youth on You-Tube. *Kids' Informal Learning with Digital Media: An Ethnographic Investigation of Innovative Knowledge Cultures.* Retrieved October, 15, 2006, from http://digitalyouth.ischool.berkeley.edu/node/49.

Beach R., Anson, C., Breuch, L., & Swiss, T. (in press). *Engaging digital literacies in the classroom.* Norwood, MA: Christopher-Gordon Publishers.

Black, R. W. (2007). Digital design: English language learners and reader feedback in online fanfiction. In M. Knobel & C. Lankshear (Eds.), *A New Literacies Sampler* (pp. 115–136). New York: Peter Lang.

Castells, M. (1996). *The rise of the network society.* Cambridge, MA: Blackwell.

Farrell, F. E. (2006). Judging roommates by their FaceBook cover. *Chronicle of Higher Education, 53*(2), A 63–64.

Gee, J. P., Hull, G., & Lankshear, C. (1996). *The new work order.* Boulder, CO: Westview Press.

Jones, R. (2005). Sites of engagement as sites of attention: Time, space, and culture in electronic discourse. In S. Norris & R. Jones (Eds.), *Discourse in action: Introducing mediated discourse analysis* (pp.141–154). London: Routledge.

Lam, W. S. E. (2004). Second language socialization in a bilingual chat room. *Language Learning and Technology, 8*(3), 44–65.

Lankshear, C., & Knobel, M. (2003). *New literacies: Changing knowledge and classroom learning.* Philadelphia: Open University Press.

Leander, K. M. (2007). "You won't be needing your laptops today": Wired bodies in the wire-less classroom. In M. Knobel & C. Lankshear (Eds.), *A new literacies sampler* (pp. 25–48). New York: Peter Lang.

Leander, K. M., & McKim, K. (2003). Tracing the everyday "sitings" of adolescents on the Internet: A strategic adaptation of ethnography across online and offline spaces. *Education, Communication, & Information, 3,* 211–240.

Leander, K. M., & Lovvorn, J. (2006). Literacy networks: Following the circulation of texts, bodies, and objects in the schooling and online gaming of one youth. *Cognition and Instruction, 24*(3), 291–340.

Lemeul, J. (2006). Why I registered on FaceBook. *Chronicle of Higher Education, 53*(2).

Lenhart, A., Madden, M., & Hitlin, P. (2005). *Teens and technology: Youth are leading the transition to a fully wired and mobile nation.* Washington, DC: Pew Internet & American Life Project.

Lewis, C. (2007). New literacies. In M. Knobel & C. Lankshear (Eds.), *A new literacies sampler* (pp. 229–238). New York: Peter Lang.

Lewis, C., & Fabos, B. (2005). Instant messaging, literacies, and social identities. *Reading Research Quarterly, 40*(4), 470–501.

Ling, R., & Yttri, B. (2002). Hyper-coordination via mobile phones in Norway. In J.E.K.M. Aakhus (Ed.), *Perpetual contact: Mobile communication, private talk, public performance* (pp. 139–169). Cambridge: Cambridge University Press.

Livingstone, S. (2002). *Young people and new media.* London: Sage.

Livingstone, S., & Bober, M. (2004). Taking up online opportunities? Children's uses of the Internet for education, communication, and participation. *E-Learning, 1,* 395–419.

Lucasarts (2003). Star Wars Galaxies: An Empire Divided [Computer software]. San Francisco, CA: LucasArts Entertainment Company LLC.

Merchant, G. (2001). Teenagers in cyberspace: An investigation of language use and language change in internet chatrooms. *Journal of Reading Research, 24*(3), 293–306.

Miller, D., & Slater, D. (2000). *The internet: An ethnographic approach.* New York: Berg.

MocoNews.net. (2006, February). MySpace mobile to debut on Helio; details on handsets. Retrieved July 6, 2007, from http://www.helio.com/live files/1/1145986889291/1145986889304/MocoNews_021606.pdf

New London Group. (2000). A pedagogy of multiliteracies: Designing social futures. In B. Cope & M. Kalantzis (Eds.), *Multiliteracies: Literacy learning and the design of social futures* (pp. 9–37). New York: Routledge.

Rodgers, J., & Gauntlett, D. (2002, October). *Teenage intercultural communications redeployment of the Internet Activist Model.* Paper presented at the Conference of the Association of Internet Researchers, Maastricht, Holland.

Sarrio, J. (2007, January 18). Teachers fear text effect. *The Tennessean.* Available at http://www.tennessean.com/apps/pbcs.dll/article?AID=2007701180385

Thiel, S. (2005). "IM Me": Identity construction and gender negotiation in the world of adolescent girls and instant messaging. In S. Mazzarella (Ed.), *Girl wide web: Girls, the Internet, and the negotiation of identity* (pp. 179–202). New York: Peter Lang.

Thomas, A. (2004). Digital literacies of the cybergirl. *E-Learning, 1,* 358–382.

Watrall, E. & Ellison, N. (2006). *Blogs for learning: A case study.* Screencast available at http://www.higheredblogcon.com/index.php/blogs-for-learning-a-case-study/

Wellman, B. (2004). The three stages of Internet studies: Ten, five and zero years ago. *New Media and Society, 6,* 123–129.

Wittenberg, K. (2006). Beyond Google: What next for publishing? *Chronicle of Higher Education, 52*(41).

Chapter Fourteen

LINKING POPULAR CULTURE TO LITERACY LEARNING AND TEACHING IN THE TWENTY-FIRST CENTURY

Margaret C. Hagood

Literacy Rap

It's not like it's literacy that we hate,
It's all those methods that are outta date.
Give us something we like to do,
And you better believe we'll succeed too.
Before school's been just a bore,
And language arts is always a chore,
Then some teachers gave us what we're lookin' for.
We love hip-hop music and rap,
Not some old worn-out textbook full of crap.
If you'll only teach us using what we know,
You'll see our literacy knowledge really start to grow.
We like using African-American Vernacular,
But no one at this school thinks it's so spectacular.
Just give us a chance to teach you how to rhyme,
And we'll learn about literacy while having a good time.
If you'll start using hip-hop in our class,
We'll be sure to come and sure enough we'll pass.
Somebody give me a rhythm fast or slow,
Let us rhyme and let us start to flow.
(Beat Box)
Teacher, look I'm an in-divid-ual,
So quit using practices that are so re-sid-u-al.
Believe it or not, I'm smarter than you'd know,
Give me a shot, and I'll let it show.
Old school practices are to blame,

They treat everyone as if they are the same.
All right, here I stand, ready when you are,
Let's get together and change the way things are.

Rachel Kahn, an undergraduate preservice teacher in an elementary education program, wrote this rap at the end of a semester-long course on teaching literacy in the twenty-first century. While in this class, she learned that literacy is all about the social context and must be coupled with students' interests and experiences to be meaningful to them. If students cannot, do not, or will not connect to the text and content being taught, then they run the risk of disconnecting from school and from learning the literacy content important for success in school.

This chapter discusses how to teach literacy in schools while valuing the personal literacies that students bring with them. This chapter covers three points. First, I describe the current context of teaching literacy in the United States. Then I examine how the teaching of literacy is enhanced with the inclusion of students' literacies, as seen in various literacy activities. Finally, I share examples of how to draw from students' out-of-school literacies related to popular culture to understand the connections to school-based literacies and classroom instruction. Assumed within this discussion is the premise that the educational process can be enhanced when teachers learn about the everyday lived contexts of their students' lives.

WHAT'S THE BIG DEAL ABOUT STUDENTS' LIVES?

U.S. classrooms today are more diverse than ever and are projected to become more so. Not only are there significantly more children in schools today than compared to populations from 1970, but the student population is more diverse (Feller, 2005). In 2005, nearly 20 percent of the U.S. population lived in a household where a second language (other than English) was spoken (Provasnik & Dorfman, 2005). Also, 22 percent of students had at least one foreign-born parent, including 91 percent of Asian children and 66 percent of Hispanic youngsters (Feller, 2005). That number differs tremendously from the student population of the 1970s, where only 2 out of 10 students recorded any status other than white. As of 2003, the kindergarten through grade 12 population in U.S. schools comprised 60 percent white non-Hispanic and nearly 40 percent minority (nearly 16% black, nearly 18% Hispanic, 1% American Indian/Native Alaskan, and 3% Asian/Pacific Islander; National Center for Education Statistics, 2006).

The teaching profession in the United States is faced with a huge dilemma. In contrast to the rich ethnic and racial diversity of the population of students prevalent in U.S. classrooms, most teachers are ill prepared to teach children with diverse cultures, languages, and academic abilities. Currently, the teaching population in K–12 U.S. schools is 75 percent female (Provasnik & Dorfman, 2005), and 83 percent of all teachers are white, while 17 percent are minority (National Center for Education Statistics, 2006). In short, most teachers are white and monolingual (Davis-Wiley, 2002). The experiences they draw on to teach their students often differ widely from students' own lives. One such area of difference involves students' multiliteracies. Multiliteracies include both a multiplicity of different forms of communication and media and the cultural and linguistic diversity of the ways that learners use these literacies to live and work in their communities (Cope & Kalantzis, 2000). A specific strand of these multiliteracies is considered *new literacies.*

New literacies have been conceptualized in many different ways. For the purpose of this chapter, I implement Lankshear and Knobel's (2003) definition of new literacies based on two overarching categories: (1) posttypographic new literacies associated with digital literacies and (2) "literacies that are comparatively new in chronological terms and/or that are (or will be) new to being recognized as literacies" (p. 25). These literacies may or may not have anything to do with digital technologies. It is this second category of new literacies, and specifically the literacies associated with popular culture, that I will address in this chapter.

Popular culture is the culture of the people. It differs by groups of people and comprises the daily practices that hold people together. It can include any number of texts, from music to clothing to entertainment (such as movies and sports) and literature. People use popular culture as a way to connect with others, to be a part of a group, and to take on identities and to construct their own perceptions of self or ideas about who they would like to be through their uses of popular culture. Often contrasted with the literacy practices considered as high culture that are found in school curricula (e.g., reading Shakespeare, listening to Bach, creating realistic art), popular culture is seen in conjunction with the mass circulation of texts and ideas, which run counter to school-based literacies that address high culture (see Alvermann & Xu, 2003).

The popular culture texts children use in the twenty-first century are the new literacies texts of today's learners. From a new literacies perspective, it is no longer appropriate to think of reading as the ability to read print-based text. Instead, literacy must be understood in light of the kinds of texts children use on a daily basis. These texts include television, Internet, movies, music, magazines, text messages, and video games. Children spend an average of six and one-half hours a day using these texts (Rideout, Roberts, & Foehr, 2005).

Today's teachers must consider these literacies and teach literacy standards with all sorts of texts (print, audio, visual, Internet, video, etc.) and use these texts to help children understand, construct, and create comprehension of the world around them. Thus a broadened notion of text—one that encapsulates texts of popular culture—acknowledges how the subject of *reading* has shifted to the subject of *literacy* and has changed for students. Rather than focus solely on reading and writing print-based texts, an approach with new literacies builds on students' out-of-school competencies in all literacies: reading, writing, listening, speaking, and viewing. Many of these literacies are associated with popular culture.

Often, teachers assume that their students' out-of-school literacies do not reflect valid school-based literacy practices. Teachers rarely connect students' interests in and uses of media and popular culture texts to their in-school reading abilities (Vasquez, 2003). When teachers do not realize the sophisticated literacy competencies that their students exhibit in out-of-school contexts, they miss valuable opportunities to tap into the out-of-school literacy practices that students have at their disposal. Moreover, teachers often overlook important literacy competencies that could assist in developing their students' in-school reading performance.

Research shows that many teachers are unaware of new literacies and the best practices that couple learning strategies with students' sociocultural literate identities to improve their literacy performance (Marsh & Millard, 2006). Research suggests, however, that when teachers understand and respect students' cultural backgrounds and draw on their out-of-school literacies, they can build on students' cultural resources to improve their academic performance and higher-order thinking skills (Mraz, Heron, & Wood, 2003). For example, Brown (2003) documented how urban teachers designed culturally responsive styles that included showing care for all students, while at the same time acting with authority. Brown further noted the importance of using communication patterns that matched students' cultural backgrounds.

More specifically, research has shown that when teachers draw on adolescents' out-of-school literacies as scaffolds for learning, students' in-school reading interest and proficiency increase significantly (Hull & Schultz, 2002). For example, Morrell (2002) drew on his urban students' cultural backgrounds and interests to improve their comprehension of poetry by relating the genre to their competencies with understanding hip-hop culture. Chandler-Olcott and Mahar (2001) drew on adolescents' interests in writing fan fiction (author's use of published texts for the jumping off point of their own creative writing of a new story line) to teach them how to write particular academic texts. Other research in new literacies has addressed how using adolescents' out-of-school media and popular culture interests improve their engagement with and uses of in-school learning tasks (e.g., Guzzetti & Gamboa, 2004; O'Brien, 2001; Skinner, 2006).

Another challenge in the literacy classroom is the perceived or real disconnect between teachers and students (Noguera, 2006). This disconnect is often related to issues of sociocultural identity (e.g., race, class, gender, or ethnicity) and to the mismatch between literacies used outside of school and those that are taught and valued in school (Mahiri, 2004). A new literacies perspective recognizes that students' identities are closely tied to their out-of-school and personal literacies (Gee, 2000), which they use to build relationships with others and to demonstrate their literacy competencies among peers (Dimitriadis, 2002).

So what does all this mean? Teachers need to be more aware of and in tune with students' out-of-school literacies, and those specifically related to popular culture, to help them make connections to in-school literacies and standards that must be taught.

CONNECTING THE NEW TO THE KNOWN: IT IS REALLY NOT A NEW IDEA

Attention to students' out-of-school literacies—their new literacies—in school is actually not novel or unusual. The idea of bridging students' own lives and knowledge with those of school curricula standards is not unlike other well-known, respected, and successful approaches. Examples such as the use of the funds of knowledge language experience approach and invented spelling all point to ways to connect in- and out-of-school literacy competencies for teachers' and students' benefit. Below, I briefly define and describe these approaches and then connect them to approaches of acknowledging literacy competencies through students' popular culture interests in schools.

The Funds of Knowledge for Teaching Project (Gonzalez, Moll, & Tenery, 1995) is a well-known and supported research design that helps teachers better understand their students' literacy lives. Begun in Arizona, this project was designed to help teachers connect better with students. Teachers conduct home visits for the sole purpose of identifying and documenting the repositories of knowledge used in Latino homes so that this information can augment and enrich classroom practices. Classroom teachers use ethnographic research methods whereby they study closely and in depth the child through home context observing, interviewing, and reflecting on their detailed notes taken to glean a deeper understanding of the child's and family's multiliteracies.

The teacher researchers in the project found that these home visits, coupled with their reflections from regular meetings with other teacher researchers, gave rise to transformative shifts in relationships between teachers and parents and ultimately between schools and homes/communities. What teachers found through their inquiries into students' out-of-school literacies became known as funds of knowledge. *Funds of knowledge* refers to historically developed and accumulated strategies (e.g., skills, abilities, ideas, practices) and practical bodies of knowledge that are essential to a household's functioning and well-being (Moll, 1994). Thus funds of knowledge are central aspects of life in the home and are the tools children bring to school for understanding and engaging in a different environment.

The concept of using children's personal, out-of-school literacies both to understand their rich literacy lives and to connect with school-based literacy practices has been used in other projects, too. For example, Dworin (2006) found that 4th-grade Latino students in a bilingual classroom were more successful with school-based literacy writing tasks when prompted to write stories that involved their home lives and use of their native language. He noted that the children's biliteracy to write in both Spanish and English was a central social and cultural tool in the process that made the assignments relevant to their lives, facilitated their comprehension, and ultimately, promoted their writing abilities.

A second approach that has been well regarded and used in early childhood literacy instruction as well as with English as a second language (ESL) students is the language experience approach (LEA). This approach was developed almost a half century ago as a means to capitalize on students' oral language to connect to writing (Dixon & Nessel, 1983). A LEA draws on students' natural language, which has developed in their out-of-school lives, and on their language development to facilitate school-based literacy activities. This approach to literacy instruction values children's desires to discuss the matters of their world. A more knowledgeable other (the teacher) then scribes the students' words, helping the children see the relationship between speech and print. It is a small steps approach to help the students see the connections between their world and schooling, starting with their overall ideas, then moving on to spoken words, and ultimately to printed messages. These small steps always begin with the students' thinking, which is most often a reflection of their out-of-school identities and experiences. Like students' funds of knowledge, this approach validates students' literacy tools and resources to engage in the print-based literacy activity. The teacher in this approach provides the support for the students, assisting them in their thinking and writing students' thoughts.

This approach to literacy instruction is prevalent in early childhood classrooms and with ESL students, where children have much to add orally to the literacy discussion but do not yet have the conventional print skills to relay their detailed thoughts in writing. This approach has also been successful for struggling readers and writers. Fisher and Frey (2003) found that through a gradual release of responsibility, struggling 9th-grade students made significant gains in their reading and writing abilities over a semester. In this class, the authors began using LEA to help students begin writing and focus their thoughts. What they found was that the students' discussions before writing often related to their personal lives, their cultural identities, and their views of the world. Using LEA allowed the teachers to work with the students' natural language and help the students translate oral language conventions into standards-based print conventions.

Finally, this approach is helpful when teachers are working with students of various backgrounds to ascertain the personal connections that the students make to the text (Dorr, 2006). As Dorr found when working with 3rd-grade students, language experience helped the teacher grasp the students' background knowledge and connect their prior experiences with the information to be written. Bringing together students' personal, out-of-school literacies with in-school writing offers opportunities to create meaningful connections between individual learners and course content.

A third approach that capitalizes on students' own knowledge to connect to schooled, conventional modes of communication is the use of invented spelling in classrooms. Invented spelling (also known as developmental spelling) has become a method for assisting children in spelling development, while also fostering their writing. In this approach, researchers and teachers let children show what they can do and what they know, rather than what they have not yet mastered. Clark's (1988) research indicated that children's writing and the ability to spell words conventionally are developed by invented spelling. Closely connected to this positive emphasis is the idea that children are empowered by teachers' acceptance of their invented spelling. They are able to write purposefully and with communicative intent from the very beginning of school (Sipe, 2001). When students use invented spelling in their writing, they bring to bear their current understanding of sound and letter relationships. The students' approximations of conventional spellings are accepted by the teacher, while at the same time, the teacher must assist in furthering students' understandings of the principles of spelling (Bear, Invernizzi, Templeton, & Johnston, 2003). In this way, invented spelling shows the developmental process of learning to write conventionally. The teacher does not just accept the students' approximations, but rather uses students' spellings to teach and assess phonemic awareness and regular phonics patterns, while also assisting the student in identifying key sounds or patterns that will be addressed to spell conventionally (Gentry, 2000).

All three of these approaches to literacy share a few common traits. First, all strive to connect children to school-based literacy learning, and more specifically, to affirm children's cultural identities and help them understand their experiences in relation to school practices. Second, all share a foundation in the sociocultural nature of knowledge development and the connection between personal identities and school identities. These approaches recognize that children's broad base of knowledge and experiences comes first and, primarily, from their everyday lives, and not from the classroom. Third, teachers in all these approaches have a responsibility to help bridge students' out-of-school literacies to help students see connections to their in-school literacy learning. In short, educators who enact these practices believe that it is crucial to connect course content to students' lives.

These premises are also central to the premise of studying children's literacies related to popular culture. Often adults, and consequently, children, take a narrow view of literacy and think that literacy only applies to reading and writing print-based texts. With the prevalence of this viewpoint, children begin to believe similarly, and the literacies of reading, writing, listening, speaking, and viewing outside of school are seen as subordinate to school texts and are likely to be perceived not as the reading of texts at all, but as visual and auditory entertainment. Actually, research has shown that students' identities and self-perceptions are often tied up with out-of-school literacy interests (Chandler-Olcott & Mahar, 2003; Mahar, 2003). If those interests are only engaged and expounded on in out-of-school contexts, children often lose motivation to engage with literacy activities in school.

TEACHING USING POPULAR CULTURE AND YOUTH CULTURE

Many literacy researchers and educators advocate for making use of children's personal literacies, promoting different types of literacies as strengths, rather than as deficits (e.g., Au, 1993; Heath, 1983; Moll, 1994). One of these forms of personal literacies happens to be popular culture. Children use popular culture in their everyday lives to create meaning of the world and of themselves. Students' interests in popular culture reflect their cultural and social perceptions and give insight into students' identities, both those used at school and those used outside of school.

What are the connections between popular culture and school-based learning? What follows is a description of a preservice teacher candidate's popular culture project, which was for partial fulfillment of a literacy course for teaching in grades 2–8. A preservice teacher's final project using the televisual text *The Suite Life of Zack and Cody* illustrates the connections between out-of-school and in-school literacies. *The Suite Life of Zack and Cody* is a sitcom that appeals to children between the ages of 8 and 14 and stars a set of adolescent, white twin boys who live in an upscale Boston hotel as a result of their mother's job there (Kallis & Geoghan, 2005).

Teaching Literacies Grades 2–8 is a course that I teach to students who are studying to become classroom teachers. In this course, students learn about new literacies theories, research, and related literacy instructional practices and engage in several new literacies projects. One project includes the in-depth study of children's out-of-school popular culture literacies and connections to in-school literacy standards. During a 14-week field experience that meets for three hours once a week in a local urban school that is coupled with the course, class participants study children's popular culture lives. Goals of this project include development in several areas: (1) ethnographic inquiry of children's popular culture interests, (2) reflective analyses of similarities and differences between teacher and student identities related to their popular culture literacy interests (based on age, race, gender, and ethnicity), (3) in-depth research on one popular culture text that is selected from the children's interests but is relatively unknown to the teacher candidate, and (4) analyses of the popular culture texts for relations between literacies used with the text and school-based literacy standards.

Preservice teachers begin this project by conducting a survey. They first answer the survey themselves, then they query the children in their field placement classroom, and finally, they ask their cooperating teacher the same questions, recording the answers on a questionnaire table (see Table 14.1).

Afterward, the preservice teachers analyze the similarities and differences between and among the groups, examining how identities of each of the groups (preservice teacher, students, cooperating teacher) factor into each group's affinities for its popular culture interests. Preservice teachers must analyze the data to see how much or little they have in common with their cooperating teacher and with the children they have to teach that semester.

Table 14.1
Popular Culture Survey

Popular Culture Survey

Your name _____ Date: _____

Student demographics: ____ female ___ male School: _____

Races represented: _____ Grade level ____

SES represented: _____

	Your interests	Students' interests	Cooperating teacher's interests	Analyses of similarities and differences
TV shows				
Movies				
Music				
Best sellers				
Magazines				
Web sites				
Video games				
Trading cards				
Other (computer, shopping/fashion, hobbies, sports)				

One example illustrates this process. Elizabeth was a white, middle-class, mid-twenties preservice teacher whose field placement, which was coupled with the literacy course, was in a combined 4th/5th-grade class in an urban, public charter school. The classroom teacher was a 60-year-old African American woman. Of the 17 students in the class, 11 were female and 6 were male. All were African American. From the survey data, Elizabeth found few similarities between her students', her cooperating teacher's, and her own popular culture interests. Of all the categories, she shared overlapping interests with her students in music, magazines, and Web sites, but really shared no interests with her cooperating teacher. Likewise, the cooperating teacher had no similar interests with her students. Elizabeth's analyses revealed that the differences in preferences likely resulted from differences in gender, age, race, and ethnicity.

In the next part of the project, the preservice teacher candidates choose a popular culture text from the students' survey, one that is unfamiliar to them. They spend several weeks researching this text (which could be a print or media text). They interview the students in the classroom, asking and recording answers to the following questions: (1) What do you like about this text? (2) Who uses this text with you? (3) What don't you like about this text? (4) Who might not like this text? Why do you think that?

This source of data gathering helps preservice teachers determine how critically aware students are of various identities and engagement with the text. For example, the preservice teachers must consider from the interview how aware the child is of multiple perspectives of who might be offended by a text or might not like it because of a person's affiliation with a particular identity (e.g., older people might not like a Disney sitcom because they have a different sense of humor).

Afterward, preservice teachers research the students' text on their own, as part of their out-of-school literacy practice. They watch related movies and/or television shows, read reviews, blogs, and magazine and newspaper articles, listen to podcasts, play video games, surf the Web, and discuss the text with others (children, teachers, parents) to develop a deeper understanding and multifaceted perspective of the text. They record their findings in a learning log, describing how they researched the text, their findings from their research, when they used it, for how long they engaged it, and what they thought of it.

Elizabeth chose the television show *The Suite Life of Zach and Cody*. In her learning log, she wrote,

> Zach and Cody are twin, White boys who live in a hotel. The boys are raised by their mother (also White), their dad has appeared in one episode. The hotel is the center of all the action. It has a variety of characters that either work or live in the

hotel. Maddie (White girl) works in the hotel and is the typical girl next door. Landon's father owns the hotel, and Landon (White boy) is spoiled. Both Maddie and Landon are friends with Zach and Cody. The story follows a common story line of plot, setting, character development, problem, and resolution.

When interviewing a group of students, Elizabeth recorded the following:

ELIZABETH: What do you like about *The Suite Life?*
STUDENT: Zach is funny, does crazy things and a funny dancing thing [which he demonstrated]. Cody is smart, talented and like being the school leader. Cody wanted to be the president, and Zach won. Landon has a lot of credit cards and likes clothes.
ELIZABETH: Why do you like this show better than other shows?
STUDENT: Not boring, like news, and everyone is nice to everyone.
ELIZABETH: Who do you watch it with?
STUDENT: When I go to nanny's house [grandmother]. With my mom and brother.
ELIZABETH: What don't you like about the show?
STUDENT: Cody tries to be president and Zach takes over.
ELIZABETH: So you don't like that particular show?
STUDENT: No.
ELIZABETH: Are there many black people in it?
STUDENT: No. Oh, Mr. Mosely, the hotel man.
ELIZABETH: Is that OK with you?
STUDENT: Yeah.
ELIZABETH: Are there a lot of adults?
STUDENT: No. I want more kids than adults.
ELIZABETH: Who might not like *Suite Life?*
STUDENT: Nanny doesn't like it because they sing and talk too much.
ELIZABETH: Anyone else?
STUDENT: My teacher.
ELIZABETH: Why?
STUDENT: She don't like the comedy shows like that cuz she don't like too much little kids. It's a boring show for old people.

Preservice teachers then use their findings from the interviews with students and their research on students' text choices to analyze the kinds of literacy activities children engage in when they use the texts in out-of-school settings. Then they take the children's out-of-school uses and connect the text to curriculum standards. They engage in this portion of the project to understand the implicit literacy links between out-of-school and in-school literacies and to better understand how students engage literacies with texts beyond reading and writing print. Finally, they use this analysis to consider ways that they can assist their students in connecting school-based literacy standards to students' personal literacy competencies, which are often ignored at school.

Table 14.2 is an example of Elizabeth's analyses of out-of-school literacy uses of *The Suite Life of Zach and Cody* compared with the state standards and to hypothetical in-school literacy uses of reading, writing, listening, speaking, and viewing.

Finally, preservice teachers reflect on the overall project and on their perceptions of the value of inquiring into students' literacies related to popular culture. Elizabeth wrote the following:

> I believe popular culture is a powerful medium with kids. However, I feel it must be used appropriately and strategically. Like any other activity, in excess or without thought, popular culture can be as ineffective as drill and kill worksheets. None-

Table 14.2
Out-of-School and In-School Literacy Connections in *Suite Life*

Out-of-school literacy uses	SC state literacy standards (4th and 5th grades)	In-school literacy uses
Watch the show.	The students will recognize, demonstrate, and analyze the qualities of effective communication.	Discuss the show as a group; address how characters communicated to solve a problem, and why it was good or bad.
Predict how the show will end.	The student will comprehend and analyze information received from nonprint sources.	In a journal, predict how a situation using Zach and Cody will end, and give reasons for their thinking.
Talk with parents and friends about their views of the show.	Demonstrate a variety of strategies to derive meaning from texts.	Do prereading of a show on the Internet and gather multiple predictions of what might happen.
Summarize the show to friends/family who missed the episode.	Demonstrate the ability to summarize the main idea of a particular text. Demonstrate the ability to recall details in texts.	Watch the show and summarize it as a homework assignment, and then review as a class.
Send fan mail (e-mail on the Web site) and ask specific questions about the show.	Demonstrate the ability to ask and answer questions about texts.	Make a list of questions using the language experience approach to ask online. Students role-play the answers before posting the questions online.
Watch the show, and discuss the problem and solution with other episodes.	Demonstrate the ability to identify conflict in a literary work; begin comparing and contrasting conflicts in a variety of literary works.	Compare and contrast conflict and resolution in several episodes in a small-group discussion.

theless, I think overall it is a great way to reach kids and empower them to be the experts. . . . If they can help chart their learning through texts they are more versed in, they will be more dedicated and loyal to the process of learning. Unfortunately, the perceived "wildness" of popular culture turns adults away from using it. Kids are no different from adults, in that they want to connect, to understand and respond to someone who is giving back on the other end. How can we commend students' respect and attention without some curiosity and compassion for their life? (p. 9).

Delving into Popular Culture As Literacy Texts: Why Do It?

Researchers and educators of new literacies describe the necessity of acknowledging and addressing the increasingly diverse cultural contexts that students and teachers encounter. As Lankshear and Knobel (2003) explained, one form of the new literacies is perhaps not new at all, but is new to being a form of literacy. Popular culture fits that description. Like the other approaches to literacy described earlier (funds of knowledge, LEA, and invented/developmental spelling), examining popular culture as a form of literacy recognizes the holistic, cultural, and social nature of literacy learning that must be included when living and teaching in a diverse world. In all these approaches, children's worldviews, interests, and schemas are accounted for as children show more engagement with school literacy when their identities are considered. Teachers take strides to acknowledge the richness of out-of-school literacies and connect them to in-school practices, and teachers act as pattern recognizers by scaffolding children's learning to make explicit connections between their sociocultural understandings—whether those are based on language or visual texts—and their in-school literacy learning.

These approaches to teaching and learning can only occur when teachers explore how social and cultural tools and activities mediate learning and development across contexts. As demonstrated across these methods, and in the literacy rap that opens this chapter, teachers must be vigilant in their efforts to value students' out-of-school literacy practices.

As Gee (2004) explained,

> learning does not work well when learners are forced to check their bodies at the schoolroom door like guns in the old West. School learning is often about disembodied minds learning outside any context of decisions and actions. (p. 39)

What children read is often related to their out-of-school literacies and to their popular culture interests. As forms of new literacies, students implicitly understand that they are working with non-print-based media. These new literacies and the practices children use need to be considered in school so that students' in-school literacy competencies can be as bountiful as their out-of-school literacy lives.

REFERENCES

Alvermann, D. E., & Xu, S. (2003). Children's everyday literacies: Intersections of popular culture and language arts instruction. *Language Arts, 81,* 145–154.

Au, K. (1993). *Literacy instruction in multicultural settings.* Fort Worth, TX: Harcourt Brace.

Bear, D., Invernizzi, M., Templeton, S., & Johnston, F. (2003). *Words their way* (3rd ed.). New York: Prentice Hall.

Brown, D. (2003). Urban teachers' use of culturally responsive management strategies. *Theory into Practice, 42*(4), 277–282.

Chandler-Olcott, K., & Mahar, D. (2001). A framework for choosing topics for, with, and by adolescent writers. *Voices from the Middle, 9*(1), 40–47.

Chandler-Olcott, K., & Mahar, D. (2003). Adolescents anime-inspired fanfictions: An exploration of multiliteracies. *Journal of Adolescent and Adult Literacy, 46*(7), 556–566.

Clark, L. K. (1988). Invented versus traditional spelling in first graders' writings: Effects on learning to spell and read. *Research in the Teaching of English, 22,* 281–309.

Cope, B., & Kalantzis, M. (2000). *Multiliteracies: Literacy learning and the design of social futures.* London: Routledge.

Davis-Wiley, P. (2002). A demographic profile of diversity in the United States: Who are the newcomers of the 21st century? *International Education, 32,* 49–57.

Dimitriadis, G. (2002). Trying to make a dollar out of fifteen cents: Pedagogies of racial affiliation in black popular culture. *Journal of Curriculum Theorizing, 18,* 99–107.

Dixon, C., & Nessel, D. (1983). *Language experience approach to reading (and writing): Language experience reading for second language learners.* Hayward, CA: Alemany.

Dorr, R. E. (2006). Something old is new again: Revisiting language experience. *Reading Teacher, 60,* 138–146.

Dworin, J. E. (2006). The Family Stories Project: Using *funds of knowledge* for writing. *Reading Teacher, 59,* 510–520.

Feller, B. (2005). *U.S. student population soars to record.* Retrieved December 1, 2006, from http://azbilingualed.org/News%202005/US%20student%20population%20soars%2 0to%20record.htm

Fisher, D., & Frey, N. (2003). Writing instruction for struggling adolescent readers: A gradual release model. *Journal of Adolescent and Adult Literacy, 46,* 396–405.

Gee, J. P. (2000). Teenagers in new times: A new literacy studies perspective. *Journal of Adolescent and Adult Literacy, 43*(5), 412–420.

Gee, J. P. (2004). *What video games have to teach us about learning and literacy.* New York: Palgrave Macmillan.

Gentry, J. R. (2000). A retrospective on invented spelling and a look forward. *Reading Teacher, 54,* 318–332.

Gonzalez, N., Moll, L., & Tenery, M. (1995). Funds of knowledge for teaching in Latino households. *Urban Education, 29,* 443–470.

Guzzetti, B., & Gamboa, M. (2004). Zines for social justice: Adolescent girls writing on their own. *Reading Research Quarterly, 39*(4), 408–436.

Heath, S. B. (1983). *Ways with words.* Boston: Cambridge University Press.

Hull, G., & Schultz, K. (Eds.). (2002). *School's out: Bridging out-of-school literacies with classroom practice.* New York: Teachers College Press.

Kallis, D., Dreager, I., & Geoghan, J. (Producers). (2005). *Suite life of Zach and Cody* [Television series]. Burbank, CA: Disney Channel.

Lankshear, C., & Knobel, M. (2003). *New literacies: Changing knowledge and classroom learning.* London: Open University Press.

Mahar, D. (2003). Bringing the outside in: One teacher's ride on the anime highway. *Language Arts, 2,* 110–117.

Mahiri, J. (Ed.). (2004). *What they don't learn in school: Literacy in the lives of urban youth.* New York: Peter Lang.

Marsh, J., & Millard, E. (2006). *Popular literacies, childhood and schooling.* New York: Routledge.

Moll, L. C. (1994). Literacy research in community and classrooms: A sociocultural approach. In R. B. Ruddell & H. Singer (Eds.), *Theoretical models and processes of reading* (4th ed., pp. 179–207). Newark, DE: International Reading Association.

Morrell, E. (2002). Promoting academic literacy with urban youth through engaging hip-hop culture. *English Journal, 91* (6), 88–92.

Mraz, M., Heron, A., & Wood, K. (2003). Media literacy, popular culture, and the transfer of higher order thinking abilities. *Middle School Journal, 34,* 51–56.

National Center for Education Statistics. (2006). *Characteristics of schools, districts, teachers, principals, and school libraries in the United States: 2003–2004 schools and staffing survey.* Retrieved November 30, 2006, from http://nces.ed.gov/pubs2006/2006313.pdf

Noguera, P. (2006). *Closing the racial achievement gap: What it takes to leave no child behind.* Paper presented at Overcoming the Achievement Gap Conference: Strategies for Eliminating Educational Disparities in Our Public Schools. Charleston, SC.

O'Brien, D. (2001, June). "At-risk" adolescents: Redefining competence through the multiliteracies of intermediality, visual arts, and representation. *Reading Online, 4*(11). Retrieved January 30, 2006, from http://www.readingonline.org/newliteracies/lit_index.asp?HREF=/newliteracies/obrien/index.html

Provasnik, S., & Dorfman, S. (2005). *Mobility in the teacher workforce: Findings from the Condition of Education 2005* (Report No. NCES 2005-114). Washington, DC: National Center for Educational Statistics.

Rideout, V. J., Roberts, D. F., & Foehr, U. G. (2005). *Generation M: Media in the lives of 8–18 year-olds.* Menlo Park, CA: Kaiser Family Foundation.

Sipe, L. (2001). Invention, convention, and intervention: Invented spelling and the teacher's role. *Reading Teacher, 55,* 264–273.

Skinner, E. N. (2006). *Reconnecting with adolescents' lives: Popular culture texts as mentor texts in an after-school writing club.* Unpublished doctoral dissertation, Teachers College, Columbia University, New York, NY.

Vasquez, V. (2003). What Pokemon can teach us about learning and literacy. *Language Arts, 81,* 118–125.

Chapter Fifteen

IN THEIR WORDS, SOUNDS, AND IMAGES: AFTER-SCHOOL LITERACY PROGRAMS FOR URBAN YOUTH

Eliane Rubinstein-Avila

Although later literacy development is often associated with school-based forms of literacy, some after-school programs are playing a pivotal role in "widen[ing] the lens of what we consider literacy and literate activities" (Schultz & Hull, 2002, p. 11). The four programs highlighted in this chapter also reveal the essential role literacy practices play in young people's construction of identities and in broadening their conceptions of citizenship. In fact, the following statement by a young woman is illustrative of the power of organized after-school programs to broaden adolescents' and young adults' horizons—especially low-income youth, who are often also students of color and the most likely to attend crowded, underresourced, and low-performing schools:

> At [high] school, my body was in the classroom, but my mind and heart were nowhere to be found.... Then, I walked into Youth Radio. (Chavez & Soep, 2005, p. 411)

Kate, a 17-year-old participant in another after-school program, a journalism apprenticeship, provided a glimpse of her evolving understanding of citizenship. As a result of her inquiry into a local activist group comprising solely young people, Kate wrote an article titled "Imagining a Better World." The following excerpt from her article was published in the second annual issue of *110 Degrees* magazine (Thompson, 2002):

> After seeing such enthusiasm about peace here in Tucson, I realize that I don't have to join the Peace Corps to make a positive difference in this world. Many Tucsonans realize they can make a difference. Among them are many young people. (p. 10)

These excerpts illustrate the power of literacy-based after-school programs to enact alternative pedagogies (Chavez & Soep, 2005) that are meaningful and potentially transformative such as the participatory approach suggested by Alvermann (2004); this approach relies on learners' authentic involvement in and ownership of the learning process across an array of modalities: print, aural, visual, and digital. Literacy-based programs, such as the ones highlighted in this chapter, foster urban adults' feelings of recognition and inclusion by acknowledging and building on their cultural and linguistic funds of knowledge (Moll & Gonzalez, 1994) and provide young adults with opportunities to negotiate their layered identities as they find and hone their voices through multiple media. Informal but structured literacy learning environments recognize, value, and build on urban youth's experiences. The mentors across these sites value participants' metalinguistic resources, such as the command of two or more languages or codes; the rhetorical strategies they employ; and the many ways in which urban adolescents engage creatively with language in and out of school (Lee, 2004).

The Proliferation of Informal Learning Environments

While investment in urban public schools was stymied during the 1990s, a federal initiative, the Twenty-first-Century Community Learning Centers (CCLC), allocated $1 billion for after-school programs. The goal was to supplement the educational experiences and improve the academic performance of children and youth attending low-performing urban and rural schools (Miller, 2001). This initiative resulted in the proliferation of citywide after-school programs across large urban centers. The initiative also facilitated unprecedented partnerships among the federal government, states, cities, corporations, and private foundations for funding nonprofit organizations and community centers to serve low-income youths after school hours.

Since budget cuts practically decimated arts programs, including literacy-based creative writing and performing arts programs in low-income schools, after-school programs and community arts spaces have become one of the few outlets for creative expression in many urban communities (Miller, 2001). In fact, within the past five years, there has been a sizable increase in both school- and community-based after-school programs that aim to support positive youth development, that is, to encourage academic, physical, social, and emotional well-being among urban and rural youths (Hamilton & Hamilton, 2004).

After-school programs that target young people vary in size, foci, goals, objectives, and the ways in which they are implemented. Most programs rely on open enrollment, where participants are welcome to drop in. Other programs recruit participants to engage in particular projects, according to certain criteria stipulated by funding agencies. Although participation is voluntary, these programs expect a commitment from participants for the duration of the program cycle (anywhere from several weeks to one academic year). Programs that include a career development component sometimes offer youth a stipend for their continuous participation.

Theoretical Roots (Often Implicit)

Rather than viewing literacy as a set of individual cognitive skills measured through tests, these programs approach literacy from a broader sociocultural perspective that takes into account the multiple roles literacy plays in communities' day-to-day social practices. As suggested by the new literacy studies (NLS), this broader view of literacy entails not only blurring "communicative boundaries—spoken, and written language, performance and other semiotic modes of communication" (Street, 2005, p. 420), but also addressing the social uses, meanings, and power dimensions of literacy practices. Rather than viewing its participants as at risk, the adults across these programs recognize that urban youth's expertise, strategies, and cultural capital are often overlooked, and even marginalized, across the formal educational system.

Literacy-Based After-School Programs

Given the surge in organized but informal learning settings after school, researchers from several fields, such as human development, family studies, community psychology, sociology, and education, have been exploring the conditions that yield positive youth development. Studies on these informal contexts vary as much as the programs that they portray. Although many studies seem to evaluate the degree to which the programs influence participants' academic achievements and high school completion rates, more scholars have begun to explore the processes, not only outcomes, by which after-school programs are supporting what has come to be known as the five Cs of positive youth development: competence, confidence, connections, character, and caring (Hamilton & Hamilton, 2004).

More recently, scholars in the field of language and literacy have underscored the role of particular after-school programs in supporting urban youth's meaning making through language and literacy (e.g., Blackburn, 2003; Rubinstein-Ávila, 2006). The four urban after-school programs I describe in this chapter engage young people in authentic, multimodal, and purposeful literacy practices. Through researching, photographing, videotaping, and writing, participants are encouraged to express their feelings, reflect on their identities, explore their concerns and those of their communities, and share their work with a broader audience.

Across the programs described below, participants work in collaboration with adult mentors to complete a final product: a radio program, a zine (an author-published alternative to commercial magazines), a digital story, or a 100-page published magazine.

YOUTH RADIO, SAN FRANCISCO, CALIFORNIA

The mission of Youth Radio is to provide young people with professional training by teaching them the basics of broadcasting and other media-related careers. The goal is to strengthen youth's verbal and written expression, access to technology, critical thinking, and conflict resolution through journalism education. Youth's interests and concerns are the major focus of Youth Radio.

For those who cannot reach the primary site, Youth Radio offers several workshops after school and during the summer months in schools and community-based organizations. One such workshop is for incarcerated young men at Camp Sweeney, in San Leandro, California. Other workshops include a six-month community action program (CAP), during which local youth are trained as peer educators in radio broadcast, music production, journalism, and graphic production, and an eight-week program for young women in San Francisco's Mission district, Mission Girls, focusing on creative writing and providing participants an opportunity to address issues such as sexuality, race, and identity.

During the summer of 2006, Youth Radio's first Spanish language workshop took place in Oakland's Fruitvale Public Library. Nine participants explored the ways in which mainstream media covered issues addressing the Latino immigrant community. Participating youth produced several bilingual service announcements, addressing issues such as immigration protests and learning English as an additional language; the youth also broadcasted a story on the United States–Mexico border on May 24, 2004, through All Things Considered, one of the leading programs heard on National Public Radio.

HORIZON YOUTH PROGRAM (CENTER ON HALSTED), CHICAGO, ILLINOIS

The increased visibility of gay, lesbian, bisexual, and transgender (GLBT) people in our society has no doubt encouraged GLBT youth to find the courage to reveal their gender identities at younger ages. Nevertheless, GLBT youth are not immune to negative reactions, which sometimes result in rejection from their family members and friends. GLBT youth are overrepresented in dropout rates and suicide attempts and make up 25–40 percent of the homeless youth population in New York City and many other large cities across the country. In fact, they also suffer from greater levels of violence and trauma and higher rates of HIV infection.

Horizon Youth Program is located in the Center on Halsted in Chicago; this large space offers the GLBT community a myriad of services such as a cyber center, health screening and education, basketball courts, a library, a café, meeting spaces, and so on. The program was designed to serve GLBT youth and allies 13–24 years of age by providing a safe and supportive space for youth to meet, express their feelings, develop self-esteem, access health information, learn communication skills, and develop leadership skills. The program is open to youth during after-school hours on weekdays and on Saturday afternoons. Funding is provided by the city of Chicago and several private foundations.

Although participants are welcome to drop in, the Horizon Youth Program offers weekly scheduled programs and activities. For example, once a week, on Wednesday evenings, the Young Women's Group of the Horizon Youth Program offers lesbian, bi, and transgender women ages 14–24 a space to meet, discuss, and share their writing. This program is one of the few to target young GLBT women of color.

Recently, the members of the Young Women's Group collected their compositions into a 30-page personal zine, also available electronically (http://www.centeronhalsted.org). The zine, titled *Reflections of Herself*, features an array of personal texts such as collages, drawings, poems, photos, short essays, and excerpts of interviews with its members. The following is an example of and excerpt from an interview published in the zine. The interview was conducted between two group members and addressed "views on being in the closet." LaToya, the young woman who was interviewed and is quoted below, was asked to explain her decision not to come out to her peers in college:

> Yeah, since it [engineering] is a predominately white male field, and I'm a black woman; I'm kind of like a triple threat minority. Because I'm black, I'm female and I'm gay! I have enough hurdles to jump as it is, and I feel like being gay is only going to make things harder than it has to be. (p. 12)

A collage addressed the issue of women's body image from the perspective of young women of color, and another interview addressed dating a transgender person. This illustrates the power of the zine to provide the participating young women with an opportunity to be heard. These topics, of great importance to the young women, are not encouraged or sanctioned within the confines of the classroom.

VOICES: COMMUNITY STORIES PAST AND PRESENT, TUCSON, ARIZONA

Voices Inc. is a small nonprofit organization founded by Regina Kelly of Tucson, Arizona. Kelly's intent was to train low-income youth (14–21 years old) to document local stories, preserve and celebrate local cultures, and facilitate the improvement of young people's academic, artistic, and professional skills. Two of their projects, which involved youth at all steps in the process, sought to deepen intergenerational relationships and tighten youth's connection to the communities in which they lived. *Snapped on the Street* (1999), the first book published as a result of Voices' youth and the staff collaborative inquiry, reported on the heyday of downtown Tucson, Arizona, during the mid-twentieth century, prior to urban sprawl. It included over 200 street photographs taken between the 1930s and 1960s. Another book, *Don't Look at Me Different/No Me Veas Diferente* (2001), published entirely in both English and Spanish, conveyed the oral history of Tucson's first housing projects through interviews and historic and contemporary photographs shot by the young participants. This account from young and senior residents dispelled the mostly negative stereotypes about public housing, revealing the complexities of an intricately connected community from the perspective of the adolescents, some of whom resided in public housing.

Moreover, Voices Inc. has been extremely successful with the ongoing after-school youth program 110 Degrees, now in its sixth year of operation. The main goals of this program are to apprentice low-income young adults as staff writers. In collaboration with two youth workers/mentors, a freelance writer/editor, and a photographer, the participants compose and publish an annual issue of a magazine titled *110 Degrees*.

Every fall, 20 low-income youth are recruited at local public high schools and hired through stipends contingent on their continuous participation. The program operates Monday through Thursday afternoon through an eight-month cycle. The young staff writers research, photograph, and write about topics that impact their peers and communities. They conduct journalistic research on their own neighborhoods, often addressing issues such as gentrification, revitalization, and racial profiling. Full-feature magazine articles rely on interviews and archival sources that address topics such as the United States–Mexico border, youth homelessness, teen parenthood, and young people's participation in the democratic process.

The young staff writers are also provided opportunities to present their work in local bookstores and invited presentations. Within the past few years, the *Arizona Daily Star* has printed a special newspaper issue entirely composed by the young participants, in collaboration with their mentors. The publication is now free and has a broad readership. Each annual issue is celebrated in an evening performance by the youth that draws a large and diverse crowd, including city officials.

DIGITAL UNDERGROUND STORYTELLING FOR YOUTH (DUSTY), OAKLAND, CALIFORNIA

This after-school program for middle and high school youth is a partnership between the College of Education at the University of California at

Berkeley and Oakland's Joseph Prescott Center for Community Enhancement. The program brings together low-income, underserved, mostly (about 75%) black youth and an expanding population (about 20%)of Latinos with university undergraduates, graduate students, and community members, who serve as tutors and mentors for the participants. According to the Digital Underground Storytelling for Youth (DUSTY) Web site (http://oakland dusty.org/index), 80 percent of participating youth "struggle with literacy," and 25 percent are either learning English as an additional language and/or have parents who are non–English speakers.

This program's four main goals are (1) to provide underserved youth access to new digital technologies not available to them at school or at home for self-expression; (2) to encourage and foster literacy development and creativity through a technology-rich context; (3) to bridge the dichotomous worlds of formal and informal learning; and (4) to foster intergenerational communication and community building. In this informal learning environment, participants, with the assistance of youth workers, combine print literacy, photography, video, and audio to create digital stories.

At DUSTY, young people learn how to use programs such as iMovie, Adobe Premiere, Fruity Loops, and Acid Pro to compose their digital stories. DUSTY not only provides participating youth with access to new technologies, but the tutors and mentors also provide youth with the necessary support to use the technologies in culturally relevant and empowering ways that resonate with youth's concerns and lives. The designers of this program realized that in spite of the crucial role that visualization plays in reading and writing, schools are not likely to provide students with sustained attention to the visual aspect of new literacies (Hull, 2003, p. 231).

This program encourages adolescents to compose multimodal and personal digital accounts, which in Hull's (2003) words "challenge logocentric habits of mind" (p. 230). This often entails removing text, images, and sounds from their historical or original contexts and repositioning and appropriating them. For example, one young man's multimedia composition included juxtaposition and what Hull calls the "recontextualization of images" (such as images of pyramids, Malcolm X, Tupac Shakur, and Marcus Garvey, among others) to create a context with a "powerful authorial agency" through which to express his own social world in Oakland (23).

These new literacies, afforded by the rapid introduction of new technologies, not usually available in low-income, underresourced schools, encourage youth to create multimodal texts "without denying the importance of traditional alphabetic literacies" (Hull, 2003, p. 233). DUSTY's participants are also provided opportunities to share their digital, multimedia compositions with their extended families, members of their communities, and university affiliates.

THE ROLE OF YOUTH WORKERS ACROSS INFORMAL LEARNING CONTEXTS

Studies across organized but informal learning environments underscore the role of the rapport established between youth workers and participating youth. Youth workers are staff hired by programs as mentors, informal instructors, and coaches. Youth workers are more likely than teachers to share the youth's racial, ethnic, and socioeconomic backgrounds and experiences; to live in the same communities as the youth they serve; and to be closer in age to the youth. As one youth worker said, youth workers "know where the kids are coming from" (Halpren, Barker, & Mollard, 2000, p. 490). In fact, in their examination of six youth programs deemed successful by the youth who participated in them, McLaughlin, Irby, and Langman (1994) found that youth workers' personalities, charisma, and the rapport that they established with the youths they served were essential to determining a program's success.

For many youths, informal learning environments provide a unique opportunity to engage with caring adults, who are neither family members nor teachers, and who make a positive impact in their lives (McLaughlin & Heath, 1993). Nevertheless, it is also important to understand the conditions that support the successful bond between youth workers and youth and explore potential limitations. For example, Halpren and colleagues (2000) pointed out that too often, youth workers' own experiences with formal education are at times limited to high school completion and that youth workers' experiences with the public school system are often marred by mixed or negative experiences. Thus it is suggested that potential inexperience with higher education may limit the type of guidance and social networks that youth workers are able to provide to the participants. High rates of mobility among youth workers, while understandable, are also likely to be barriers for forging long-lasting and caring relationships. Given the low pay, the low status, the absence of medical benefits, and the lack of training opportunities and job advancement, programs struggle to keep stability among hired staff (Halpren et al., 2000).

The role of youth workers is accepted as a key to the success of youth programs. Nevertheless, little is known about the nature of the relationships that youth workers forge with the young adults they serve. One of the most solid findings across the literature is that youth workers are likely to view youth from a perspective of strength than from a perspective of deficit and are highly sensitive to power relations and the constant changing dynamics in their interactions with youth. In fact, mentors often describe their relationships with young people as ones in which roles alternate; a youth worker may act as a guide or mentor, but at other times, he or she may fulfill the role of a friend, a counselor, a parent, a teacher, or simply a sounding board.

The relationships between participants and mentors in after-school programs are not free from the power relations that exist between youth and adults, nor are these relationships free from the co-constructed, social representation of gender, race, and class, but they are intense, dynamic, and reciprocal. In my ethnographic study of a literacy-based youth program (Rubinstein-Ávila, 2006), a highly educated youth worker who was a freelance photographer described his interactions with participants as a sensitive balancing act. Evoking the imagery of jugglers as he reflected on his four years with the program, he described his and their cocreation of the final product (the publication of a magazine) as "moment-to-moment" scenes between a group of jugglers who together manipulate several objects at once, most of which are, or at least seem to be, suspended precariously in midair (Rubinstein-Ávila, in progress).

BRIDGING OF INFORMAL AND FORMAL LEARNING

While the goals of these after-school programs do not include replicating school curricula or pedagogies, support for youth's academic achievement is included in their objectives. To extend youth's exposure to schools' rather narrow, and even limiting, literacy experiences, two of the programs described in this chapter attempt to bridge informal and formal learning through partnerships with schools that are willing to adopt alternative pedagogies. For example, the staff at Youth Radio have recently released an online curriculum resource that provides interested classroom teachers with suggestions about aligning the stories produced by the participants to national standards across content areas. This Internet resource also provides tips on media production techniques and the biographies of the young reporters. The pilot program also invites teachers who are using the Youth Radio curriculum to submit their students' stories, inspiring students' writing through authentic practices and thereby enabling students to reach broader audiences.

Another example of a partnership between informal and formal learning is Tucson's Voices Inc.'s collaborative project with a local public middle school. For several years, once a week, several staff members of Voices Inc. worked with a teacher and approximately 40 of her students on an oral history project in which students interviewed over 100 local seniors who had served in World War II. The process of this authentic inquiry and its results—the many intergenerational lessons learned by the students and the participating seniors—are reported in a culminating book titled *They Opened Their Hearts: Tucson Elders Tell World War II Stories to Tucson Youth* (2005).

CONCLUSION

Although the objective of after-school programs may be to supplement formal learning, successful youth programs and successful schools seem to share a great deal of characteristics. They provide youth opportunities to partake in effective leadership; maintain a unique identity structure; maintain a strong and productive peer culture; and establish clear, fair, and articulate goals and rules. They engage youth in challenging activities of significance to them and their communities, and they engage young people in structured, open-ended activities. They provide adolescents with exposure and access to a world outside their immediate boundaries. In essence, what makes both types of institutions successful is their ability to "reach, motivate and promote young people, who many dismiss as unreachable, irredeemable, or hopeless" (McLaughlin et al., 1994, p. xvii).

The four youth programs highlighted in this chapter view participating urban youth as knowers; young adults are defined by their strengths, creativity, talents, and amazing perseverance, not labeled as students who resist mainstream schooling nor defined by the competencies they may lack. These youth programs encourage youth-centered inquiry and youth decision making. They celebrate and encourage multimodal, critical literacy practices by encouraging students to question the texts of their worlds. Across these four programs, youth and adult mentors work together to cocreate narratives that resonate with a broader audience—beyond the participants' own peer or geographical communities. In addition, mentors and youth workers in these programs understand that young people's identity work is inextricable from their learning and becoming. More importantly, these programs accomplish a great deal more than encouraging the five Cs of positive youth development (competence, confidence, connection, character, and caring).

Unlike the uncritical color/class-blind approach to multicultural education commonly found in schools, the youth programs highlighted in this chapter support discussions on issues pertaining to race and discrimination that are outside of the mainstream comfort zone. These after-school programs provide a safe and fertile space for urban youth to tackle issues that impact their day-to-day lives and the well-being of their communities. I argue that these programs are successful precisely because they encourage critical inquiry into the intersections of race, ethnicity, culture, class, sexuality, and issues of power, discrimination, and marginalization.

Implications for the Development of (New) Literacies and Active Citizenship

Even if not explicitly stated in their goals, ultimately, the four after-school programs presented in this chapter are committed to unleashing, supporting, encouraging, and broadening youth's literacies within youth's sociocultural and sociopolitical contexts. Rather than equating language and literacy proficiencies with privilege and class, and rather than devaluing the interactional nature of spoken language and visual literacies, these programs, in line with the theoretical conceptualization of NLS, embrace school literacy and the literacies in youth's everyday lives. These programs also support interactive talk and the cocreation of knowledge among youth peers and between adults and youth. In addition, these programs have appeal because they embrace young people's integration of popular culture (Alvermann, Hagood, & Williams, 2001).

In the spirit of Paulo Freire, the late Brazilian educational philosopher, these programs provide urban youth with opportunities to have their views expressed and their voices heard, read, and viewed by a broad audience. Just as these programs have demonstrated, after-school, multimodal youth spaces can move beyond supporting adolescents' reading of the word and the world, as was suggested by Freire and Macedo (1987). They can also provide the world with an alternative view into urban youth's words, images, and worlds. Thus after-school, literacy-based youth programs are able to accomplish a great deal more than raising urban youth's test scores. Some after-school programs may be better equipped than schools to support and develop youth's technological, visual, and informational literacies and inter-textual understandings or the competencies to make meaning from an array of texts.

Finally, I hope that this chapter helped underscore the important role literacy-based after-school programs can play in broadening youth's language and literacy practices, in encouraging young people's expressions of their agen-tive selves (Hull & Katz, 2006), and in expanding young people's democratic participation and pursuit of social justice.

REFERENCES

Alvermann, D. E. (2004). Adolescent aliteracy: Are schools causing it? *Voices in Urban Education: Adolescents Literacy, 3*, 26–35. Available at http://www.annenberginsti tute.org/VUE/index.html

Alvermann, D. E., Hagood, M. C., & Williams, K. B. (2001). Image, language and sound: Making meaning with popular culture texts. *Reading Online, 4*(11). Retrieved March 3, 2007, from http://www.reading.org/newliteracies/lit_index. asp?HREF=?newliteracies/action/alvermann/index.html.

Bailey, L. (2005). Views of being in the closet. In *Reflections of herself. Young women's program.* (pp. 12-13). Center on Halsted; Chicago. Retrieved March 3, 2007, from http://www.centeronhalsted.org.

Blackburn, M. V. (2003). Disrupting the (hetero)normative: Exploring literacy perfor-mances and identity work with queer youth. *Journal of Adult and Adolescent Literacy, 46*, 312–324.

Chavez, V., & Soep, E. (2005). Youth Radio and the pedagogy of collegiality. *Harvard Educational Review, 54*(4), 409–434.

Freire, P., & Macedo, D. (1987). *Literacy: Reading the word and the world.* South Hadley, MA: Begin and Garvey.

Halpren, R., Barker, G., & Mollard, W. (2000). Youth programs as alternative spaces to be: A study of neighborhood youth programs in Chicago's west town. *Youth and Society, 31*, 469–506.

Hamilton, S. F., & Hamilton, M. A. (Eds.). (2004). *The youth development handbook: Coming of age in American communities.* Thousand Oaks, CA: Sage.

Hull, G. (2003). At last: Youth culture and digital media: New literacies for new times. *Research in the Teaching of English, 38,* 229–233.

Hull, G., & Katz, M. (2006). Crafting an agentive self: Case studies of digital storytelling. *Research in the Teaching of English, 41*(1), 43–81.

Lee, C. D. (2004). Literacy in the academic disciplines and the needs of adolescent struggling readers. *Voices in Urban Education: Adolescents Literacy, 3,* 14–25.

McLaughlin, M. W., & Heath, S. B. (1993). Casting the self: Frames for identity and dilemmas for policy. In S. B. Heath & M. W. McLaughlin (Eds.), *Identity and inner-city youth: Beyond ethnicity and gender* (pp. 210–240). New York: Teachers College Press.

McLaughlin, M. W., Irby, M. A., & Langman, J. (1994). *Urban sanctuaries: Neighborhood organizations in the lives and futures of inner-city youth.* San Francisco: Jossey-Bass.

Miller, B. M. (2001). The promise of after-school programs. *Educational Leadership, 58,* 6–12.

Moll, L. C., & Gonzalez, N. (1994). Lessons from research with language minority children. *Journal of Reading Behavior, 26,* 439–456.

Rubinstein-Ávila, E. (2006). Publishing "Equinox": An ethnographic tale of youth literacy development after school. *Anthropology and Education Quarterly, 37,* 255–272.

Rubinstein-Ávila, E. (in progress). *Ethnographic insights into youthwork: Balance, meaningful collaboration and a tangible product.*

Schultz, K., & Hull, G. (2002). Locating literacy theory in out-of-school contexts. In G. Hull & K. Schultz (Eds.), *School's out! Bridging out-of-school literacies with classroom practice* (pp. 11–31). New York: Teachers College Press.

Street, B. V. (2005). At last: Recent applications of new literacy studies in educational contexts. *Research in the Teaching of English, 39,* 417–423.

Thompson, K. (2002). Imagining a better world. *110 Degrees: Tucson Youth's Tell Tucson's Stories, 2,* 10.

Chapter Sixteen

BRIDGING THE CONTINENTS OF DIFFERENCE: FAMILY LITERACY WITH ADOLESCENTS

Sharon Kane

INTRODUCTION: THE NEED FOR BRIDGES

"Carried down on the … escalator, mother and daughter, one step apart, but separated by a continent of difference" (Smith, 2005, p. 103). When I read this description of a shopping expedition in Alexander McCall Smith's *44 Scotland Street*, I thought it captured perfectly the distance almost universally felt by the parents and teens I know. Though I have only sons, I have been there, walking in the mall a few steps behind a boy who needs his mother's credit card but certainly does not want the world to think we belong together.

Although I understood the need for my teenagers to separate from me, I still felt nostalgic for those times when they would sit on either side of me, squishing me as they peered at pictures of storybook characters: Tigger and Piglet, Lucy and Aslan, or the Boxcar children. I was especially unnerved when I realized that Patrick had reached a stage where he was embarrassed even by his mother's *literacy*. "You're the only mother who comes to my soccer games with magazines," he'd say scornfully. "The other parents watch the game." Didn't he understand about time-outs? I could read whole articles when there was no action on the field.

Literacy had been a strong bond between me and each of my sons before adolescence robbed me of my library buddies. I learned I could no longer greet new friends they brought home with, "So, what's your favorite book?" When I came home from conferences with books autographed by Jane Yolen, Avi, Theodore Taylor, Jerry Spinelli, Walter Dean Myers, and Sharon Creech, the boys did not respond as ecstatically as they had in years past. Had I made a mistake by attaching such importance to books through their childhood years? Would they reject reading and writing in an effort to establish their own identities?

I turned to my literary mentors for answers as to how I might narrow the distance I felt growing between my children and me. Katherine Paterson (1981) provided one answer:

> It occurs to me that I have spent a good part of my life trying to construct bridges.... There were so many chasms I saw that needed bridging—chasms of time and culture and disparate human nature—that I began sawing and hammering at the rough wood planks for my children and for any other children who might read what I had written.... I discovered gradually and not without a little pain that you don't put together a bridge for a child. You become one—you lay yourself across the chasm. (p. 113)

The scholarly literature on adolescent literacy confirms that our teenagers need adults in their lives who will lay the planks, be the bridges. One of the principles of the International Reading Association's (1999) position statement on adolescent literacy states, "Adolescents deserve homes, communities, and a nation that will support their efforts to achieve advanced levels of literacy and provide the support necessary for them to achieve" (p. 9). The variety of teens in our nation and their concerns is great; some of our teens are in drug rehabilitation, others in prison. Some teens literally have no family or home; for others, family literacy is taking on new meaning as they read Dr. Seuss to their own infants and toddlers. Much of the research and other scholarly literature relating to family literacy have focused on young children. This chapter will explore some of the ways families can nurture literacy during the crucial developmental stage of adolescence. Though I will use the term *parents* throughout, I really mean to extend that term to guardians, grandparents, siblings, aunts and uncles, teachers, and other adults who interact in caring ways with teens.

BRIDGING THROUGH BOOKS

Books have been connecting the generations for centuries; they certainly can continue this function now. Rather than parents fretting over their children leaving the world of children's literature that they have inhabited together for so long, they can welcome their children into adolescence through the genre of young adult literature. Parents can communicate with teachers to find out what their children will be reading in their middle and high school classes and read along so that they can discuss the literature with their daughters and sons, sharing perspectives and evaluations. Many teachers are happy to invite parents to read along with their children who participate in reading-writing workshops; they will send home reading lists, Internet sources, and newsletters highlighting students' responses and recommendations. They will let families know where audio versions or Spanish translations of the books can be procured.

In addition, parents can provide books for pleasure reading. I still remember the pride I felt in 8th grade when my mother deemed me ready to read her favorites: *Jane Eyre* (Bronte, 1987), *Rebecca* (du Maurier, 1993), *The Silver Chalice* (Costain, 1952). Today, the choices might include *The Da Vinci Code* (Brown, 2003), John Grisham books, and treasures by Barbara Kingsolver and Isabelle Allende. Parents can get the audio versions of books so that family members can enjoy them together in the car as adults transport teens to sports practice, school events, jobs, college visits, and recreational activities. Books can be chosen based on mutual interests. They can be fiction, such as *The Curious Incident of Dog in the Night-time* by Mark Haddon (2003), whose narrator lets us into his mind as an adolescent with autism. Others can be nonfiction, such as *The Lady and the Panda* (Croke, 2005), the adventure of a woman who overcame many obstacles to capture a live panda in Tibet and subsequently faced an ethical dilemma she had to resolve. Both of these are examples of what librarians call *crossover* books, which appeal to both older children and adults. Or parents and teenagers can listen to Selected Shorts on National Public Radio (also available on CD). Teenagers will let their parents know what types of literature they prefer for shared listening.

One family tradition could be to celebrate the end of each school year with a gift of books for summer reading involving main characters who are in the grade the adolescent will be entering in the fall. Imagine Mario, who has just graduated from middle school. He comes home to find the following books on his bedside table: *Speak*, by Laurie Halse Anderson (1999), narrated by 9th-grader Melinda, who finds herself excluded by her peers and struggling to recover from a traumatic event that happened over the summer; *Nothing but the Truth*, by Avi (2004), a story told in multiple voices about 9th-grader Philip Malloy, who has been suspended from school after disobeying the school rule requiring silence during the playing of the national anthem; and *Sleeping Freshmen Never Lie*, by David Lubar (2005), whose main character writes about his school year in his journal. Table 16.1 shows titles of books whose settings are in the middle and high school grade levels.

One of my former students began a family book discussion club when she was in my methods course for preservice teachers. Heather's parents, cousins, grandparents, aunts, and uncles meet monthly to discuss a book read in common. The book club is now in its third year, and the responsibility and privilege of selecting the books rotates among the members. An age range of several decades is represented, so the chosen titles represent great variety. There is potential for benefits on many levels when intergenerational family members

Table 16.1
Books about Characters in Various Grade Levels

GRADE 7

Bloor, E. (1997). *Tangerine.* San Diego: Harcourt Brace.

Boles, P. M. (2006). *Little divas.* New York: HarperCollins/Amistad.

Goldschmidt, J. (2005). *The secret blog of Raisin Rodriguez: A novel.* New York: Razorbill.

Howe, J. (2001). *The misfits.* New York: Simon and Schuster/Aladdin.

Howe, J. (2005). *Totally Joe.* New York: Atheneum.

Pollet, A. (2004). *Nobody was here: Seventh grade in the life of me, Penelope.* New York: Orchard Books.

Rosenbloom, F. (2005). *You are so not invited to my bat mitzvah!* New York: Hyperion.

Spinelli, J. (2004). *Space station seventh grade.* New York: Little, Brown.

Vega, D. (2005). *Click here: (to find out how I survived seventh grade), a novel.* New York: Little, Brown.

Wallace, R. (2006). *Southpaw.* New York: Viking.

GRADE 8

Evangelista, B. (2005). *Gifted.* New York: Walker.

Feinstein, J. (2005). *Last shot: A final four mystery.* New York: Knopf.

Little, J. (1989). *Hey, world, here I am!* (S. Truesdell, Illus.). New York: Harper and Row.

Mills, C. (2005). *Makeovers by Marcia.* New York: Farrar, Straus, and Giroux.

Peck, R. (2006). *Here lies the librarian.* New York: Dial Books.

Pollett, A. (2005). *The pity party: 8th grade in the life of me, Cass.* London: Orchard Books.

Van Draanen, W. (2001). *Flipped.* New York: Alfred A. Knopf.

Wittinger, E. (2005). *Sandpiper.* Simon and Schuster.

GRADE 9

Bernstein, M. W., & Kaufmann, Y. (Eds.). (2004). *How to survive your freshman year.* Atlanta, GA: Hundreds of Heads Books.

Naylor, P. R. (2000). *The grooming of Alice.* New York: Atheneum Books.

Voigt, C. (2006). *When bad things happen to bad people.* New York: Atheneum Books.

Yavin, T. S. (2007). *All-star season* (C. Orback, Illus.). Minneapolis, MN: Kar-Ben.

GRADE 10

Atkins, C. (2003). *Alt ed.* New York: G. P. Putnam's Sons.

Graham, R. (2005). *Thou shalt not dump the skater dude and other commandments I have broken.* New York: Viking.

Koja, K. (2003). *Buddha boy.* Waterville, ME: Thorndike Press.

Portman, F. (2006). *King dork.* New York: Delacorte Press.

Serros, M. (2006). *Goy crazy.* New York: Hyperion.

Spinelli, J. (2000). *Stargirl.* New York: Knopf.

Vail, R. (2006). *You, maybe: The profound asymmetry of love in high school.* New York: HarperCollins.

Walters, E. (2005). *Juice.* Victoria, BC: Orca.

(Continued)

Table 16.1
(*continued*)

GRADE 11

Brashares, A. (2001). *The sisterhood of the traveling pants.* New York: Delacorte Press.

Hemphill, S. (2005). *Things left unsaid: A novel in poems.* New York: Hyperion.

Kulpa, K. (Ed.). (1996). *Juniors: Fourteen short stories by eleventh graders.* East Greenwich, RI: Merlyn's Press.

Myracle, L. (2006). *Ttfn.* New York: Amulet Books.

GRADE 12

Anderson, L. H. (2002). *Catalyst.* New York: Viking.

Anderson, L. H. (2005). *Prom.* Waterville, ME: Thorndike Press.

Nelson, R. A. (2005). *Teach me: A novel.* New York: Razorbill.

Sanchez, A. (2001). *Rainbow boys.* New York: Simon and Schuster.

Sanchez, A. (2003). *Rainbow high.* New York: Simon and Schuster.

gather, formally or informally, to discuss books, whether they be fantasy or informational; political or romantic; humorous or apt to evoke tears and sobs; or any combination of the above. Everyone can feel valued and listened to; new insights about the literature and about each other are almost bound to occur. One of my students, Diana, wrote about a memory that demonstrates this:

> One moment that always sticks in my mind is when I had to stay at my grandmother's house while my parents were out of town. I was probably twelve or thirteen and I was really into Stephen King. I had just finished reading *The Shining* [1977] and my grandmother picked it up and read the whole thing that night. While some of the language may have been offensive to her, she thought he was a terrific writer who used very vivid descriptions. I was surprised that my sixty-something Latin-teaching grandmother was so cool.

Adolescence is a time of questioning, of figuring out one's identity in relation to peers, family, society, and the world. Parents can provide books that deal with many facets of relationships, including those between parents and teens, whose values do not always match. There are many ways authors let us know about the tensions between teens and parents, but the shopping and clothing metaphors seem to be prevalent. For example, the title of Deborah Tannen's (2006) nonfiction book about mother-daughter communication says it all: *You're Wearing That?* In the fictional *The Second Summer of the Sisterhood* (Brashares, 2003), Lena feels trapped as she reluctantly accompanies her mother on errands. "This was how her mom secured quality mother-daughter time—through stealth and trickery" (p. 26). At one point, Lena waits in the car, but that is no fun, either. "It was too hot for sunroofs. It was too hot for parking lots. It was too hot for mothers" (p. 26). In the store, Lena's perception of her mother is reflected in her disdain for everything involved in the event:

> Her mother went right for the racks of beige-colored clothing. On the first pass she picked out a pair of beige linen pants and a beige shirt. "Cute, no?".... Lena shrugged. They were so boring they made her eyes glaze over.... Her mother's clothing vocabulary made her wince. "Slacks ... blouse ... cream ... ecru ... taupe." Lena fled to the front of the store. (p. 27)

Sometimes the parents in novels are truly horrible; in Chris Crutcher's (1995) *Ironman,* for example, Bo Brewster's father is abusive. In *Speak,* Melinda's parents are busy with their own lives to the point of being negligent, completely unaware of her pain and her needs. In other novels, parents are loving but flawed. There are several novels in which a teen needs desperately to learn about a parent who is gone (through death or abandonment), yet the remaining parent refuses to talk about the missing person. These include *Following Fake Man* by Barbara Ware Holmes (2001), *Because of Winn-Dixie* by Kate Di Camillo (2003), *A Solitary Blue* by Cynthia Voigt (2005), and *Park's Quest* by Katherine Paterson (1988). In each of these stories, the main character comes to realize that the parent who is the caregiver is also dealing with grief and is not deliberately behaving in ways to make the adolescent's life miserable.

In many young adult novels, the parents as well as the teen protagonists develop throughout the plot, resulting in better understanding and improved relationships. In others, the parent is unwilling or unable to grow, but the teen learns to accept the parent's limitation or to get beyond the sorrow of the untenable or unattainable relationship and approach adulthood with the help of other mentors. Books can help our teen readers perceive parents as real people and think about their own family relationships in more complex ways. Table 16.2 gives additional titles of novels and nonfiction works that deal with parent-teen relationships.

Nonfiction books can be very helpful as we strive to keep both literacy bridges and emotional bridges between ourselves and our teenagers intact, as illustrated in books about teen-parent relationships such as those written by Amy Tan and Tim Russert. There are many more ways to connect with teenagers through literature. It might be difficult to keep up with children's devouring of the thousands of pages of Harry Potter's adventures at Hogwarts Academy or their travels to an alternative universe in the popular fantasy series *His Dark Materials,* by Philip Pullman. Besides, they might not want us to go along for the total ride. But our contribution could be, while admitting we are the Muggles that J. K. Rowling pokes fun at, bringing home informational books, such as *The Science of Harry Potter* by R. Highfield (2002) and *The Science of Philip Pullman's His Dark Materials* by M. Gribben and J. Gribben (2003), which can offer new insights and extend the conversation among family members

Table 16.2
Books Dealing with Parent-Teen Relationships

Brashares, A. (2001). *The sisterhood of the traveling pants*. New York: Delacorte.
 Four girls help each other with problems involving parents—suicide, divorce, new baby.

Fensham, E. (2005). *Helicopter man*. New York: Bloomsbury.
 Father is homeless and schizophrenic.

Gantos, J. (2002). *What would Joey do?* New York: Farrar, Straus and Giroux.
 Both mother and father have so many personal problems that they are unable to be good parents.

Gillot, S., & Sibiril, V. (2005). *Dealing with mom: How to understand your changing relationship* (T. Shaw, Ed., & A. Tschiegg, Illus.). New York: Amulet Books.

Henkes, K. (2003). *Olive's ocean*. New York: Greenwillow Books.
 Teenager wants to be a writer, like her father.

Johnson, A. (2003). *The first part last*. New York: Simon and Schuster/Pulse.
 Narrated by a 16-year-old father.

Mackler, C. (2003). *The earth, my butt, and other big round things*. Cambridge, MA: Candlewick Press.
 Parents pressure young girl to be thin and successful according to their traditional norms.

McBride, J. (1996). *The color of water: A black man's tribute to his white mother*. New York: Riverhead Books.
 Describes author's relationship with his mother.

McCourt, F. (1996). *Angela's ashes: A memoir*. New York: Scribner.
 Describes author's relationship with his mother.

Mikaelsen, B. (2001). *Touching spirit bear*. New York: HarperTrophy.
 Father has been abusive.

Picoult, J. (2004). *My sister's keeper: A novel*. New York: Atria.
 Main character sues when her parents ask her to donate a kidney to her sister.

Russert, T. (2004). *Big Russ and me: Father and son, lessons of life*. New York: Miramax Books.
 A memoir written by a son.

Russert, T. (2006). *Wisdom of our fathers: Lessons and letters from daughters and sons*. New York: Random House.

Ryan, P. M. (2004). *Becoming Naomi Leon*. New York: Scholastic.
 Mother only wants one of her children, and that is for an ulterior motive.

Stratton, A. (2004). *Chanda's secrets*. Toronto: Annick Press.
 A teen in Africa cares for her mother, who has AIDS.

Weeks, S. (2004). *So B. it*. New York: Scholastic.
 Mother has a developmental disability.

---

about the fantasy books themselves. There are also numerous articles written about both the Rowling and Pullman series such as "What American Schools Can Learn from Hogwarts School of Witchcraft and Wizardry" (Booth & Booth, 2003), "Harry Potter and the Magic of Mathematics" (McShea, Vogel, & Yarnevich, 2005), and "Moving beyond Censorship: What Will Educators Do If a Controversy over *His Dark Materials* Erupts?" (Glanzer, 2005).

 If children pick up these materials parents have left around and show an interest in discussing the issues, parents can be available. Parents can also have books lying around that could help initiate discussion on topics our teens might find sensitive or be reluctant to talk about. In addition, books, magazines, music, art, and Web sites can offer ways to help adolescents learn about their heritage and the lands and cultures of their parents, grandparents, or more distant ancestors. Table 16.3 gives examples of nonfiction titles relating to topics of potential interest to teenagers and to curricular topics they may be studying in school.

BRIDGING THROUGH MULTILITERACIES

Everyday experience, along with the scholarly literature from experts (e.g., Alvermann, 2004; Leu, Leu, & Coiro, 2004; Masny, 2005; New London Group, 1996), makes it clear that literacy is changing rapidly and that looking

Table 16.3
Nonfiction Books to Match the Needs and Interests of Teenagers

Bardin, M., & Fine, S. (2005). *Zen in the art of the SAT: How to think, focus, and achieve your highest score.* Boston: Houghton Mifflin.

Borden, S., Miller, S., Strikeleather, A., Valladares, M., & Yeltonwrote, M. (2005). *Middle school: How to deal* (Y. Hatori, Illus.). San Fancisco: Chronicle.

Brockman, J. (2004). *Curious minds: Twenty-seven scientists describe what inspired them to choose their paths.* New York: Pantheon Books.

Budhos, M. (1999). *Remix: Conversations with immigrant teenagers.* New York: Henry Holt.

Burnett, B. (2002). *Cool careers without college for math and science wizards.* New York: Rosen.

Carlson, L. M. (Ed.). (2005). *Red hot salsa: Bilingual poems about growing up Latino in the United States.* New York: Henry Holt.

Chopra, D. (2006). *Teens ask Deepok: All the right questions.* New York: Simon Pulse.

Gelb, M. J. (2003). *Discover your genius: How to think like history's ten most revolutionary minds.* New York: Quill.

Goldsmith, C. (2006). *Invisible invaders: Dangerous infectious diseases.* Minneapolis, MN: Twenty-first Century Books.

Hill, J. B. (2000). *The legacy of Luna: The story of a tree, a woman, and the struggle to save the redwoods.* San Francisco: HarperSanFrancisco.

Huegel, K. (2003). *GLBTQ: The survival guide of queer and questioning teens.* Minneapolis, MN: Free Spirit.

Kidder, T. (2003). *Mountains beyond mountains: The quest of Dr. Paul Farmer, a man who would cure the world.* New York: Random House.

Kittleson, M. J. (Ed.), Haley, J., & Stein, W. (2005). *The truth about abuse.* New York: Facts on File.

Zimmerman, K., Hyneman, J., & Savage, A. (2005). *Mythbusters: The explosive truth behind 30 of the most perplexing urban legends of all time.* New York: Simon Spotlight Entertainment.

at teenagers' out-of-school literacies is very important if we want to under-stand them and support them in their academic and personal growth. Parents can find ways to relate to their children as teens react to and create multimodal texts and as they negotiate the world of pop culture they inhabit, participate in, and contribute to.

Computer technologies have made it possible for our children to lay some planks from their end of the parent-child bridge. For the first time in history, children often know more than their parents about digital literacies, a major part of the present world, thus providing a unique opportunity for a role reversal as they teach their parents about the new literacies (Dresang, 1999). Many parents are humbly, and with good humor, asking for help as they search the Internet, join the instant messaging (IM) crowd, try text messaging, and download music and images. If parents are lucky, their adolescent children will allow them, at least to some extent, into their world of blogging, fan fiction, manga and anime (Japanese forms of comics and animation), multimedia digital storytelling, and game playing. I have several friends who tell me that their teenagers will talk about issues with them through text messaging or IM that they would not dis-cuss with them in person.

Denny Taylor's (1997) *Many Families, Many Literacies* reminds us to think of family literacy broadly, beyond just print media. Keene (2003) exempli-fies this as she shares a story of a visit she and her daughter made to the National Gallery of Art. They entered together but toured the Van Gogh exhibit separately, the daughter with artist's pad to sketch, the mother with journal to write down reflections. They met up later and talked about their experiences as well as their understanding of Van Gogh and his subjects. Keene concludes,

> I would argue that our verbal, written, and artistic struggle to understand better rep-resented what it is to understand than any packet the museum might have created to guide us. I would argue that the conversation, our writing, her art, and the content of the exhibit—so worthy of our struggle to understand—helped us develop insights that influence our thinking to this day in ways seen and unseen. (p. 29)

I would argue that the experience Keene describes and analyzes shows fam-ily literacy at its best. There is no competition involved, no pressuring to con-form. There is a respect for each other's need for space; there is mutual giving of flexibility and freedom in terms of modes of learning and expressing what has been learned.

Any time adults share reading, writing, speaking, listening, or viewing in any form with their children, they are engaged in family literacy. Watching a movie together and then talking about the issues, the characters and actors, the visual effects, and emotional responses can support relationships and nur-ture thinking on everyone's part. (Actually, my sons started monitoring and censoring my film watching. Patrick once said, "You have to rent *Saving Private Ryan,* but fast forward through the first half hour; you couldn't handle the violence.") Shooting one-line e-mails back and forth each day, or forwarding jokes and cartoons, or giving compliments and encouragement can strengthen bonds. Sharing newspaper articles (whether hard copy or online) on topics related to the interests of family members is an authentic way to enhance literacy. Searching Web sites together for information on sporting equipment, concerts, a sports-related injury, college scholarships, a vacation destination, used cars, local politics, or other issues that come up during the family's daily routine can be beneficial. Clothing catalogues and college catalogues can be perused together or looked at individually and left around the house for others to explore.

Advances in technology can assist parents as they support their children with their academic responsibilities. Many schools have some sort of homework hotline, and many teachers have Web sites parents can visit to find out the curriculum being taught, assignments and projects, and possibly even avenues for interaction with the teacher and/or class. Giulia is a young girl who tends to freeze when her parents stand over her shoulder or look at her homework in progress, but she willingly e-mails drafts of papers via attachments to her father at his workplace and accepts the editing suggestions that he sends back electronically.

Literacy can be instrumental as families confront issues of social justice, whether those issues involve individuals or groups being treated disrespectfully at school, or countries in other parts of the world. My son Christopher encouraged me to write to my state representatives before the start of the war in Iraq and to attend rallies for peace, at which literacy was present in the form of posters and placards, speeches, and circulating petitions. Chris now forwards me information on issues relating to sustainable farming, poverty and politics, and animal rights.

There are dangers connected with the Internet, and children need to be cognizant of them and protected from them. Preaching and giving warnings will not always work, especially since teenagers often think that they know more than their parents—and in the case of technology, this may be true. The best way to deal with the potential for harm might be to investigate the Internet together. A parent I know asked her daughter to show her a sample of what she reads and writes on the popular blogging site MySpace.com. She was able to explain rationally some of the potential ramifications of posting personal information and messages. Parent and child communicated as two people weighing the plusses and drawbacks of a technology. The key to communication was that the mother let the adolescent lead the way; the discussion was contextualized, not forced on the daughter, and not laced with threats or demands.

CONCLUSION

Some caveats relating to family literacy are in order. One caution is that it is possible, in an effort to remain close to teens, to try too hard, thereby pushing them more than they wish. It is important to remember that adolescents need to separate from their parents, and in some ways, they need to find, or craft, their own identities. Where they go, parents are not always welcome to follow. For example, rock musician Kurt Cobain died when my Christopher was a teen. He did not need me to mourn in the same way he and his friends did. Later, however, I cut out newspaper editorials written by columnists about Cobain's death and its effect on his family, friends, fans, and the music industry; I left the articles lying around for him. That effort gave the message that I cared and that I knew he was hurting, even though I had not been a fan of the musician in the same way he had been. He gave signals that he did not want me encroaching on his personal grief, so I stayed apart, but connected through a literacy bridge. Most teens do not want parents to be a friend, an equal—they do not want parents to IM them and their friends or wear their clothes. So it stands to reason that the literacies of parent and child will not be identical, or totally shared.

We must also be careful not to turn literacy opportunities into lessons. Parents should try to refrain from giving lame or didactic books and must not try to tell teens what a text is supposed to mean, for, as Katherine Paterson (1997) states,

> A good story is alive, ever changing and growing as it meets each listener or reader in a spirited and unique encounter, while the moralistic tale is not only dead on arrival, it's already been embalmed.... [Children] may not behave, but they certainly already know what is meant by behaving. And a book that tries to rub it in succeeds only in rubbing them the wrong way. (pp. 7–8)

Here is a final example of a mother and daughter shopping, one which conveys a hint that underneath all the tension between parents and teens, we are all *trying* to accommodate the other, and there is really much that is positive. In Lynne Rae Perkins's (2005) Newbery winner *Criss Cross*, two friends are changing clothes in the rhododendrons on the way to school. One of them, Debbie, had been shopping with her mother for jeans recently and found that her mother "was opposed to spending money on something that was going to drag on the ground and get ruined. She could not hear the siren call of the dragging jeans" (p. 45). After trying on many, many pairs of jeans that were wrong, Debbie finally tried on a pair that, while they did have an embroidered bunny nibbling on a bunch of carrots, were at least the right length by her standards:

> "I can hem them," she said.... She was fibbing, but it was a noble fib, because she was really saying, "I love you. I want us to be having fun." She was also saying, "If you really love me, you won't make me hem them." (p. 48)

This family could have used a copy of *The Blue Jean Book: The Story Behind the Seams* by T. L. Kyi (2005). The good news is that teenagers are only teenagers for seven years; adolescence is self-limiting. In an article I wrote when my boys were young teens, I recommended sneaking literacy into home discussions by paying attention to newspaper articles relating to individual interests of our children, nonchalantly saying, "Hey, listen to this!" and proceeding to read the beginning of an article on an eclipse, a field trip to an amusement park to study the physics of rides, or a pop culture figure (Kane, 1995). Now, these adult sons employ a similar strategy as they communicate to me through e-mail. Recently, Patrick, a law school student at Wake Forest University, sent a message saying only "Check this out" and giving a link to a Web site advertising the Southern Writers Festival hosted by Duke University. I not only checked out the site, I went to North Carolina, meeting Patrick and his wife there to hear lectures on literature together. From another part of the country, Christopher kept connected electronically as he volunteered with the Buffalo Field Campaign, a group based in Montana and dedicated to rescuing the wild buffalo living in Yellowstone from harassment and slaughter. He put me on the organization's e-mail list, he sent me a video, and he asked me to write letters and make phone calls to politicians. Here is the text of his most recent e-mail to me, which mentions books we read together during his childhood and taps into our lifelong shared interest in illustration:

> Do you know my friend Jeff Mack? I met him last night. He grew up in Skaneateles, graduated from SUNY Oswego, and now illustrates children's books for a living. Most recently he did the illustrations for the new Bunnicula series.

So at this point, the boys are using multimodal forms of literacy to communicate with me. Traffic is going both ways on the literacy bridge—a bridge that leads us to surprising new places, none of which, thank heaven, is a shopping mall.

REFERENCES

Alvermann, D. (2004). *Adolescents and literacies in a digital world.* New York: Peter Lang.

Booth, M. B., & Booth, G. M. (2003). What American schools can learn from Hogwarts School of Witchcraft and Wizardry. *Phi Delta Kappan, 85*(4), 310–315.

Dresang, E. (1999). *Radical change: Books for youth in a digital age.* New York: H. W. Wilson.

Glanzer, P. (2005). Moving beyond censorship: What will educators do if a controversy over *His Dark Materials* erupts? *Phi Delta Kappan, 87*, 166–168.

Gribben, M., & Gribben, J. (2003). *The science of Philip Pullman's* His Dark Materials. New York: Alfred A. Knopf.

Highfield, R. (2002). *The science of Harry Potter: How magic really works.* New York: Viking.

International Reading Association. (1999). *Adolescent literacy: A position statement.* Newark, DE: Author.

Kane, S. (1995). "Hey, look at this! Meeting the challenge of family literacy with adolescents. *State of Reading: Journal of the Texas Reading Association, 2*(1), 13–17.

Keene, E. O. (2003). To understand. In L. Hoyt (Ed.), *Spotlight on comprehension: Building a literacy of thoughtfulness* (pp. 22–39). Portsmouth, NH: Heinemann.

Leu, D., Leu, D. D., & Coiro, J. (2004). *Teaching with the Internet K–12: New literacies for new times.* Norwood, MA: Christopher-Gordon.

Masny, D. (2005). Multiple literacies: An alternative OR beyond Freire. In J. Anderson, M. Kendrick, T. Rogers, & S. Smythe (Eds.), *Portraits of literacy across families, communities, and schools: Intersections and tensions* (pp. 171–184). Mahwah, NJ: Lawrence Erlbaum Associates.

McShea, B., Vogel, J., & Yarnevich, M. (2005). Harry Potter and the magic of mathematics. *Mathematics Teaching in the Middle School, 10,* 408–414.

New London Group. (1996). A pedagogy of multiliteracies: Designing social futures. *Harvard Educational Review, 66,* 60–92.

Paterson, K. (1981). Newbery Medal acceptance, *Bridge to Terabithia.* In K. Paterson (Ed.), *Gates of excellence: On reading and writing for children* (pp. 112–115). New York: EP Dutton.

Paterson, K. (1997). Family values. *New Advocate, 10*(1), 5–14.

Smith, A. M. (2005). *44 Scotland Street.* New York: Anchor Books.

Tannen, D. (2006). *You're wearing that? Understanding mothers and daughters in conversation.* New York: Random House.

Taylor, D. (Ed.). (1997). *Many families, many literacies: An international declaration of principles.* Portsmouth, NH: Heinemann.

Literature Cited

Anderson, L. H. (1999). *Speak.* New York: Farrar, Straus and Giroux.

Avi. (2004). *Nothing but the truth: A documentary novel.* London: Orchard Books.

Brashares, A. (2003). *The second summer of the sisterhood.* New York: Delacorte.

Bronte, C. (1987). *Jane Eyre* (H. Bloom, Ed.). New York: Chelsea House.

Brown, D. (2003). *The Da Vinci code.* New York: Doubleday.

Costain, T. (1952). *The silver chalice.* Garden City, NY: Doubleday.

Croke, V. C. (2005). *The lady and the panda: The true adventures of the first American explorer to bring back China's most exotic animal.* New York: Random House.

Crutcher, C. (1995). *Ironman.* New York: Greenwillow Books.

Di Camillo, K. (2000). *Because of Winn-Dixie.* Cambridge, MA: Candlewick Press.

Du Maurier, D. (1993). *Rebecca.* New York: Doubleday.

Haddon, M. (2003). *The curious incident of the dog in the night-time.* New York: Doubleday.

Holmes, B. W. (2001). *Following fake man.* New York: Random House/Dell Yearling.

King, S. (1977). *The shining.* Garden City, NY: Doubleday.

Kyi, T. L. (2005). *The blue jean book: The story behind the seams.* Toronto: Annick Press.

Lubar, D. (2005). *Sleeping freshmen never lie.* New York: Dutton Books.

Paterson, K. (1988). *Park's quest.* New York: Lodestar Books.

Perkins, L. R. (2005). *Criss cross.* New York: Greenwillow Books.

Voigt, C. (2005). *A solitary blue.* Waterville, ME: Thorndike Press.

Chapter Seventeen

RESOURCES FOR ADOLESCENT LITERACY

Thomas W. Bean and Jennifer J. Wimmer

Adolescent literacy is the new kid on the block within the larger and well-established fields of content area literacy and secondary reading. In this chapter, we chronicle the relatively recent history of adolescent literacy and consider the impact of globalization and technology on adolescents' literacy lives. In addition, we list critical resources that will be useful in supporting work with adolescents and provide annotated recommended readings and key Web sites for adolescent literacy. Specifically, we provide selected resources and annotations for the following topic areas: adolescent literacy books, Web sites, funding sources, and program examples; policy documents; adolescents and new literacies; struggling readers; adolescent literacy journals; and young adult literature and critical literacy.

Briefly defined, adolescent literacy refers to extending literacy beyond school and textbook-based literacy to include multiple literacies such as reading online material as well as multiple texts including popular music, instant messages, blogs, television, magazines, and other text forms (Readence, Bean, & Baldwin, 2004). Thus adolescent literacy acknowledges both in-school and out-of-school literacies and, as a field, argues for better connections between the two.

ADOLESCENTS AND ADOLESCENT LITERACY

Nearly 10 years ago, the International Reading Association created the Commission on Adolescent Literacy, resulting in the publication of "Adolescent Literacy: A Position Statement" (Moore, Bean, Birdyshaw, & Rycik, 1999). At that point in time, adolescent literacy initiatives were largely without the funding support typical of K–3 literacy efforts, and the commission set out to highlight the plight of adolescent learners. Professional organizations offered themed journal issues devoted to adolescent literacy (e.g., Bean & Readence, 2002), and edited collections began to appear, aimed at helping educators work with struggling adolescent readers (e.g., Moore, Alvermann, & Hinchman, 2000). All these resources remain valuable; the realm of adolescent literacy continues to flourish with a growing array of published articles, books, and documents.

Clearly some of the impetus for the growing interest in adolescent literacy is due to the high-stakes testing movement and greater scrutiny of adolescents' performance on state achievement measures. For example, the National Assessment of Educational Progress data revealed that adolescent learners are proficient at decoding predictable words and answering factual-level questions (Sturtevant et al., 2006). They are far less able to engage the advanced levels of reading necessary for understanding more complicated subject area texts, however. In addition, recent analyses of adolescents' dropout rates are cause for alarm. More than 3,000 students drop out of high school in the United States each day (Biancarosa & Snow, 2004). While alternate routes to graduation (e.g., credit recovery, GED, etc.) are possible, and large-scale intervention efforts, funded by programs like the U.S. Department of Education Striving Readers (USDOE, 2006) grants, as well as funded projects devoted to the integration of science, mathematics, and content area literacy (e.g., Bean, 2006) may help, these dropout data suggest that adolescents are struggling under the weight of assessments, second language acquisition, and increasingly complex and multimodal texts (Wilder & Dressman, 2006).

A recent review of research on marginalized adolescent readers found that effective programs for these students (often referred to as struggling readers) were characterized by a departure from traditional literary texts and a move toward using shorter, youth-friendly materials and curricula (Franzak, 2006). Greater student choice in reading material that interested and engaged struggling readers, particularly boys, included magazines, ads, music lyrics, comics, cartoons, and Internet-based texts. The use of multiple texts in teaching English, economics, and other subject areas contributes to students' ability to make conceptual connections across texts (Walker, Bean, & Dillard, 2005). This ability to read and link ideas across texts is crucial given the vast array of material available on the Internet and the increasing emphasis on information- and knowledge-related careers. Being able to analyze and critique multiple perspectives on an issue or problem requires teachers skilled in orchestrating lessons that encompass a variety of materials ranging from traditional print-based texts to nonprint media, including videos, television clips, ads, music, and so on (Sturtevant et al., 2006). In addition, in the case of struggling readers, the use of multiple texts that include high-interest materials produces a sense of competence and control that is often missing when students are only permitted to read traditional texts (Franzak, 2006).

To get a better picture of the changing nature of literacy and the increasing demands of advanced literacy, definitions of both adolescent literacy and content area (subject-based literacy) are needed. For example, the National Council of Teachers of English (NCTE) has a glossary of terms devoted to adolescent literacy stating that "this term includes the idea that adolescents have multiple literacies, expanded ideas about texts, their literacies shape their emerging sense of self, and they need school-based opportunities to explore multiple literacies."

Bean (2001) acknowledged the need for a definition of content area literacy that accounts for the multiple forms of texts adolescents encounter in and out of school:

> Content area literacy is a cognitive and social practice involving the ability to read and write about multiple forms of print. These multiple forms of print include textbooks, novels, magazines, Internet material and other sociotechnical sign systems conveying information, emotional content, and ideas to be considered from a critical stance. (para. 3)

What these definitions of adolescent literacy and content area literacy suggest is the changing and expanding scope of what it means to be literate in the twenty-first century. Communications technology and multimedia forms of text, including the Internet, smart phones that include calendars, e-mail capability, and other features such as navigational aids, instant messaging (IM), text messaging, wireless communication, and extensive music and video files on iPods, present contemporary adolescents with a huge array of information (Bean & Harper, in press). Although often bypassed in school curricular contexts, pop culture interests in music and other pop culture forms intersect with literacy development through adolescents' critical reading and writing (Guzzetti & Gamboa, 2004). Being able to make intertextual connections across multiple forms of texts (e.g., print and film) will be crucial (Walker, Bean, & Dillard, 2005). More importantly, being able to discern critically important, accurate, and reliable information from misinformation as well as being able to deconstruct the underlying ideologies and positions represented in various forms of texts will be essential for functioning as global citizens (Harper & Bean, 2006; Stevens & Bean, 2007).

ADOLESCENT LITERACY IN THE NEW TIMES AND NEW LITERACIES

Globalization and the changing nature of work both suggest a critical need for more advanced literacy development for adolescents. The award-winning

New York Times columnist Thomas Friedman (2005) argued that twenty-first-century citizens must be able to critique the propaganda that is widely disseminated on the Internet. Environmental disasters, including tsunamis, global warming, bird flu, and other worldwide risks, demand a world citizenry capable of careful, detailed reading, analysis, and critique. The nature of involvement in a democratic society will be influenced by adolescents' literacies, literacies that call for more sophistication than those literacy abilities tested on standardized reading tests. Indeed, democracy is complex and requires world citizens who not only manipulate huge quantities of information, but also know how to question effectively the value and underlying beliefs in any form of discourse (Harper & Bean, 2006).

Toward that end, we offer recommended readings at the close of the chapter that will help advance adolescents' critical literacy through the use of young adult literature and other forms of text. This is especially important given the rapid increase in new forms of texts. Often labeled new literacies (Kist, 2005), these newer forms of texts include IMing, blogging, e-zines, and various Internet Web pages (O'Brien, 2006). Although the term *new literacies* encompasses much more than information and communication technologies (ICT), advances in technology greatly impact how adolescents read. O'Brien (2006) noted that adolescents' multimodal channel switching, evidenced when young people seamlessly shift in and out of real and virtual worlds through such simultaneous processes as word processing, using multiple screens, making cell phone calls, and playing MP3 music files, produces new competencies.

Kress (2003) noted a shift from print-based reading as a dominant form to reading on the online screen as predominant. He argued that the dominance of the screen has changed literacy; reading is now a distinctly different activity from what it was in the era of the traditional print literacy. With each day, technologies are outdated, Web sites are shut down, and software is updated. Therefore literacy education must be receptive to these changes and willing to keep up with the "neckbreak speed" at which technologies are occurring (International Reading Association, 2002). Yet it is likely that new literacies of technology (sometimes called technoliteracies) are not new to adolescents. ICT continues to be such an integral part of adolescents' lives that they are likely to take these elements for granted. Moorman (2006) distinguished immigrant from native users of technology. Immigrant users are those individuals from the Baby Boomer generation who did not grow up with digital literacies. Adolescents with access to technological devices have, in many cases, grown up with these tools as native users. Although adolescents may not make connections between the reading and writing they engage in as they navigate chat rooms, Web pages, and IM, the literacies they use are extensive as they read, critique, and make meaning while interacting with computer-based texts.

The shift from the page to the screen has greatly impacted what it means to read. The movement from print-based texts to the incorporation of new literacies has expanded current definitions of text and reading. Kress (2003) defined a text as any form of communication. Given this definition, the traditional linear reading path in Western culture, with a direct sequence from top to bottom and left to right, is not sufficient or effective when reading on the Internet, particularly because of the dominance of images. Kress (2003) argued that "*the world told* is a different world to *the world shown*" (p. 1). The texts of today's world are reliant on image and use text as a support. Because images do not need to be read in the traditional reading path of left to right and top to bottom, other reading paths are made possible. Reading paths are determined by the reader's sense of what is relevant on the screen (Kress, 2003). As a result, the number of reading paths is infinite. The reader has greater opportunities to construct his or her own knowledge that is most relevant for the issue or problem under consideration. McNabb (2006) cautioned that online texts require sophisticated and often idiosyncratic navigational paths that are quite different from predictable and familiar print-based text structures. In addition, the sheer volume of texts and information on any topic available online offers multiple perspectives and multiple biases, calling for careful reading and critique.

Advances in technology present limitless learning opportunities for students. Information is now available with a click of a button. With the daily advances of ICT, the possibilities are challenging yet offer exciting opportunities for classrooms. To investigate further the occurrence of new literacies in the classroom, Kist (2000) sought to define and characterize new literacies classrooms across the United States and Canada. Kist's (2005) most recent work is a book containing multiple case studies, describing new literacies classrooms and practices. In defining new literacies, Kist looked for the following five classroom characteristics: (1) daily work in multiple forms of representation; (2) explicit discussions of the merits of using certain symbol systems; (3) metadialogues by the teacher who models problem-solving; (4) a mixture of individual and collaborative activities; and (5) engaging contexts where students achieve flow state.

Using these characteristics, Kist (2005) was able to identify and observe classrooms where teachers were drawing on students' knowledge of technology and extending their learning through collaboration, creativity, and higher-level thinking skills. Among many elements present in the classrooms Kist observed, collaboration was paramount to the success of students' multimedia projects. Thus learning how to work effectively and productively with others was an important byproduct of being a student in a new literacies classroom. In addition, students reported a stronger sense of agency and voice when they were engaged in collaboratively constructing a product such as a film festival at San Fernando High School in southern California. From a teacher's perspective, working on new literacies projects is likely to improve students' communication skills as well as their ability to plan and manage time. Multiple text forms were present in these classrooms such that students saw a link between their video productions and the supporting material underpinning these productions (e.g., written rationales and title cards explaining the intent of a video, sometimes in both English and Spanish).

Current research offers a glimpse of what is possible when new literacies are part of classroom instruction. Adolescents using these technologies are collaborating, using technology, creating, and exploring their worlds in multiple forms (Alvermann & Hagood, 2000; Alvermann & Heron, 2001; Kist, 2000, 2002, 2005; O'Brien, 2006). Students in these classrooms are engaging in meaningful learning and are bringing their outside literacies into the school. Adolescents who may have been previously marginalized by print-based literacies may be enabled to find a space in a new literacies classroom because multiple ideas and skills are needed (Leu, Castek, Henry, Coiro, & McMullan, 2004). Adolescents must learn the needed literacy knowledge, skills, and dispositions to participate in their future lives, and therefore technology is not something that can be an add-on to a lesson every now and then; rather, technology must be infused into the daily curriculum (Lankshear & Knobel, 2004). Nevertheless, traditional print literacy skill influences how struggling readers engage digital texts. For example, Wilder and Dressman (2006) conducted a study of six 9th-grade students in a cultural geography class. Three of the students were struggling readers reading below grade level, while three were in the college preparation curriculum. On the basis of this study, the researchers cautioned that print literacy remains an important prerequisite for successful navigation of Web-based sites. When one of the struggling readers misspelled the name of an international island site, his search bogged down in misinformation. Struggling readers in the study, when confronted with extensive information and lengthy text passages, began skimming. They ultimately opted out of these sites for shorter, often less informative Web sites. Wilder and Dressman concluded that although most students were proficient in the mechanics of conducting searches or typing in URLs of Web sites, the level of (print) literacy demanded by a particular Web site visited or searched closely matched their general level of literate proficiency.

READING AND BOYS

Recent and somewhat alarmist concern about boys and their reading achievement has prompted a developing area of research and resources devoted to this topic. Although much less voluminous than the array of studies on girls and reading produced in the 1990s, research around adolescent masculinity and reading is developing rapidly. For example, Brozo (2002) recommended directly introducing adolescent boys to archetypal literature featuring male characters who challenge narrow notions of what it means to be male. Well-known novels and films like *Holes* (Sachar, 1998), with its healer archetype, or the freedom-loving archetype in *Brian's Winter* (Paulsen, 1996) are but two examples. Others recommend using young adult literature as a vehicle for critiquing gendered practices (e.g., men do not cry; Bean & Harper, in press). In interviews with Australian adolescent boys, many of the students mentioned that they wanted to read books that dealt realistically with relationships in their lives (Martino & Pallotta-Chiarolli, 2003), suggesting that books that simply valorized rugged individuals and loners failed to capture their broader interests. Similarly, work by Smith and Wilhelm (2002) countered the notion that boys see reading as a feminine pursuit. Their study, involving interviews with adolescent boys, showed that these students had a broad array of literacy interests that were not well represented in school. Some wrote poetry, others music, film scripts, and a host of other literacy-related practices, yet many struggled with school-sanctioned literacy practices and high-stakes testing. The developing work on boys and reading, particularly in the United States, Canada, and Australia, is likely to tap into a curriculum that acknowledges provisions for extra literacy support. A number of programs already exist that, while not centered exclusively on boys and reading, offer support mechanisms that encourage adolescents to think seriously about further study, particularly at the college and community college levels.

Support for adolescents' print-based literacies, especially for adolescents who may not have access to computer-based new literacies tools, remains crucial. Support programs like project Advancement Via Individual Determination (AVID) and Gaining Early Awareness and Readiness for Undergraduate Programs (GEAR-UP), aimed at building adolescents' cultural capital (or dominant cultural resources) and school-based skills, offer a strong bridge to college study. Both funded projects are designed to assist students in mastering studying, time management, test-taking strategies, and ways of talking to teachers about their progress in a class. AVID is designed to ensure that underrepresented youth in high school develop the literacy and social skills needed to attend and graduate from college. GEAR-UP offers adolescents an array of summer programs, financial support, and information on college admissions and other resources. These programs are listed in the annotated bibliography at the close of the chapter, and their Web sites offer information on the characteristics of both programs.

Within a new literacies framework, an increasing number of virtual or hybrid online high schools coexist with more traditional high schools. Hybrid online high schools generally have one on campus face-to-face day with teachers, while the remainder of the week is devoted to online subject area study. Often developed as online charter schools, the advent of virtual schools offers students who are homebound, wary of bullying in traditional high schools, incarcerated in jail or prison, or simply interested in the rich array of content area information available in digital formats an alternative learning experience. Research on the impact of virtual schools on student achievement shows that these alternative offerings are at least as good as face-to-face settings (Blomeyer & Dawson, 2005).

CRITICAL RESOURCES FOR SUPPORTING ADOLESCENT LITERACIES

A growing number of policy documents, books, book chapters, articles, and Web sites are devoted to supporting adolescent literacy (Franzak, 2006). While by no means exhaustive, the following annotated resources should provide a good springboard for additional exploration in adolescent literacy. In addition, the reference list for this chapter includes articles that chronicle ongoing work in adolescent literacy.

ANNOTATED BIBLIOGRAPHY

Adolescent Literacy Books

Alvermann, D. L., Hinchman, K. A., Moore, D. W., Phelps, S. F., & Waff, D. R. (Eds.). (2006). *Reconceptualizing the literacies in adolescents' lives* (2nd ed.). Mahwah, NJ: Lawrence Erlbaum Associates.
   This recent edited volume addresses major topics in adolescent literacy, including supporting research and promising practices. The voices of many key figures in adolescent literacy are included, and the volume extends the ideas begun in the 1998 edition of this widely quoted book.

Jetton, T. L., & Dole, J. A. (Eds.). (2004). *Adolescent literacy: Research and practice.* New York: Guilford Press.
   This comprehensive edited volume looks at the teaching of subject area literacy in a variety of areas, including English and science. In addition, there are sections and chapters on working with struggling readers and a consideration of critical issues in adolescent literacy, including assessment.

Rycik, J. A., & Irvin, J. L . (2001). *What adolescents deserve: A commitment to students' literacy learning.* Newark, DE: International Reading Association.
   This edited volume features a wealth of information on programs for adolescents as well as foreshadowing more recent work in multiple literacies and new literacies. Information on second language learners, struggling readers, and middle school readers is included.

Sturtevant, E. G., Boyd, F. B., Brozo, W. G., Hinchman, K. A., Moore, D. W., & Alvermann, D. E. (2006). *Principled practices for adolescent literacy: A framework for instruction and policy.* Mahwah, NJ: Lawrence Erlbaum Associates.
   Supported by a Carnegie Corporation grant, this volume chronicles vignettes of content area classrooms across the country where teachers of adolescents demon-

strated successful practices in literacy related to mathematics, science, English, and other subjects. These vignettes offer readers classroom examples of teachers using multiple texts and various approaches to engage adolescent learners in complex material.

Adolescent Literacy Web Sites

The 2006 International Reading Association Annual Convention featured an Institute on Praxis in Adolescent Literacy Instruction: The Interplay of Theory and Practice, cochaired by Jill Lewis and Gary Moorman. The Web site that grew out of this institute has a wealth of information applicable to policy issues and recommendations for practice. The Web site can be found at http://moormangb.ced.appstate.edu/ira_institute_06.

The more general International Reading Association Web site has numerous resources for adolescent literacy. This site can be found at http://www.reading.org.

The NCTE has a policy document on adolescent literacy available via the organization's homepage or at http://www.ncte.org/library/files/Middle/NolanBrief.pdf.

A Web site devoted to boys and reading is http://guysread.com.

Adolescent Literacy Funding Sources and Examples

The U.S. Department of Education (DOE) supports grants to states to improve teaching in science and mathematics. Formerly called Eisenhower grants, this funding source now supports projects that integrate content area literacy with mathematics and science teaching (e.g., Bean, 2006). Information on application procedures for these grants (termed NeCoTIP in Nevada) can be located at the U.S. DOE Web site under Mathematics and Science Partnerships: http://www.ed.gov/programs/math-sci/index.html.

Striving Readers Grants information can be found at the U.S. DOE site: http://www.ed.gov/programs/strivingreaders/faq.html. The Striving Reader Grants center on middle and secondary struggling reader interventions. Approximately nine grants were awarded to projects in Chicago, New Jersey, and elsewhere. It is expected that funding for this grant category will increase but remain highly competitive, with educational labs and other professional grant writing agencies developing proposals.

Adolescent Literacy Policy Documents

Moore, D. W., Bean, T. W., Birdyshaw, D., & Rycik, J. (1999). Adolescent literacy: A position statement. *Journal of Adolescent and Adult Literacy, 43*, 97–112.

This is the original policy document supporting work in adolescent literacy. Developed by the International Reading Association Adolescent Literacy Commission, the document is widely cited and used by school districts, principals, and literacy leaders. It can be retrieved online at http://www.reading.org/pdf/1036.pdf

In addition to this document, both the NCTE and the National Middle School Association have policy documents underpinning adolescent literacy. The NCTE document can be found at http://www.ncte.org/edpolicy/literacy/about/122379.htm

Adolescents and New Literacies

Alvermann, D. E. (Ed.). (2004). *Adolescents and literacies in a digital world.* New York: Peter Lang.

>This edited text details the literacies that are necessary for adolescents to partici-pate effectively in today's technologically advanced world. Each chapter discusses the challenges and possibilities that adolescents face as they interact with infor-mation and communication technologies both inside and outside the classroom.

Berge, Z. L., & Clark, T. (2005). *Virtual schools: Planning for success.* New York: Teachers College Press.

>This edited volume features chapters detailing the impact of virtual learning. Hybrid models where students engage in both online and face-to-face learning configurations seem to result in high completion rates and learning that parallels face-to-face learning alone. The book is a good resource for educators planning to implement online learning.

Kist, W. (2005). *New literacies in action: Teaching and learning in multiple media.* New York: Teachers College Press.

>This book provides a detailed description of the practices used in new literacy class-rooms. Through multiple case studies, Kist describes the experiences of both teachers and students as they work with new literacies in various content areas.

Kress, G. (2003). *Literacy in the new media age.* London: Routledge.

>This book describes the changes occurring in literacy as the emphasis shifts from print-based texts to the computer screen. Kress reports that traditional reading skills are insufficient to meet the needs of students as they interact with multimedia texts. Classroom examples are provided.

Lankshear, C., & Knobel, M. (2003). *New literacies: Changing knowledge and classroom learning.* Berkshire, UK: Open University Press.

>This book argues for a shift in mind-set among educators due to the technological revolution. The authors argue that the use of new literacies in classrooms is essential to students' current and future lives.

Levesque, S. (2006, June). *Virtual historian.* London, ON: University of Western Ontario Faculty of Education.

>This demonstration software project involved the development of a virtual learning environment that immerses students in the actual sites of historical events through interactive inquiry. A variety of multimedia supports students' learning of history. Students can manipulate visual links and move objects and troops in battle scenes to compare their thinking to that of leaders in history. In an age of interactive video games, this form of learning is a powerful alternative to static textbooks. For a look at this project, see http://www.virtualhistorian.ca.

McNabb, M. L. (2006). *Literacy learning in networked classrooms: Using the Internet with middle-level students.* Newark, DE: International Reading Association.

>On the basis of research in middle-level classrooms, McNabb finds that more sophisticated navigation and critical reading skills are needed to prepare students for life in the networked world of the twenty-first century. Print-based literacy skills alone are inadequate in light of global networks. The book offers a number of useful Web sites related to digital literacies.

Adolescent Struggling Readers
Advancement via Individual Determination (AVID)

>The AVID project is designed to ensure that underserved students increase their enrollment in four-year colleges to "become educated and responsible participants

and leaders in a democratic society" (p. 1). In terms of literacy support, AVID uses vocabulary concept mapping and comprehension strategies like "What I *know*, What I *want* to know, What I *learned*" (KWL), along with various note taking approaches, to scaffold students' learning and develop independence. Students are served from grades 5–12 as they prepare for college. The program targets students who are not meeting their academic potential (i.e., receiving B grades or lower). Although AVID is not specifically designed to target struggling readers, it offers support mechanisms for increasing students' likelihood of success in pursuing a college education. Schools associated with the AVID program receive extensive professional development and learn the writing, inquiry, collaboration, and reading (WIC-R) method to better meet the needs of students in content area classes. Research studies have shown that the implementation of the AVID program increases students' test scores and also increases the number of students attending college. AVID is currently part of 2,200 middle schools and high schools in 36 states and 16 countries. More general information about AVID can be found at http://www.avidonline.org. To view an example of an AVID program, use your search engine to locate multiple sites, for example, http://sths.ltusd.k12.ca.us/STHS%20AVID/shatisavid.htm

Franzak, J. K. (2006). *Zoom:* A review of the literature on marginalized adolescent readers, literacy theory, and policy implications. *Review of Educational Research, 76,* 209–248. This review looks closely at three instructional approaches for struggling adolescent readers: reader response, strategic reading, and critical literacy. The author evaluates each approach with an eye toward advantages and disadvantages. Recommendations for policy changes aimed at serving adolescent struggling readers are advanced, including greater attention to adolescents' expressed competencies and interests in literacy.

GEAR-UP Program: Gaining Early Awareness and Readiness for Undergraduate Programs

The GEAR-UP Program offers students support services to prepare for college, including summer internships, information on college admissions, and a host of other activities designed to interest adolescents in college enrollment. For an example, see http://www.sccedu.org/gearup.

Houge, T. T., Peyton, D., Geier, C., & Petrie, B. (in press). Adolescent literacy tutoring: Face-to-face and via web-cam technology. *Reading Psychology 28* (3), 1–18. This innovative tutorial program, developed at Northern State University in South Dakota, combines a content area literacy course for undergraduates with long-distance tutoring of struggling adolescent readers throughout rural South Dakota and beyond. The article reports on recent research comparing face-to-face and online tutoring in terms of adolescents' reading growth. The value added dimensions of this distance-tutoring model using technology is supported in the study.

Moore, D. W., Alvermann, D. E., & Hinchman, K. A. (Eds.). (2000). *Struggling adolescent readers: A collection of teaching strategies.* Newark, DE: International Reading Association. This edited volume includes a wealth of articles on vocabulary and comprehension development and other topics that will be useful to educators interested in advancing struggling readers' development.

NovaNET: Pearson Digital Learning

NovaNET is an online, standards-based curriculum for middle and high school learners offering a credit recovery program aimed at successful completion of content area courses. See additional information at http://www.PearsonDigital.com.

Journals

Journal of Adolescent and Adult Literacy

Published eight times a year by the International Reading Association, this is the premier journal devoted to adolescent literacy issues. It offers educators consistently valuable resources for working with adolescent learners, and it includes regular reviews of young adult novels and promising books.

Journal of Content Area Reading

This journal is supported by the Secondary Special Interest Group of the International Reading Association and features articles on promising practices in subject areas for adolescent literacy. The articles are generally short and highly readable.

Themed Issues of Selected Journals Devoted to Adolescent Literacy

Reading Research and Instruction

The spring 2001 issue of the College Reading Association's *Reading Research and Instruction* was a themed issue edited by John Readence and Tom Bean. It featured articles on second language learners, identity, and critical literacy, to name a few topics.

Reading Psychology

The fall 2006 issue of the international journal *Reading Psychology* was a themed issue on adolescent literacy. It included refereed articles on a variety of topics useful to educators working with adolescents. For example, the topic of boys and reading was considered, along with other topics in adolescent literacy.

Canadian Journal of Education

A 2007 themed issue of this journal will be coedited by Wayne Martino and Michael Kehler and devoted to boys, literacies, and schooling. Articles will include H. Harper's "Reading Masculinity in Books about Girls."

Young Adult Literature and Critical Literacy

The wealth of young adult literature now available to adolescent readers can be found at the American Library Association Web site as well as at the Web sites for the International Reading Association, the NCTE, and commercial bookstores, including Amazon.com and Barnes and Noble. Ongoing work in critical literacy centered on adolescents can be found in recent books, including the following:

Stevens, L. P., & Bean, T. W. (2007). *Critical literacy: Context and practice in the K–12 classroom.* Thousand Oaks, CA: Sage.

This book provides classroom examples and lists numerous other texts and Web sites aimed at developing students' understanding and application of critical literacy to a variety of print- and media-based texts carrying ideological content to be carefully scrutinized and critiqued.

This annotated bibliography is selective and is by no means meant to be an exhaustive list of all that is under way in the burgeoning area of adolescent literacy. By looking over these resources and sites, the reader can gain a working knowledge of essential policy issues and practices related to adolescent literacy. These resources show that this is an exciting era for adolescent literacy and a hopeful time for adolescents as learners in both traditional and nontraditional classroom settings.

REFERENCES

Alvermann, D. E., & Hagood, M. C. (2000). Fandom and critical media literacy. *Journal of Adolescent and Adult Literacy, 43*, 436–446.

Alvermann, D. E., & Heron, A. H. (2001). Literacy identity work: Playing to learn with popular media. *Journal of Adolescent and Adult Literacy, 45*, 118–122.

Bean, T. W. (2001). An update on reading in the content areas: Social constructivist dimensions. *Reading Online, 5*(5). Retrieved May 16, 2006, from http://www.readingon line.org/articles/handbook/bean/index.html

Bean, T. W. (2006). *Professional development of science and mathematics teachers through systematic integration of literacy practices.* Las Vegas: Nevada Collaborative Teaching Improvement Program, Nevada System of Higher Education.

Bean, T. W., & Harper, H. J. (2007). Reading men differently: Alternative portrayals of masculinity in contemporary young adult fiction. *Reading Psychology 28*(1), 11–30.

Bean, T. W., & Harper, H. J. (in press). Content area reading: Current state of the art. In D. Lapp & J. Flood (Eds.), *Content area reading and learning* (3rd ed.). Mahwah, NJ: Lawrence Erlbaum Associates.

Bean, T. W., & Readence, J. E. (2002). Adolescent literacy: Charting a course for successful futures as lifelong learners. *Reading Research and Instruction, 41*(3), 203–210.

Biancarosa, G., & Snow, C. (2004). *Reading Next—A vision for action and research in middle and high school literacy: A report to the Carnegie Corporation of New York.* Washington, DC: Alliance for Excellent Education.

Blomeyer, R. L., & Dawson, M. (2005). Virtual schools: Policy and practice considerations. In Z. L. Berge & T. Clark (Eds.), *Virtual schools: Planning for success* (pp. 61–76). New York: Teachers College Press.

Brozo, W. G. (2002). *To be a boy, to be a reader: Engaging teen and preteen boys in active literacy.* Newark, DE: International Reading Association.

Franzak, J. K. (2006). *Zoom:* A review of the literature on marginalized adolescent readers, literacy theory, and policy implications. *Review of Educational Research, 76*, 209–248.

Friedman, T. (2005). *The world is flat: A brief history of the twenty-first century.* New York: Farrar, Straus and Giroux.

Guzzetti, B., & Gamboa, M. (2004). Zines for social justice: Adolescent girls writing on their own. *Reading Research Quarterly, 39*, 408–437.

Harper, H. J., & Bean, T. W. (2006). Fallen angels: Finding adolescents and adolescent literacy in a renewed project of democratic citizenship. In D. E. Alvermann, D. W. Moore, S. F. Phelps, & D. R. Waff (Eds.), *Reconceptualizing the literacies in adolescents' lives* (2nd ed., pp. 147–160). Mahwah, NJ: Lawrence Erlbaum Associates.

International Reading Association. (2002). *Integrating literacy and technology in the curriculum: A position statement of the International Reading Association.* Retrieved October 14, 2005, from http://www.reading.org/pdf/technology-pos.pdf

Kist, W. (2000). Beginning to create the new literacy classroom: What does the new literacy look like? *Journal of Adolescent and Adult Literacy, 43*, 710–718.

Kist, W. (2002). Finding "new literacy" in action: An interdisciplinary high school Western civilization class. *Journal of Adolescent and Adult Literacy, 45*, 368–377.

Kist, W. (2005). *New literacies in action: Teaching and learning in multiple media.* New York: Teachers College Press.

Kress, G. (2003). *Literacy in the new media age.* London: Routledge.

Lankshear, C., & Knobel, M. (2004). Do we have your attention? New literacies, digital technologies, and the education of adolescents. In D. E. Alvermann (Ed.), *Adolescents and literacies in a digital world* (pp. 19–39). New York: Peter Lang.

Leu, D. J., Jr., Castek, J., Hentry, L. A., Coiro, J., & McMullan, M. (2004). The lessons that children teach us: Integrating children's literature and the new literacies of the Internet. *Reading Teacher, 57,* 496–503.

Martino, W., & Pallotta-Chiarolli, M. (2003). *So what's a boy? Addressing issues of masculinity and schooling.* Maidenhead, UK: Open University Press.

McNabb, M. (2006). *Literacy learning in networked classrooms: Using the Internet with middle-level students.* Newark, DE: International Reading Association.

Moore, D. W., Alvermann, D. E., & Hinchman, K. A. (Eds.). (2000). *Struggling adolescent readers: A collection of teaching strategies.* Newark, DE: International Reading Association.

Moore, D. W., Bean, T. W., Birdyshaw, D., & Rycik, J. (1999). Adolescent literacy: A position statement. *Journal of Adolescent and Adult Literacy, 43*(1), 97–112.

Moorman, G. (2006). *Text messaging, blogs, wikies, and online gaming: What adolescents can teach educators about literacy.* Paper presented at the Annual Convention of the International Reading Association, Chicago, IL.

O'Brien, D. (2006). "Struggling" adolescents' engagement in multimediating: Countering the institutional construction of incompetence. In D. E. Alvermann, K. A. Hinchman, D. W. Moore, S. F. Phelps, & D. R. Waff (Eds.), *Reconceptualizing the literacies in adolescents' lives* (pp. 29–46). Mahwah, NJ: Lawrence Erlbaum Associates.

Paulsen, G. (1996). *Brian's winter.* New York: Bantam Doubleday Dell.

Readence, J. E., Bean, T. W., & Baldwin, R. S. (2004). *Content area literacy: An integrated approach* (8th ed.). Dubuque, IA: Kandall/Hunt.

Sachar, L. (1998). *Holes.* New York: Farrar, Strauss and Giroux.

Smith, M., & Wilhelm, J. D. (2002). *"Reading don't fix no Chevy's": Literacy in the lives of young men.* Portsmouth, NH: Heinemann.

Stevens, L. P., & Bean, T. W. (2007). *Critical literacy: Context and practice in the K–12 classroom.* Thousand Oaks, CA: Sage.

Sturtevant, E. G., Boyd, F. B., Brozo, W. G., Hinchman, K. A., Moore, D. W., & Alvermann, D. E. (2006). *Principled practices for adolescent literacy: A framework for instruction and policy.* Mahwah, NJ: Lawrence Erlbaum Associates.

U.S. Department of Education (2006). *Striving readers initiative.* Retrieved from www.ed.gov/programs/strivingreaders/index.html

Walker, N. T., Bean, T. W., & Dillard, B. (2005). Two experienced content teachers' use of multiple texts in economics and English. In B. Maloch, J. V. Hoffman, D. L. Schallert, C. M. Fairbanks, & J. Worthy (Eds.), *54th yearbook of the National Reading Conference* (pp. 416–427). Oak Creek, WI: National Reading Conference.

Wilder, P., & Dressman, M. (2006). New literacies, enduring challenges? The influence of capital on adolescent readers' Internet practices. In D. E. Alvermann, K. A. Hinchman, D. W. Moore, S. F. Phelps, & D. R. Waff (Eds.), *Reconceptualizing the literacies in adolescents' lives* (pp. 205–229). Mahwah, NJ: Lawrence Erlbaum Associates.

INDEX

ABOUT THE CONTRIBUTORS

BARBARA J. GUZZETTI is a professor of language and literacy at Arizona State University in the Mary Lou Fulton College of Education. She is also an affiliated faculty member in the College of Liberal Arts and Sciences in Women's and Gender Studies. Her research interests include gender and literacy, science education and literacy, adolescent literacy, popular culture, and new literacies, including digital literacies.

DONNA E. ALVERMANN is University-Appointed Distinguished Research Professor of Language and Literacy Education at the University of Georgia. Her research focuses on adolescent literacy, especially as it interfaces with young people's interests in digital media and popular culture. Her coauthored/edited books include *Content Reading and Literacy: Succeeding in Today's Diverse Classrooms* (5th ed.), *Reconceptualizing the Literacies in Adolescents' Lives* (2nd ed.), *Popular Culture in the Classroom: Teaching and Researching Critical Media Literacy*, and *Adolescents and Literacies in a Digital World*.

THOMAS W. BEAN is a professor of reading/literacy in the Curriculum and Instruction Department at the University of Nevada, Las Vegas. He directs the doctoral program and conducts research in young adult literature in the content areas and research on content teachers' use of multiple texts in traditional and online teaching. Bean can be contacted via e-mail at beant1@unlv.nevada.edu.

HEATHER BLAIR is an associate professor in the faculty of education at the University of Alberta in Canada, where she teaches language, literacy, and reading to undergraduate and graduate students. Her research interests focus on the intersections of literacy, gender, ethnicity, race, and class. She has just finished a five-year longitudinal study with four adolescent boys.

JAMES BLASINGAME JR. is an associate professor of English at Arizona State University. He has served as coeditor of *The ALAN Review* (2003–2008) and has created the Books for Adolescents pages of the *Journal of Adolescent and Adult Literacy* (2002–2008). He is the author of *Books That Don't Bore 'Em: Young Adult Literature for Today's Generation* (2007) and *Teaching Writing in Middle and Secondary Schools* (2004).

DIANA J. DURBIN is a doctoral student and teaching assistant in the elementary education program at the University of Georgia. Her research interests include literacy and teacher reading groups.

BOB FECHO is an associate professor in the reading program of the Language and Literacy Education Department at the University of Georgia in Athens. To date, his work has focused on issues of language, identity, sociocultural perspectives, practitioner research, and critical inquiry pedagogy as they relate to adolescent literacy, particularly among marginalized populations. His book *"Is This English?" Race, Language, and Culture in the Classroom* was awarded the James Britton Award for Teacher Research from the National Council of Teachers of English, and a second book, *No Deposit, No Return: Enriching Literacy Teaching and Learning through Critical Inquiry Pedagogy* was recently published by the International Reading Association.

SHAWN M. GLYNN is a Josiah Meigs Distinguished Teaching Professor of Educational Psychology and Instructional Technology at the University of Georgia. His research interests include content area reading strategies.

MARGARET C. HAGOOD is an assistant professor in the Department of Early Childhood, Elementary, and Middle Grades in the School of Education at the College of Charleston. She teaches undergraduate and graduate courses in early childhood, elementary, and middle-grade literacies, focusing on sociocultural and poststructural theories relevant to new literacies. She is the primary researcher for the Center of the Advancement of New Literacies in Middle Grades, studying how middle-grade educators and students understand new literacies and utilize out-of-school literacies to improve their literacy performance in teaching and learning in in-school settings.

STEVEN HART is an assistant professor in the Literacy and Early Education Department at California State University–Fresno. Hart teaches adolescent and elementary literacy education courses that focus on critical approaches. His research is focused on using service learning as an approach to critical literacy education with adolescents.

SHARON KANE is a professor in the School of Education at the State University of New York at Oswego, where she teaches English methods, young adult literature, and literacy courses. She is the author of *Literacy and Learning in the Content Areas,* 2nd ed. (2007), and *Using Literature to Teach in the Content Areas* (in press).

JAMES R. KING is a professor of literacy studies at the University of South Florida in Tampa, where he teaches literacy and qualitative research methods. He is currently working in media literacies and analysis of visual texts. King can be contacted via e-mail at king@tempest.coedu.usf.edu.

DEBORAH KOZDRAS, enrolled in the PhD program in the College of Education at the University of South Florida, after teaching elementary school for 11 years in Canada, is currently in her third year of studies. Her research interests lie in the area of literacy and technology, including critical literacy and technology, multimedia discourse, hypermedia reading and writing, and technology-infused literacy education. Her publications include journal articles, conference proceedings, book chapters, and research-based lesson plans.

KEVIN LEANDER is an associate professor in the Department of Teaching and Learning at Vanderbilt University, Nashville. Prior to his work at Vanderbilt, Leander taught high school English and French in the United States and Italy. Leander's research interests include digital literacies, social space and literacy, and the relations of literacy to identity.

CYNTHIA LEWIS is a professor of English education at the University of Minnesota. Her research focuses on the connection between literacy practices and social identities, specifically as related to new literacies, response to literature, and classroom discourse. Her books include *Literary Practices As Social Acts: Power, Status, and Cultural Norms in the Classroom* and *Reframing Sociocultural Research on Literacy: Identity, Agency, and Power* (coedited with Patricia Enciso and Elizabeth Moje).

CHRISTINE A. MALLOZZI is a PhD student in the Language and Literacy Education Department at the University of Georgia, where her research interests include teacher education, feminist theories, policy issues, and globalization. These foci are influenced by the five years she spent teaching 5th and 6th grades and earning her master's degree in literacy at the University of Cincinnati. Currently, she is researching the constructions of gender by, for, and among female teacher education students.

DAVID W. MOORE is a professor of education at Arizona State University, where he teaches secondary school teacher education courses and specializes in adolescent literacy. His vita shows a 25-year publication record that balances research reports, professional articles, book chapters, and books.

K. DENISE MUTH is a professor of middle school education at the University of Georgia. Her research interests include middle school content area reading, with a particular focus on reading in mathematics.

DAVID O'BRIEN is a professor of literacy education in the Department of Curriculum and Instruction and an associated faculty member at the Minnesota Reading Research Center, University of Minnesota, Twin Cities. O'Brien has taught junior high reading (7th grade) and high school at-risk students in a literacy lab setting (grades 9–12) and has served as a district reading curriculum coordinator, Title I reading project director, and Title I reading teacher (grades 1–8). His scholarship and teaching focus on the literacy practices of adolescents, particularly the engagement of struggling readers and how adolescents use literacy to learn content across the disciplines.

ELIANE RUBINSTEIN-AVILA was a bilingual teacher in California (early 90s). She is currently an assistant professor in the Department of Language Reading and Culture at the University of Arizona. Her main research interests focus on the language and literacy practices of immigrant and nondominant youths in and out of school, and she has published several academic articles on this topic. She was recently awarded the Elva Knight Research Grant by the International Reading Association to explore the ways in which English language learners use L1 and L2 to reason and develop mathematical arguments.

LESLIE S. RUSH is an assistant professor of English education in the Department of Secondary Education at the University of Wyoming in Laramie, Wyoming. A former high school English teacher, she teaches courses in English methods, adolescent literacy, and young adult literature; she also supervises secondary English preservice teachers during their student teaching semester.

Rush's research interests include multigenre writing, multiliteracies, and the work of literacy coaches with secondary content area teachers.

TERRY SALINGER is a managing director and chief scientist for reading research at the American Institutes for Research. Currently the project director for an Institute of Education Studies (IES) study of the effectiveness of reading interventions for adolescent struggling readers, her specific areas of focus are reading and literacy research and assessment. Additionally, Salinger provides content expertise on studies investigating preservice teachers' preparation to teach beginning reading, developing a curriculum for adult English as a second language learners, and monitoring the implementation of the Reading First program.

KATHERINE SCHULTZ is an associate professor of education and director of the new Center for Collaborative Research and Practice in Teacher Education. Her research focuses on the preparation and ongoing support of new teachers in urban public schools and addresses adolescent literacy practices, pathways into teaching, and international teacher education. Her recent book, *Listening: A Framework for Teaching across Differences,* suggests that teachers build their pedagogy and practice by listening closely to students.

JEANNE SWAFFORD is an associate professor of literacy education in the Donald R. Watson School of Education, Department of Elementary Middle Level and Literacy Education at the University of North Carolina, Wilmington. She is also a former elementary school and middle school teacher. Her research focuses on content area literacy in the elementary grades and nonfiction children's literature.

RACHEL THROOP is a doctoral student in the teaching, learning, and curriculum program at the University of Pennsylvania. Before coming to Penn, Throop taught middle and high school science in Arizona and EFL courses in southern Mexico. One of her research interests is preparing teachers to work in linguistically diverse classrooms.

LALITHA VASUDEVAN is assistant professor of technology and education at Teachers College, Columbia University, where she conducts research on education in the lives of urban youth outside the school walls, in between institutional spaces, and across new literacies and technologies. Awarded a PhD in education from the University of Pennsylvania, where she studied the stories, literacy practices, and technology engagements of adolescent boys, she is coeditor of a volume of essays titled *Media, Learning, and Sites of Possibility* (with Marc L. Hill), which critically examines the integration of media and technologies in teaching/learning spaces with youth.

XIQIAO WANG is a doctoral student in language, literacy, and culture at Vanderbilt University. She studies the language, literacy, and cultural practices of young adolescents, focusing particularly on adolescents' composition activities and identity performances in digital multimedia environments.

AMY ALEXANDRA WILSON is a doctoral student in the Department of Language and Literacy Education at the University of Georgia. A former high school and middle school teacher, she received the International Reading Association's Teacher as Researcher Grant and is interested in continuing her studies of adolescent literacy. In addition, her research addresses secondary teacher education in the field of content area literacy.

JENNIFER J. WIMMER is a doctoral student in reading/literacy in the Curriculum and Instruction Department at the University of Nevada, Las Vegas. Her research centers on the intersection of content area literacy and new literacies, including hybrid online high schools and secondary schools where multimedia is an integral part of teacher and student learning. Wimmer can be contacted via e-mail at wimmerj2@unlv.nevada.edu.